EROS
TOWARD THE
WORLD

EROS
TOWARD THE WORLD

*Paul Tillich and the
Theology of the Erotic*

Alexander C. Irwin

FORTRESS PRESS
MINNEAPOLIS

EROS TOWARD THE WORLD:
Paul Tillich and the Theology of the Erotic

Scripture quotations unless otherwise noted are from the Revised Standard Version of the Bible, copyright © 1946, 1952, and 1971 by the Division of Christian Education of the National Council of Churches.

Portions of chapter 2 originally appeared as "The Faces of Desire: Tillich on Essential Libido, Concupiscence, and the Transcendence of Estrangement," in *Encounter* 51, no. 4 (Autumn 1990). Portions of chapter 5 originally appeared as an article written with Sandra Friedman, "Christian Feminism, Eros, and Power in Right Relation," in *Cross Currents* (Fall 1990). Both are used by permission.

Cover design: Judy Swanson
Internal design: Karen Buck

Library of Congress Cataloging-in-Publication Data

Irwin, Alexander C., 1960–
    Eros toward the world : Paul Tillich and the theology of the
erotic / Alexander C. Irwin.
        p.   cm.
    Includes bibliographical references and index.
    ISBN 0-8006-2494-7 (alk. paper)
    1. Tillich, Paul, 1886–1965—Contributions in theology of the
erotic.   2. Erotica—Religious aspects—Christianity—History of
doctrines—20th century.   I. Title.
BT708.4.I78   1991
233'.5—dc20   91-23936
                                                        CIP

The paper used in this publication meets the minimum requirements of American National Standard for Information Sciences—Permanence of Paper for Printed Library Materials, ANSI Z329.48-1984.   ∞™

Manufactured in the U.S.A.   AF 1-2494

95   94   93   92   91   1   2   3   4   5   6   7   8   9   10

To A. E., Catherine Ann, and Janet,
who taught me what I know of philia and agape

And to Sandra,
who introduced me to the "great daimon"

Contents

Preface

Christianity has not been kind to eros. Hostility toward feelings and behavior associated with the erotic has been one of the most consistent hallmarks of Christian thought through the ages. As recently as the middle of this century, neo-orthodox theologians solemnly affirmed that the overcoming of eros through the superhuman power of agape is the very essence of the Christian message.

In the past few years, however, a reappraisal of eros has begun in progressive theological circles. New understandings of the erotic have appeared in the work of feminist and womanist authors. For many feminists, eros is not the enemy of the Christian life, but a creative force exerting a positive influence in all areas of human existence, including religion. Feminist and womanist writing on the erotic opens new and exciting theological perspectives.

But if orthodox Christian theology has been uniformly hostile to eros, then dialogue would seem impossible between the theological tradition and those who have begun to shape a new understanding of the life-giving power of the erotic. If its leading thinkers can offer no help in interpreting and assimilating these new ideas, Christianity may reject them as alien and destructive. It may turn away, refusing to learn and to change. Can traditional Christian theology find within itself elements enabling it to acknowledge, affirm, and learn from new interpretations of eros? Looking back over the history of mainstream Christian thought, can we hear voices that celebrate the erotic, alongside those that denounce it?

In this book, I try to furnish elements of a response to this question. My study focuses on Paul Tillich, a theologian whose work has been described as paradigmatic of the liberal Christian theological tradition. In looking at the theme of eros in Tillich, my aim is to draw the issue of the relationship between eros and established Christian theology out into the open and to give it the full, explicit importance it deserves. Taking eros as a key to Tillich's thought yields both new insights into Tillich, and new hope for creative dialogue between today's radical theologies and the tradition. I am convinced that such creative exchange around the topic of the erotic is necessary if Christianity is to function as a viable and credible spiritual force in the contemporary world.

The idea for this approach to Tillich's theology originated in the course of my graduate studies at Union Theological Seminary in New York. The text I provide grew and evolved over a period of roughly two years, changing substantially as my familiarity both with Tillich's writings and with the work of feminist and womanist authors deepened. To all those teachers and friends who contributed to this deepening process, I owe a debt of gratitude.

Several persons at Union and elsewhere read part or all of the manuscript and made helpful suggestions. Among these persons, I would like to extend special thanks to Tom Driver, Victoria Erickson, Sandra Friedman, Beverly Harrison, Tom Kelly, Vivian Lindermayer, and Judith Plaskow. Without their generous support and alert criticism, the project could never have been completed. Judith in particular was unfailingly gracious in giving time, attention, and insightful criticism.

I would also like to thank my friends and instructors at the Faculté de Théologie Protestante de Paris, particularly Olivier Abel, Olivier Déaux, Laurent Gagnebin, Yann Morvant, Raphael Picon, and Ailean and Anna Vater. It was under their influence that I first began to take a serious interest in Tillich. Their friendship has been a source of inspiration and enrichment on many levels.

Part of the research for this project was financed through a summer study grant from the D.A.A.D. (German Academic Exchange Service), which enabled me to enhance substantially my familiarity with Tillich's early writings.

Thanks are due, finally, to Cindy Beal, Andrea Kannapell, Marguerite Lukes, Sandra Friedman, and Cathy and Janet Irwin for moral support at crucial moments.

Abbreviations

To avoid an unnecessary proliferation of footnotes, the following abbreviations have been used in the text to identify citations from the works of Paul Tillich.

BR   *Biblical Religion and the Search for Ultimate Reality.* Chicago: University of Chicago Press, 1955.

D   *Dogmatik: Marburger Vorlesung von 1925.* Edited by Werner Shüßler. Düsseldorf: Patmos, 1986.

DF   *Dynamics of Faith.* New York: Harper & Row, 1957.

GW   *Gesammelte Werke.* 14 vols. Stuttgart: Evangelisches Verlagswerk, 1959–74.

IH   *The Interpretation of History.* New York and London: Charles Scribner's Sons, 1936.

LPJ   *Love, Power, and Justice.* New York and London: Oxford University Press, 1954.

MB   *Morality and Beyond.* New York: Harper & Row, 1963.

NB   *The New Being.* New York: Charles Scribner's Sons, 1955.

OB   *On the Boundary.* New York: Charles Scribner's Sons, 1966.

PE   *The Protestant Era.* Chicago: University of Chicago Press, 1948.

SD   *The Socialist Decision.* New York: Harper & Row, 1977.

SF   *The Shaking of the Foundations.* New York: Charles Scribner's Sons, 1952.

ST	*Systematic Theology.* 3 vols. Chicago: University of Chicago Press, 1951–63.
TC	*Theology of Culture.* New York: Oxford University Press, 1959.

In addition, the following frequently cited secondary sources are also annotated parenthetically in the text, listed by the last name of the author (except Plato).

Brock	Rita Nakashima Brock. *Journeys by Heart: A Christology of Erotic Power.* New York: Crossroad, 1988.
Heyward	Carter Heyward. *Touching Our Strength: The Erotic as Power and the Love of God.* San Francisco: Harper & Row, 1989.
Lorde	Audre Lorde. "The Uses of the Erotic: The Erotic as Power." Essay in *Sister Outsider: Essays and Speeches.* Trumansburg, N.Y.: The Crossing Press, 1984.
May	Rollo May. *Paulus: Reminiscences of Friendship.* New York: Harper & Row, 1973.
Nygren	Anders Nygren. *Agape and Eros.* Translated by Philip Watson. Philadelphia: Westminster Press, 1953.
Pauck and Pauck	Wilhelm and Marion Pauck. *Paul Tillich: His Life and Thought.* New York: Harper & Row, 1976.
Plaskow	Judith Plaskow. *Standing Again at Sinai: Judaism from a Feminist Perspective.* San Francisco: Harper & Row, 1990.
Symposium	Plato. *Symposium.* In *The Dialogues of Plato,* translated by Bernard Jowett. Oxford: Clarendon, 1953.
H. Tillich	Hannah Tillich. *From Time to Time.* New York: Stein & Day, 1973.
Ulanov	Ann Belford Ulanov. "Between Anxiety and Faith: The Role of the Feminine in Tillich's Theological Thought." Essay in *Paul Tillich on Creativity,* edited by Jacquelyn Ann K. Kegley. Lanham, Md.: University Press of America, 1989.

1 Eros in Context

The Ontological Unity of Love

"What then is Eros?" I asked; "Is he mortal?"
"No."
"What then?"

—Plato, *Symposium*

And you whose spirits are sad or unsure, try to remember the very best parts of your life, the loveliest feelings in your bodyself, occasions of bold delight and quiet confidence. . . . Try to remember when you have believed passionately in something or someone, human or divine.

—Carter Heyward

"We have, following Plato," Paul Tillich writes in the final pages of his book *Love, Power, and Justice,* "defined *eros* as the driving force in all cultural creativity and in all mysticism." As such, Tillich continues matter-of-factly, "eros has the greatness of a divine-human power" (*LPJ,* 117).

It seems incongruous to encounter in an eminently serious work of philosophical theology by a prominent Protestant thinker an affirmation of the "divine-human power" of the erotic. One may find the remark theologically unsound, perhaps even mildly offensive. One is not used to hearing respected representatives of the Protestant theological tradition—especially those representatives born well before the turn of the last century—celebrate erotic energies as the animating force behind cultural achievements. We are

1

even less used to hearing these theologians explicitly raise eros to the level of the "divine," or even of the "divine-human."

Attributions of divinity are not, as a rule, made lightly in works of theology. "The divine" does not belong to the class of ideas that theologians and philosophers of religion are in the habit of handling casually. Paul Tillich, even more than most of his colleagues, attached importance to an intellectual attitude of "existential seriousness." Capable of writing a hundred meticulous pages to elucidate his concepts of "reason" and "revelation," he was not an author noted for his playfulness in dealing with important theological terms.

Faced with this slightly embarrassing passage, some readers, like most students and commentators of Tillich's work in the past, will want to pass rapidly over the "divine-human eros," chalking the phrase up to poetic hyperbole or a simple error of taste. Tillich's "existential seriousness" did not stop him, after all, from getting carried away from time to time in his use of poetic language. One might also reason that as a leading Protestant thinker whose mind was focused on weighty questions of Christian doctrine and of the theological content of cultural forms, Tillich did not often find himself in the position of having to write seriously about eros. When he was obliged to discuss the topic, he probably simply pulled a few phrases from the familiar texts of Plato's *Dialogues* without giving the matter much thought. One might assume that eros was, after all, a peripheral theme in Tillich's theology, and that it is probably pointless (as well as petty) to focus obsessively on details of wording in his occasional allusions to the topic.

The centrality of eros in Tillich's thought

The way of reasoning just described would account in a sensible manner for Tillich's reference to the "divine-human power" of eros. It would allow us to move beyond the whole, rather trivial issue toward topics that should certainly be of greater importance in understanding the major structures of Tillich's thought. It would steer us away from the sort of pedantic nitpicking that causes scholars to become absorbed in minute details of language and to lose sight of broader and more significant issues. Such an approach would be reasonable, measured, mature, and satisfying in practically every respect.

Unfortunately, it would also be wrong, and for a variety of reasons. First of all, the erotic is not a theme that appears only occasionally in

Tillich's theological writings. Eros is, on the contrary, a topic that Tillich discusses frequently, and in detail. Second, and more seriously, eros is not an idea of only marginal significance in connection with the substance of Tillich's theology. It is a concept of central importance to Tillich's understanding of human embodiment and selfhood, creativity, ethics, and the religious impulse. Along with his various other roles and titles within twentieth-century theology—"theologian of the boundaries," theologian of existential alienation or of doubt and courage—Tillich was also a theologian of eros. Tillich's thinking in nearly every significant area of theological inquiry was decisively influenced by his theorization of eros.

In this and the following chapters, Tillich's attribution of "divine-human power" to eros will emerge as deliberate and purposeful, neither an uncritical borrowing from other sources, nor a simple flight of poetic fancy. On the contrary, such an attribution reflects, in clear and carefully weighed terms, an idea that is central to Tillich's understanding of the nature of human existence. The concept of eros also makes it possible for Tillich's theology to open itself to dialogue with some of the most progressive theological discourses in development today. At the end of this volume, one may still find Tillich's statement offensive or simply wrong-headed. One may reject vigorously and uncompromisingly his assertion about the divine-human power of the erotic. But one will have to acknowledge that Tillich is serious in what he affirms and that the theological consequences of his vision of eros are far-reaching.

Tillich's theology of eros has rarely been acknowledged by scholars. The reasons for this may include simple inattentiveness, the conviction that there were more "serious" topics in Tillich which need to be dealt with first, hesitation to provoke discussion on a subject that, given the character of Tillich's personal life, could easily lead in unpleasant directions. Basic, old-fashioned prudishness may have also played a role. In any case, the silence that has surrounded Tillich's writing on the erotic clashes with the structure and intention of Tillich's theological understanding of love and of the nature of human being.

The clash becomes evident once one merely counts references. The topic of eros is referred to at least briefly in all of Tillich's most important published works. The frequency of such references reflects the importance that Tillich attached to eros as a theological and philosophical category.

Tillich's concern with the subject of the erotic and his development and use of a personal eros vocabulary span both his career in the

German academic system and his three decades of teaching and writing following his emigration to the United States in 1933. Eros becomes a subject of discussion in texts and lectures ranging from Tillich's Marburg lectures on dogmatics (delivered in 1925) to his famous essay on "The Demonic" (1926) to *The Socialist Decision* (published and immediately suppressed in Germany in 1933) to the main works of the American years: *Love, Power, and Justice* (1954), *Biblical Religion and the Search for Ultimate Reality* (1955), *Morality and Beyond* (1963), and each of the three volumes of his magnum opus, *Systematic Theology* (1951–63). The classroom exchanges transcribed in *Ultimate Concern: Tillich in Dialog* confirm that erotic terminology still figured in Tillich's pedagogical vocabulary in the later days of his teaching career.[1] Eros is listed in the indices of all but one of the thirteen principal volumes of the German edition of Tillich's *Gesammelte Werke*. Volume 10 alone contains sixteen references under the heading *Eros*, twice as many as appear under *Luther, Martin*, five times more than for *Dogma, Dogmatics*, and only one less than under *Christ*.

A fundamental problem, however, arises at this point. While it becomes clear on quantitative grounds that Tillich considered eros a theological idea of major importance, it is not immediately obvious just what, in his opinion, eros actually is. A rapid reading of the discussions of the erotic in some of the works just cited is more likely to generate bewilderment than quick illumination. In no single passage or chapter does Tillich offer anything claiming to be an exhaustive analysis of the concept. Furthermore, the references that reflect Tillich's thinking on the erotic appear in a host of radically different contexts, ranging from discussions of the nature of divine love to reflections on art and technology to analyses of the dynamics of secular political movements. His use of erotic terminology in these various settings and the connections he perceives among the many different areas of human experience in which eros plays a part are far from clear.

The confusions that may be provoked by Tillich's discussions of the erotic arise in part from his way of approaching the topic: often through brief, suggestive remarks rather than sustained, analytic treatments. But the difficulties are also connected with the nature of his concept of eros.

---

[1]D. Mackenzie Brown, ed., *Ultimate Concern: Tillich in Dialog* (New York: Harper & Row, 1965), 60.

At the root of the problem is, somewhat paradoxically, the immense importance that Tillich attaches to the concept of the erotic. The fact is that his conception of the erotic embraces an extraordinarily wide spectrum of experiences, cultural practices, and relationships. He explicitly theorizes eros as a shaping force in areas ranging from sexuality to mathematics to the highest forms of human spirituality. His sense of the significance and pervasive influence of eros leads him to discuss the topic in surprising and sometimes frankly confusing ways. Not only does he frequently introduce erotic terminology in unconventional contexts, but he often fails to draw sufficiently explicit connections between the widely disparate areas to which his individual discussions apply. What relationship is to be assumed, one wonders, among the "impulse for eros," one of the driving forces of the unconscious mind ("The Demonic"); the eros that guides human cognitive acts (*Systematic Theology*, 1); and the erotic forces that influence the bonding of social groups (*The Socialist Decision*)? What links exist between the "aesthetic" and the "religious" forms of eros? What does it imply to posit a single type of love as the animating force in these diverse areas? The answers to such questions require careful examination and comparison of all the principal contexts in which Tillich makes use of erotic terminology. With a sense of the full range of applications of Tillich's eros principle, we can begin to assess its descriptive value and its possible importance for current theological discussions.

The wide-ranging importance that the theologian attributes to eros creates complexities within Tillich's texts. This importance may also lead to problems in the reception of those texts dealing with the eros motif. The powers Tillich assigned to eros make certain passages hard to comprehend. Moreover, once people do understand the texts, they may consider them profoundly threatening. To recognize the full significance of eros in Tillich's thought, readers may have to make adjustments in important aspects of their understanding of Tillich's theological project. To grasp Tillich's eros doctrine and its possible implications may at the same time present a challenge to the reader's own theological framework. When Tillich links eros with the "divine," a reader may be particularly inclined to not want to take Tillich's statements at face value. The premise of this study, however, is that these statements should be interpreted as meaning just what they say. If this step is taken—if Tillich's most important treatments of eros are examined attentively and taken seriously—then significant consequences follow.

Tillich's discussions of the erotic offer a vision of the power of eros that is challenging in its complexity and audacious in its claims. Eros provides a new "way in" to Tillich's theology. It illuminates sides of that theology which have until now been neglected or suppressed. At the same time, accepting Tillich's arguments about the pervasive power of the erotic demands a serious reexamination of traditional theological world views. Tillich's thinking on eros points toward new possibilities for understanding the nature of human existence, and for naming the relationship between human beings and the divine. In dialogue with theorizations of eros and human relationality emerging today in feminist and womanist theologies, Tillich's vision of the erotic opens perspectives on the future tasks and challenges of Christian theology.

Eros and sex

The first, basic point to be raised in connection with Tillich's concept of eros does not directly concern what eros is, but rather one important thing that it is not. In many passages Tillich expressly rejects the tendency in popular language (which he detects in the work of influential scholars as well) to use "erotic" simply as a synonym for "libidinal" or "sexual." This reduction of eros to the sexual was already prevalent, he believes, in the period in which the New Testament was written, and explains why the New Testament authors were forced to avoid the term. He insists that identifying the erotic with the sexual empties the concept of eros of its distinctive content (*LPJ*, 30, 117).

Tillich affirms that libidinal drives are unquestionably present in every form of eros and contribute decisively to the power of the erotic. He insists, nevertheless, that, "eros transcends *epithymia*," or pure physical desire. It includes but reaches beyond libido in the sexual sense. Eros is not oriented primarily toward pleasure or a release of tension. Rather, eros "strives for a union with that which is a bearer of values because of the values" that that person, object, group, or idea embodies. In contrast to the so-called normal mode of genital sexuality, the erotic impulse need not be focused exclusively on the body, let alone on the genital organs of another person. The "values" toward which the erotic orients itself refer to the beauty manifested in the human form, but also "to the beauty we find in nature, to the beautiful and the true in culture, to the mystical union with that which is the source of the beautiful and the true" (*LPJ*, 30).

As Tillich's student and friend Rollo May puts it, sex has often been defined in quantitative physiological terms as a building up and release of tensions. Eros, on the other hand, is a complex and mysterious force shaping connections among persons and between human beings and the world they inhabit. Eros is characterized by the "longing to establish full relationship." It is the "drive toward union with what we belong to," or as Tillich phrases it, the "drive towards the reunion of the separated." Thus for May, there is a sense in which it is possible, especially within an alienated culture of consumerism and pornography, to see eros "in conflict with sex." In such a culture, people may indeed use "sex precisely to avoid the anxiety-creating involvements of eros," a point that Tillich also discusses in several passages.[2] True eros and essential libido are absent, Tillich states, from a situation in which "the other being" is used "not as an object of reunion but as a tool for gaining pleasure" (*LPJ*, 117).

Tillich underlines the fact that "sexual desire is not evil as desire," but becomes so only in situations in which it "bypass[es] the centre of the other person" (*LPJ*, 117). By no means does he see a necessary opposition between eros and the libidinal drives. He denies that the differences between them should be seen as reflecting a hierarchical order, that libido or *epithymia* as physical desire is somehow "lower," inferior (*LPJ*, 28). His concept of "creative eros" explicitly acknowledges and affirms the ecstasy of sex as a significant component of erotic experience (*ST* 2:54). But even though eros always includes elements drawn from the libidinal dimension of life, the erotic cannot be identified exclusively with these elements. Eros can include sex, but it is itself more than sex. For Tillich, the scope of the erotic embraces a vast horizon of other human experiences in which the "drive towards reunion of the separated" is operative.

The "urge," "desire," or "drive toward the reunion of the separated" is Tillich's well-known ontological definition of love (*LPJ*, 25–34; *ST* 1:279–80; *MB*, 38–39). If learning what the erotic *is not* means distinguishing eros from libido, beginning to understand what Tillichean eros *is* means resituating eros in the context of his overall doctrine of the nature and forms of love. It means examining more carefully the connections of the erotic to libido/*epithymia* and to the other types or facets of love. The scope and implications of Tillich's understanding of the erotic can only be grasped by examining his interpretation of

---

[2]Rollo May, *Love and Will* (New York: Dell, 1974), 71–72, 63–64.

eros in the light of his view of the role of love in human existence
and of the dynamic interplay between love's distinct but interdependent
dimensions.

The forms of love and their ontological unity

In Tillich's understanding, love is the most crucial category of Christian
theological reflection, indeed, of all human experience. Tillich describes love as "the moving power of life" (*LPJ*, 25), life's "inner
dynamics" (*ST* 3:137), the foundation of all social and political power
structures, the "ultimate moral principle" and the "source of all moral
norms" (*MB*, 38, 42). He praises it as "the infinite which is given to
the finite," the power that "rescues life from death" (*NB*, 173–74),
the cosmic essence of "being itself" (*ST* 1:279f.). He criticizes previous
Protestant theology for its failure to give sufficient attention to the
decisive role of love in all areas, from interpersonal moral relations to
the connection between human beings and God (*MB*, 93–94).

Tillich's radical interpretation of the nature and importance of love,
in particular his enthusiastic affirmation of the erotic and libidinal
qualities of love, drew criticism from more conservative thinkers. It
also awakened skepticism even among his own friends and admirers,
some of whom detected highly unorthodox elements in his approach
to the diverse aspects of love and to their functions in morality, culture,
and religion. Ironically, Tillich undertakes his analysis of love on the
basis of an almost quaintly traditional vocabulary. Most of his treatments of the theme are organized around the familiar types of love
inherited from classical philosophy and theology: libido/*epithymia*,
philia, eros, and agape. In *Systematic Theology, Love, Power, and Justice,
Morality and Beyond,* and other important texts, Tillich presents his
most probing discussions of love in terms of the interrelationships
between these four traditional categories. His conception of eros is
decisively shaped by his view of the place of the erotic among the
other types.

The discussion of "The Divine Love and the Creature" in the first
volume of *Systematic Theology* presents definitions "in abbreviated
form" of the classical types of love as Tillich understands and uses
them. "Love as libido," Tillich states, "is the movement of the needy
toward that which fulfils the need." Philia designates "the movement
of the equal toward union with the equal." Love as eros is characterized
as "the movement of that which is lower in power and meaning toward

that which is higher." In describing eros as a connection based on "power and meaning," Tillich has chosen terms so broad as to draw almost every sort of relationship into the sphere of the erotic. Anyone and anything could potentially awaken erotic interest.

It is obvious, Tillich notes, that "the element of desire is present" in each of these three types of love: libido, philia, and eros. This fact does not, however, "contradict the created goodness of being, since separation and the longing for reunion belong to the essential nature of creaturely life." It is true, however, that libido, philia, and eros are to some extent linked to "contingent characteristics which change and are partial." These types of love are thus "dependent on attraction and repulsion, on passion and sympathy." They are in that sense limited and potentially ambiguous. The fourth type of love, agape, "affirms the other unconditionally, apart from higher or lower, pleasant or unpleasant qualities." Agapic love is "universal. No one with whom a concrete relation is technically possible (the neighbor) is excluded." Agape surpasses merely human capacities. Tillich describes it as the direct creation of the divine. It is "independent" of the qualities of passion and desire which mark the other forms of love (*ST* 1:280).

Although agape "transcends" libido, philia, and eros, Tillich stresses that none of the types of love should be viewed as inherently evil. Divine love can itself be characterized, in a "metaphorical symbolic way," in terms that evoke the libidinal, philial, and erotic energies. "It is natural," Tillich claims, and not at all inappropriate that "Christian symbolism has used these types to make the divine love concrete" (*ST* 1:282, 281)

The relationship between the "lower" and "higher" forms of love, and notably between eros and agape, is not one of irreconcilable opposition or mutual exclusion. On the contrary, eros and agape must be seen as expressions of the same ontological "drive towards reunion." Otherwise, Tillich maintains, the love of the human creature for the divine cannot be made comprehensible. "Basically," he affirms, human beings' "love to God is of the nature of eros. It involves elevation from the lower to the higher, from lower goods to the *summum bonum*." The false idea that there might be an "irreconcilable conflict between eros and agape" must not "keep theologians from asserting that man reaches his highest good in God," and that human beings "long" in an erotic manner for "[their] fulfilment in God." Eros and agape cannot exclude each other; the ontological unity of the different types of love must be recognized as the basic condition of love's expression in human life. "If eros and agape cannot be united," Tillich argues, "agape toward God is impossible" (*ST* 1:281).

The project of reconciling eros and agape is an imperative of Tillich's doctrine of love, one to which he returns with regularity. It emerges in almost all of the texts in which he offers an extended discussion of the nature and functions of love: *Systematic Theology* 1, 2, and 3, *Love, Power, and Justice, Biblical Religion,* and *Morality and Beyond.* The tensions and possible reconciliation between agape and eros deeply influenced Tillich's understanding of the erotic and his efforts to integrate the "divine-human" eros into a theological framework whose basic structures are set by the tradition of Protestant dogmatics.

Tillich refined his conception of the ontological unity of love in a series of lectures delivered at the University of Nottingham, England, and at Union Theological Seminary in Virginia and published in 1954 under the title *Love, Power, and Justice.* In a chapter devoted to the "Ontology of Love," Tillich attempted to formulate a clear definition of the ontological character of love and to explore the consequences of such a definition for the understanding of the functional interrelationships between the different types or, as Tillich now preferred to call them, "qualities" of love.

"Life is being in actuality, and love is the moving power of life. In these two sentences," Tillich asserts, "the ontological nature of love is expressed" (*LPJ,* 25). Love governs the cycle of separation and reunion which structures all dimensions of human and cosmic reality. Citing Aristotle on the "pure actuality which moves the world not as a cause (*kinoumenon*), but as the object of love (*eromenon*)," Tillich identifies love as the force that catalyzes the movement from unrealized, abstract being to being actualized in the differentiated forms of existence. "Being is not actual without the love that drives everything that is toward everything else that is." Thus, it is above all in human beings' experience of love that the "nature of life becomes manifest" for them (*LPJ,* 25). Within the domain of life as actualized being, love is operative as a "drive towards the unity of the separated," functioning in all dimensions of the experience of living organisms, from the level of biological needs up to that of human beings' highest cultural achievements and most sublime spiritual aspirations.

As Tillich had already begun to argue in the first section of *Systematic Theology,* the ontological structure of love embraces both the tendency toward separation and the movement toward reunion. The concepts of separation and reunion are intentionally vast, including ontological, existential, and properly theological aspects. Separation can refer to the creation of differentiated multiplicity out of original cosmic unity and to the existential experiences of separation from one's fellow creatures and of alienation from the divine. The complementary drive toward reunion operates on all these levels as well. "Every life-process unites a trend toward separation with a trend toward reunion. The unbroken unity of these two trends is the ontological nature of love" (*ST* 1:279). "Reunion presupposes separation of that which belongs essentially together" (*LPJ*, 25). Primacy is clearly given, however, to the movement of reunion. "It would," Tillich asserts, "be wrong to give separation the same ontological ultimacy as reunion. For separation presupposes an original unity. Unity embraces itself and separation, just as being comprises itself and non-being." The essential and defining impulse of love remains the "drive toward unity" (*LPJ*, 25).

Tillich draws on this ontological definition of love to back up his claim that love is in its essence a unified phenomenon, despite the diversity of aspects through which it manifests itself. "The ontology of love," Tillich affirms, "leads to the basic assertion that love is one" (*LPJ*, 27). This claim, he is aware, "contradicts the main trend" in theological and philosophical discussions of the nature of love, which have tended to focus on the distinctions and conflicts that appear to exist among different types of love and desire. Precisely therein, however, lies the importance of the understanding of love yielded by the ontological analysis. Discussions of love which treat the various types of love, in particular eros and agape, as radically and irreconcilably different from one another have led to serious misinterpretations of the significance of love in its erotic and libidinal dimensions. Such discussions have at the same time encouraged a sanitized, puritanical misreading of the true character of the "higher" forms of love, an understanding not based on "biblical realism," but instead on "idealistic and moralistic self-deception" (*LPJ*, 117).

Attempts to distinguish the different facets of love have proved useful and constructive "insofar as they directed the attention to the different qualities of love," and helped to gain recognition for the specific powers and possibilities implicit in libido/*epithymia*, philia, and eros. However, such fragmented presentations of the nature of love "were and are misleading" insofar as they try to transform "differences of qualities" into radical and unbridgeable "differences of types." The error "was not that one distinguished the qualities of love"; indeed, Tillich suggests that "more distinctions" might in fact have been useful in understanding the broad powers of eros. Separating, in theory, the qualities of love from one another is of practical value in grasping the varied functions of love in human life. The potentially disastrous error lies in failing to found a theory of the distinct qualities of love on an underlying "understanding of love as one" (*LPJ*, 28).

"There is a strong interest," Tillich acknowledges, "on the part of philosophical and theological moralists in establishing a complete gap" between *epithymia* or libido, traditionally "considered the lowest quality of love," and those aspects of love which are "supposed to be higher and essentially different" (*LPJ*, 28). In much the same way, "love as eros is depreciated by those theologians who depreciate culture and by those who deny a mystical element" in human beings' relation to God (*LPJ*, 30). Both of these mistaken attitudes spring, Tillich claims, from the failure to recognize the ontological unity of love, which underlies and precedes love's expression through distinct qualities.

Only if the fundamental unity of love is grasped, Tillich believes, can theology come to terms with modern conceptions of human nature, in particular, with the insights into basic drives and motivations offered by psychoanalysis. Recognizing the underlying unity of the different types of love, Christianity should no longer cling desperately to the notion of a "pure," abstract, agapic love freed from all libidinal impulses and erotic feelings. Rather, Christian thinkers should begin honestly to acknowledge the connection of libido and of the "cultural eros" to religious thought, feeling, and cultic practice. They should free themselves from the paralyzing effects of the "rejection of the eros quality of love with respect to God" (*LPJ*, 31). The role of the erotic in human beings' religious lives could then be explored honestly and developed in a creative manner. In any event, Tillich states, the unified nature of love demands unequivocally that the role of eros and libido in the spiritual sphere be recognized and accepted. The only alternative is dishonesty toward oneself and others. "There is an element of libido in even the most spiritualized friendship and in the most ascetic mysticism. A saint without libido would cease to be a creature. But there is no such saint" (*LPJ*, 33).

If the underlying ontological unity of love is understood, Tillich affirms, the actual connections and divergences among the qualities of love can be put into proper perspective. "If love in all its forms is the drive toward the reunion of the separated," then "the different qualities of the one nature of love" finally "become understandable" (*LPJ*, 28). Against the background of the ontological oneness of love, Tillich develops in *Love, Power, and Justice* a bold treatment of the nature of eros and of the relationship between the erotic and the other forms of love.

Eros and the other qualities of love

In *Love, Power, and Justice,* Tillich presents an interpretation of eros which leads to the conclusion—surprising, to say the least, within the framework of Christian theology—that the erotic can legitimately be characterized as a "divine-human power." In shaping a vision of the pervasive power of eros, Tillich draws on the vocabulary of the Greek philosophers. He refers to Aristotle's "universal eros" and to the Platonic "doctrine of eros as the power which drives to the union with the true and the good itself." Eros is revealed as a powerful uniting principle that urges human beings toward connection with persons, objects, or ideas that are "bearers of values." The erotic drives us "towards union with the forms of nature and culture and with the divine sources of both" (*LPJ,* 22, 30).

A striking characteristic of the erotic in Tillich's understanding is the variety of possible objects of erotic feeling, ranging from other humans to ideas, to natural objects and those fashioned by human skill, to the divine source of all being. Eros seems capable of absorbing all human forms of love into itself. In some passages, Tillich explicitly acknowledges that the word can be used in this way, as a global term embracing and drawing together all aspects of human love experience (*ST* 3:137, 240). Eros is a "higher form" of love, recognized as such by philosophers from Plato onward. Yet eros also partakes explicitly of the libidinal/sexual quality of love, which is present in each expression of the erotic, including the most elevated and sublime (*LPJ,* 30). Eros functions for Tillich as a concept that can embrace feelings and experiences traditionally thought of in widely separated areas of human life. Eros offers a category that reconciles the "higher" and "lower" aspects of love and desire. Thus, it unites dimensions of the personality and modes of experience which dualistic theological schemes and the work of the theological "moralists" and denigrators of culture have tried to keep separate.

Tillich does continue to insist on the usefulness of making distinctions among the qualities of love. Nevertheless, he sees the relationship of eros to the other qualities in terms of mutual reinforcement and creative intermingling.

Although eros "transcends *epithymia,*" *epithymia* as the desire for physical reunion "underlies the eros as well as the philia quality of love" (*LPJ,* 30, 33). Eros is at the same time "in a polar way related" to philia. "While eros represents the transpersonal pole, philia represents the personal pole" (*LPJ,* 31). Eros aims at values that transcend the personal identities of the individuals in a particular relationship. Philia, on the other hand, signifies for Tillich a type of relation that focuses primarily on the individual personality. It is a "person-to-person love between equals" (*LPJ,* 118). However, Tillich claims, the eros and philia impulses do not oppose or negate each other. Rather, they are "in a polar way interdependent." Neither of them is "possible without the other. There is eros quality in philia. And there is philia quality in eros."

Without the "radical separation of the self-centered self," the individual integrity upon which philia is founded, "neither the creative nor the religious eros is possible." Eros, while reaching beyond the individual, depends on the affirmation of unique individual personhood that is nourished by philia. At the same time, Tillich claims that concepts such as interpersonal "participation and communion" indicate the "eros quality" that is present and necessary in "every philia relation." Person-to-person philia is itself rooted in an erotic "desire to unite with another power of being which is most separated and most understandable." This "power of being," at once mysterious and familiar, can only be expressed through human personhood, in a personal being that "radiates possibilities and realities of the good and the true in the manifestation of its incomparable individuality" (*LPJ,* 31–32). Tillich argues that every human relationship includes both "personal" and "transpersonal" elements. Each authentic relation between individuals affirms and strengthens the autonomous personhood of the participants and is dependent upon this personal element. Yet all such healthy relationships also reach beyond the personal identities of the individuals directly involved in them. Authentic, creative human relations, Tillich claims, include a dimension of value which transcends the individual concerns and private interests. This dimension of value, through which human relational connections reach toward and reflect the divine, is opened to us by eros (cf. *MB,* 60–61).

In his "ontology of love," Tillich waits until the final pages to discuss "the quality of love which dominates the New Testament, the agape quality." This is not, Tillich claims, because agape is to be regarded as the "last and highest form of love," incompatible with the other qualities, but because "agape enters from another dimension into the whole of life and into all qualities of love" (*LPJ,* 33). Agape is not irreconcilable with *epithymia,* philia, and eros. On the contrary, as an energy of divine love, "love cutting into love," agape enters into all of these forms and "elevates" them. In the "holy community" founded on divine love, agape "cuts into" eros and the other qualities of love and "raises them beyond the ambiguities of their self-centeredness" (*LPJ*, 116, 117). Thus, "one could say that in agape, ultimate reality manifests itself and transforms life and love" (*LPJ*, 33). The breakthrough of "ultimate reality" does not imply the negation or the denaturing of the existing world. Agape does not deny or do away with the other forms of love. Instead, it "enters," "transforms," and brings them to completion.

The idea of divine agape entering the human plane "from another dimension" is an intriguing one. Among Tillich's many attempts to formulate clearly his understanding of the relationship between agape and the other qualities of love, this is one of the most appealing. Yet the actual mechanics of the transforming entry of agape into human life and love are not made explicit. Tillich does not discuss the details of how a supposedly disinterested, suprapersonal, divine love can in fact manifest itself in the human realm without either abolishing the human quality of relationships, or else undergoing a modification of its own nature. Agape reshapes and elevates the other forms of love. Yet Tillich maintains that this relationship does not imply that the other forms of love are somehow "inferior." What, then, does agape contribute? How does it elevate human love without denying the original character of that love?

This problem can be addressed with the classic model of agape as a form of relationship that always involves not just two parties (lover and beloved), but three poles: the human participants and God. "Agape unites the lover and the beloved because of the image of fulfilment which God has of both" (*ST* 1:280). We love the other person in God and through the love that God instills and awakens in us. Thus, agape can be described as a "type of love which seeks the other because of the ultimate unity of being with being within the divine ground" (*ST* 1:280-81). Agape raises the other forms of human affection above their "self-centeredness" by centering them on the divine (*LPJ*, 116, 119). Yet in the idea of agape entering human life "from another dimension" and "raising" human love above its "ambiguities," echoes of a dualistic construction creep in. Purifying relationships of their ambiguity by centering them on God risks decentering and devaluing them as *human* relationships. Tillich insists that agape neither negates nor devalues the other qualities of love. Yet the otherness of agape reinstates a

hierarchy of values. The connection between human passion and dispassionate agape with its source in the divine nature remains problematic.

The tensions surrounding the relationship of agape to the other
forms of love are never fully resolved in Tillich's writings. What is
clear is that Tillich believes agape and eros, the "disinterested" divine
and the passionate human dimensions of love, can and must be united.
Whatever the conceptual difficulties connected with this view, its immediate effect is to enhance the importance of the erotic. The idea of
the necessary union of agape and eros implies that eros communicates
directly with the divine, that the erotic forms a part, at least, of a
bridge connecting human existence to the healing power of God. This
claim, as will be stressed in the next chapter, was far from routine in
the Protestant theological circles of Tillich's day (or of our own, for
that matter). It may indeed be true, as some theologians have maintained, that traditional Christian, or at least Protestant, theological
categories cannot sustain the tensions involved in the effort to reconcile
eros with agape. This effort may literally tear a traditional theological
system apart. But Tillich is willing to take the risk. He refuses to
abandon the idea that human beings' experiences of eros open for them
forms of healing connectedness to ultimate reality: connections
through which human alienation from the divine is (fragmentarily)
transcended.

The ontological perspective Tillich adopts implies not only the
underlying unity of the different qualities of love, but also a fundamental and necessary connection between love in all its forms and the
concepts of power and justice. "If love is understood in its ontological
nature," Tillich asserts, "its relation to justice and power is seen in a
light which reveals the basic unity of the three concepts" and shows
the conflicts among them to be of a contingent, "conditioned character" (LPJ, 24).

Tillich's discussion of power is conceived in explicit opposition to
interpretations that would set power equal to force or coercion. Tillich
defines power in terms of the "possibility of overcoming non-being."
Power is the mode of the natural and necessary "self-affirmation of
life" (LPJ, 40, 37). Love as the moving force of life is not opposed to
power, but intimately and inevitably bound up with it. "The power
of being is not dead identity, but the dynamic process" in which being
"separates itself from itself and returns to itself." Love is defined as
"the process in which the separated is reunited." Thus, "love is the
foundation, not the negation of power" (LPJ, 48–49).

Justice, Tillich claims, is "the form in which the power of being actualizes itself" (*LPJ*, 56). Love, then, ontologically united with power, cannot be considered in isolation from justice. Love is the "ultimate principle" of justice. "Love reunites; justice preserves that which is to be reunited." Justice "is the form in which and through which love performs its work" (*LPJ*, 71). In their ontological nature, love, power, and justice are inextricably woven together. It is impossible to understand one of these phenomena without direct reference to the others.

In *Love, Power, and Justice* and other works of philosophical theology, Tillich sets up an ontological framework in which all forms of love must be explicitly correlated with questions of justice and power, and in which the different qualities of love cannot be radically separated from one another. Agape as the "self-transcending element of love" is not cut off from the other elements: "*epithymia*—the libido quality of love, philia—the friendship quality of love, and eros—the mystical quality of love." The distinct qualities form a cohesive whole. "In all of them, what we have called 'the urge toward the reunion of the separated' is effective" (*MB*, 40).

The drawing-together of all aspects of love—passionate and dispassionate, conditioned and transcendent, sensuous and spiritual, human and divine—is the goal Tillich tries to attain with his theory of love's "ontological unity." By linking the qualities of love at the ontological level, Tillich implies that there is a profound continuity among the different types of human activity which have traditionally been associated with libido, philia, agape, and eros. The ontological framework offers a structure in which eros unfolds wide-ranging powers. The erotic does not designate for Tillich an isolated sphere of warmth and intimacy cut off from other domains of human experience. Its connections to the other qualities of love, to power, and to justice suggest that eros is a force woven through the whole fabric of human life.

Tillich makes a leap of radical theological importance by pointing to eros as a form of love in which a broad range of what have traditionally been described as "higher" and "lower" types of experience—love for God, communal ties and cultural creativity, communion with nature, libidinal desire and sexuality—are brought together in a nonhierarchical constellation. Linked with one another under the heading of eros, these forms of experience and practice—seemingly disparate, perhaps even antithetical—may in fact emerge as intimately interrelated means of connection-making within human life.

2
Chapter

Puritans, Freudians, and the Classical Eros

> But eros is a broad river that overflows its banks, carrying everything away with it, so that it is not easy, even in thought, to dam it up and make it flow in an orderly course.
> —Anders Nygren

Many of Paul Tillich's most important ideas were shaped and refined through dialogue with other leading intellectual and cultural figures of his day, from Karl Barth to Martin Heidegger, from T. S. Eliot to Albert Einstein. In his thinking about love, and in particular his inquiry into eros and its relation to the other aspects of love, Tillich did not work in an intellectual vacuum. He formed his vision of eros and libido as qualities of an ontologically unified love principle in part by reacting against the positions of two of his prominent contemporaries. These authors' ideas had exerted a powerful influence on discussions of love and sexuality both within and beyond their respective fields. The theological and cultural understandings of eros with which Tillich was familiar—and which he sought to transform—were significantly shaped by the work of these two men. The first was the Swedish bishop and theologian Anders Nygren. The second was Sigmund Freud.

Nygren and the agape–eros antithesis

Nygren's theories on the nature of love and religious experience, presented in his monumental work *Agape*

19

and Eros, exerted a deep and lasting influence on Christian, especially
Protestant, thought in the middle decades of the twentieth century.
Originally published in Stockholm in 1930, the first part of *Agape and
Eros* had within a few years been translated into German, English, and
other languages. Its impact on theological discussions within European
and North American Protestantism was powerful. Nygren's reading
of eros and agape as radically opposed principles set the agenda for a
generation of Protestant reflection on human and divine love and the
relationship between them. Even those Protestant thinkers who, like
Tillich, disagreed emphatically with Nygren's conclusions were
obliged to react to his arguments and to a certain extent to adopt his
vocabulary.

Nygren presents agape and eros not simply as qualitatively distinct
forms of love, but as historical and theological principles that by nature
are completely antithetical, one another's most "dangerous rivals."[1]
The two terms, *agape* and *eros,* designate radically opposed "general
attitudes to life," locked in a relentless struggle for dominance throughout humankind's religious history. "At every point in the history of
the spiritual life," Nygren claims, the two principles grapple in explicit
or implicit conflict as "each of them strives to put its stamp on the
spiritual life as a whole" (Nygren, 34).

The "theocentric type" of religion associated with agape has never,
Nygren writes, "been wholly lacking." Yet "not until Christianity
does it break decisively through and claim supremacy" (Nygren, 206).
For all intents and purposes, the agapic love described in the writings
of Paul "comes to us," Nygren insists, "as a quite new creation of
Christianity." Agape constitutes the "fundamental motif" that defines
the Christian message and the Christian way of life as such. Agape
"sets its mark on everything in Christianity. Without it, nothing that
is Christian would be Christian" (Nygren, 48). Christian *"fellowship
with God is distinguished from all other kinds by the fact that it depends
exclusively on God's agape."* Agapic love, which flows "downward"
from God to human beings, is *"spontaneous and unmotivated,"* having
no ground or motive outside the divine nature itself. It is *"indifferent
to value"* in its human objects, yet it can and does create value in those
who receive it. "The man who is loved by God has no value in himself;
what gives him value is precisely the fact that God loves him." In all

---

[1]Anders Nygren, *Agape and Eros,* trans. Philip Watson (Philadelphia: Westminster
Press, 1953), 162. Further references to *Agape and Eros* will be cited parenthetically in
the text.

cases, *"Agape is the initiator of fellowship with God."* There is *"from man's side no way at all that leads to God"* (Nygren, 75–81, italics in original).

The eros motif, which has characterized "practically all religious life outside of Christianity" is the "born rival of the idea of Agape" (Nygren, 59–61). "Eros and Agape are the characteristic expressions of two . . . fundamentally opposed types of religion and ethics. They represent two streams that run throughout the whole history of religion, alternately clashing against one another and mingling with one another" (Nygren, 205). Within Christianity itself, Eros "exerts its influence and shows itself throughout history" as the opponent of the agape principle, on which it consistently exerts "solvent effects" (Nygren, 49, 39). Such effects become particularly evident in those types of Christian (more specifically Catholic) theology which have attempted to reconcile eros and agape. The most conspicuous of these efforts is associated with Augustine and the medieval church. Augustine's understanding of love as *caritas* represents in Nygren's view a synthesis of eros and agapic elements, in which the eros strain is clearly predominant.

For Nygren, eros does not, of course, mean sex. "Between Vulgar Eros [sexual love] and Christian Agape," he affirms, "there is no relation at all." It would be utterly useless to attempt to correlate human sexual desire with the divine agape. Between these two themes there are no resemblances whatsoever, no points of contact that would even permit a comparison (Nygren, 51). The historical, philosophical, and religious "eros motif" that Nygren wishes to describe is itself a highly spiritualized phenomenon.

Nygren characterizes the religious attitude conditioned by the eros principle in the following terms: In the erotic or "egocentric type" of religion, "the religious relationship is dominated essentially by man. The distance between man and the Divine is not insuperable. Man is akin to the Deity, or is maybe himself a divine being." Therefore, for the human being to "come to himself" is at the same time to "come to the Divine; and therein lies man's true end, his satisfaction and blessedness." According to this erotic model of the spiritual life, "it is possible for man to mount up successively toward an ever-increasing likeness to God, and to draw step by step nearer the Divine" (Nygren, 205). Such a view of religion as rooted in human beings' own feelings, passions, and efforts contrasts radically with the theocentric model founded on agape as God's own free, unmotivated creation, that is, with the type of religious attitude which Nygren regards as specifically and authentically Christian.

"At every point," Nygren states, the opposition between the two principles makes itself felt. "Eros is acquisitive desire and longing. Agape is sacrificial giving. Eros is an upward movement. Agape comes down. Eros is man's way to God. Agape is God's way to man." The Eros principle is primarily human love. "Even when it is attributed to God," Eros is patterned on human feeling. Agape, on the other hand, "is primarily God's love." The energy of eros "is determined by the quality, the beauty and the worth of its object; it is not spontaneous, but 'evoked,' 'motivated.' " Agape, however, is "sovereign in relation to its object." It is "spontaneous, 'overflowing,' 'unmotivated' " (Nygren, 209–10).

In the second part of *Agape and Eros*, Nygren explores in detail the history of Christian teachings on the nature of love, tracing the evolution of the conflict between the "fundamental motifs" of erotic and agapic love, and examining the misguided attempts to work out a reconciling synthesis between them. He regards the shattering of this debilitating synthesis as the great achievement of the Protestant Reformation. "Luther had observed," Nygren notes, "how the whole of the Catholic doctrine of love," colored by late antique and medieval thinkers' efforts to fuse agape with eros, "displays an *egocentric perversion*." Against this "*egocentric attitude which had come to mark the Catholic conception of love, Luther sets a thoroughly theocentric idea of love*" (Nygren, 683, italics in original). By reviving and bringing forward again in its pure form the New Testament concept of agape, Luther abolished "that interpretation of Christian love which finds expression in the idea of Caritas, which fundamentally contains more Hellenistic Eros-love than primitive Christian Agape-love" (Nygren, 739). Luther "shattered" the synthetic understanding of love elaborated by Augustine and confirmed by the theologians of the Middle Ages. This radical reseparation of eros from agape is for Nygren the great triumph and the "meaning of the Reformation" (Nygren, 684).

Tillich's response to Nygren

Against the background of Anders Nygren's influential theory of the antithetical relation between eros and agape, Tillich's unconventional treatment of eros stands out boldly. While appealing, as Nygren had also done, to ideas developed in the literature of the Reformation, Tillich drew final conclusions about the nature of human erotic love and its relation to the divinely created agape which were diametrically opposed to Nygren's views.

Tillich does not mention Nygren by name in his more important discussions of the qualities of love, but his language makes perfectly clear to whom his criticisms are addressed. His treatments of the erotic bear the unmistakable marks of his vigorous polemical engagement with the Swedish bishop's ideas. Nygren's influence was at its height in the 1950s, when Tillich wrote many of his major texts on love. The depiction of agape and eros as antagonistic principles had become a point of dogma in neo-orthodox circles. Tillich missed no opportunity to criticize this idea, which he saw as a profoundly destructive misconception.

In the first volume of *Systematic Theology,* Tillich attacks the doctrine of an "irreconcilable conflict between eros and agape," which obscures theologians' understanding of the true relation between the human and the divine (*ST* 1:281). In *Love, Power, and Justice,* he lashes out once again at misguided "attempts to establish an absolute contrast between eros and agape." "If the eros quality of love with respect to God is rejected, the consequence of this rejection is that love toward God becomes an impossible concept" and must be "replaced by mere obedience to God." Obedience, however, "is not love. It can be the opposite of love." If human beings' erotic desire for reunion with their divine origin is left out of account in analyzing the religious life and the theological concepts that shape it, Tillich concludes, "then love toward God becomes a meaningless word" (*LPJ,* 30).

Although such a description does not entirely do justice to Nygren's understanding of the concept of eros, Tillich asserts that the efforts to pit eros and agape against one another "usually presuppose" an erroneous "identification of eros and *epithymia,*" the latter being interpreted primarily as the desire for sexual satisfaction. This perspective, Tillich claims, contains an element of truth in that it acknowledges the presence of *epithymia* in eros; as a direct identification it is patently false, since eros includes but at the same time transcends *epithymia.*

Even more importantly, however, Tillich suggests, such a view fails to recognize the true nature of *epithymia*/libido, presenting as a fundamentally irrational and amoral drive for sexual release what is in fact a natural and necessary "desire for vital self-fulfilment" on the part of human beings, a desire whose life-affirming aims transcend the basic physical tensions and impulses of sexual appetite. Correctly interpreted, Tillich insists, *epithymia* and eros do not clash with one another, and the two of them should not be understood as necessarily antithetical to agape. Like eros, "*epithymia* is a quality which is not lacking in any love relation," even the most elevated and spiritual (*LPJ,* 30).

Tillich's more trenchant polemical statements in response to Nygren and his followers appear in *Morality and Beyond.* Here he sounds again the theme of the ontological unity of love, insisting that, "love is one, even if one of its qualities predominates. None of the qualities is ever completely absent." Tillich takes a vigorous dig at neo-orthodox theology's condescending attitude toward classical philosophy and mysticism, which Nygren in particular portrays primarily as foreign bodies compromising the purity of New Testament Christianity. "There is," Tillich asserts, "eros in agape, and agape in eros." It is this intimate connection between the types of love that "permitted Christianity to receive into itself the eros-created classical culture, both rational and mystical." The "agape element in eros . . . prevents culture from becoming a non-serious, merely transitory entertainment, just as eros prevents agape from becoming a moralistic turning away from the creative potentialities in nature and in man." A hierarchical ranking of divine agape above the other forms of love necessarily brings about such a "turning away" from human reality and from the created world. This ultimately leads to a "commitment to a God who can only be feared or obeyed, but not loved. For without eros toward the ultimate good there is no love toward God" (*MB,* 40–41).

Tillich repeatedly insists that agape and eros are not the same thing and that agapic love cannot simply be replaced by human eros. He distinguishes between the two aspects of love, giving precedence and ultimate authority to the agape quality, which "transcends the finite possibilities of man." "Paul indicates this in his great hymn to love (1 Corinthians 13) when he describes agape as the highest work of the divine Spirit, and as an element of the eternal life, even beyond faith and hope" (*MB,* 40). As will become clear in the next chapter, some of Tillich's discussions of eros and agape break down the barriers between them to the point where it seems that the two terms are practically identical in their experiential content. Yet in the theological framework within which Tillich moves, the idea of a simple fusion of eros and agape is unacceptable. Agape, as God's love, remains distinct from eros, even if, in human life, agapic and erotic elements inevitably appear together. Tillich's passionate insistence on love's underlying unity awakens the suspicion that *agape* and *eros* might be, after all, simply two labels for what can only be, in the realm of

possible human experience, a single, undifferentiated reality. But Tillich explicitly draws back from this synthesis. While the terms *eros*
and *agape* point to expressions of a principle that is one in its essence,
the differences between these expressions of love should not, he claims,
be ignored.

Like Nygren, Tillich invokes the names of Paul and the Reformers
in discussing eros, agape, and the relation of human reality and human
love experience to the divine. He affirms the Reformation principle
that "man, in relation to God, cannot do anything without him. He
must receive in order to act." Human beings' efforts at "self-salvation"
are doomed to failure (*ST* 2:80f.). Men and women cannot control
or order their destructive "compulsions," Tillich states, "except by
the power of that which happens to [them] in the root of these compulsions," that is, through God's loving intervention and healing grace.
"This psychological truth is also a religious truth, the truth of the
'bondage of the will,' " described by Paul and Luther (*ST* 2:79–80).
The act of grace by which the healing and reuniting force of authentic
love enters the realm of human life can only be, Tillich stresses, God's
act. "Decisive in all situations" in which the different dimensions of
love interconnect is agape, the free creation of the Spiritual Presence
that as such "transcends the finite limits of human love. Therefore in
any conflict of the qualities of love, agape is the determining element"
(*MB*, 42).

In contrast to Nygren and his school, however, Tillich does not
see a "conflict of the qualities of love" as inevitable. He claims that
human eros can be joined creatively with the agape shaped by the
divine Spirit. Indeed, such a union must take place if human beings
are to know a love toward God which is more than fear or blind
obedience. He affirms that in human experience under the healing
influence of the Spiritual Presence, defined as "the presence of the
Divine Life within creaturely life" (*ST* 3:107), eros and agape unite
with and complement one another. Agape completes and heals eros,
"making the cultural eros responsible and the mystical eros personal"
(*LPJ*, 118). At the same time, the erotic forces prevent agape from
degenerating into an ascetic moralism (*MB*, 40).

The impact of divine grace does not "create a being who is unconnected with the one who receives grace" (*ST* 2:79). The rupture
between the divine and the realm of created reality and of human life
is not as radical as it is made to seem by theologians who "depreciate
culture" and "deny a mystical element in man's relation to God" (*LPJ*,

30). Feelings and decisions on the human level do not in and of themselves "bring reunion with God." Yet "even these decisions, despite the ambiguity of all the structures of life, are related to the unambiguous and ultimate" (*ST* 2:79). In the same way, the divine love that transforms and saves is not "unconnected" with human love but related to it in a positive way. Tillich's concept of the New Being points to the healing of creaturely life and the love that animates it, not to their negation. The New Being is a "restorative principle": the "undistorted manifestation of essential being within and under the conditions of existence," brought to fulfillment in Jesus as the Christ (*ST* 2:119). Our "union with God" in the New Being produces the possibility of a "new action" in our lives, including a transformation of our capacity to interact lovingly with the world, and thus to experience joy through a fulfilled relationship to the divine and to our own human being (*ST* 2:80).

Under the heading "ultimate concern," Tillich places human desire and yearning at the center of his understanding of spiritual experience. "Ultimate concern" as the fundamental religious disposition is not an independent creation of the human psyche, but is awakened, created within the human being by the impact of the Spiritual Presence. Such concern is "unconditional, independent of any conditions of character, desire, circumstance." Yet Tillich continually describes ultimate concern in a vocabulary rich with evocations of passionate desire: "The unconditional concern is total; no part of ourselves or our world is excluded from it." It is "infinite: no moment of rest or relaxation is possible." The object of such concern is "the object of total surrender," of "infinite passion and interest." Indeed, the "object of religion" cannot be known outside of the "passion and interest" that characterize ultimate concern: "We cannot speak adequately of the 'object of religion' without simultaneously removing its character as an object. That which is ultimate gives itself only to the attitude of ultimate concern" (*ST* 1:12).

Tillich moves toward what amounts to a combined theological rehabilitation of material desire and of the religious eros by claiming that the religious passion experienced as ultimate concern stands in a positive relation to other, seemingly more mundane forms of desire and appetite. The connection between these types of desire and religious passion is not presented as one of antagonism, much less of mutual exclusion. Rather, the true "relation between the ultimate concern and the preliminary concerns makes the latter bearers and vehicles of the former." Finite desires "are not elevated to infinite significance, nor [are they] put beside the infinite." However, "in and through them the infinite becomes real" (*ST* 1:13). Tillich's assertion is a daring and a deeply significant one: Our relation to God is realized, expressed, embodied "in and through" our connections to the finite world.

Tillich insists that ultimate concern with the meaning of human existence and thus with human beings' relation to the unconditioned is a spiritual disposition vastly more important than careful observation of religio-legal precepts, codes, and rituals, or intellectual adherence to a set of dogmas. Intellectual assent to creedal doctrines is not the decisive criterion for membership in the community of faith. "The criterion of one's belonging to a church and through it to the Spiritual Community is the *serious desire,* conscious or unconscious, to participate in the life of a group which is based on the New Being as it has appeared in Jesus as the Christ" (*ST* 3:175; emphasis added).

In his homiletic texts and in his books, Tillich repeats tirelessly that the passion with which one earnestly desires participation in the New Being is the proof that one has already been grasped by the Spiritual Presence. "If the question—What can I do in order to experience the New Being?—is asked with existential seriousness, the answer is implied in the question, for existential seriousness is evidence of the impact of the Spiritual Presence upon an individual." One who is "ultimately concerned about his state of estrangement and about the possibility of reunion with the ground and aim of his being is already in the grip of the Spiritual Presence" (*ST* 3:223).

It is no accident that one of the theological authorities to whom Tillich appeals regularly in developing his views on the relationship between eros and agape, between human yearning and divine love, is Augustine. Anders Nygren had criticized Augustine as in a direct way responsible for the misguided tendency to introduce personal, anthropocentric elements into Christian agape, and thus to blend agape with Platonic eros. Nygren and Tillich both responded strongly, though in diametrically opposed ways, to Augustine's evocation of *caritas* in terms of passionate human desire.

Augustine's idea of caritas is, as Nygren rightly points out, essentially based on human "love to God," a love into the poetic evocation of which Augustine "pours the whole passion of his soul" (*Agape and Eros,* 453). "Our hearts are restless, Lord, until they find repose in You."[2] For Augustine, as Roland Delattre observes, "the problem is

---

[2]Augustine, *Confessiones/Bekenntnisse* (München: Kösel, 1966), 12.

not to uproot or transcend desire, which is an essential mark of our humanity and of our belonging to God." Rather, it is necessary in Augustine's view to "order all objects of desire in accordance with their true relation to God, the *summum bonum*," in whom alone "our restless hearts will find the satisfaction of their deepest desires."[3] Tillich's understanding of ultimate concern opens a similar perspective by showing how "preliminary concerns" are not suppressed or negated but ordered in relation to the final concern, the ultimate longing awakened in the human heart by the impact of the Spiritual Presence. In contrast to Nygren, Tillich accepts as proper and indeed necessary Augustine's reconciliation of divine love with the driving power of human passion.

In a considered departure from the Augustinian position, however, Tillich attempts to conceptualize human longing for fulfillment in God in a manner that does not denigrate or render superfluous the other forms of love which govern our relations with the created world. He wishes his recognition of erotic elements in human love toward God to be read as offering both a persuasive account of the passionate character of ultimate concern and an implicit affirmation and honoring of more worldly forms of eros and desire. He explicitly condemns Augustine's identification of sinful concupiscence with sexual desire interpreted as perverted in its essence (*ST* 2:52).

Far from excluding desire and eros, Tillich argues that the highest forms of love receive erotic and libidinal elements into themselves and use these elements to draw human beings into a more perfect relation with the divine. Ultimate concern, as an erotically charged love toward God, orients human life toward its ultimate fulfillment in reunion with the unconditioned ground and source of all being. Yet this ultimate orientation should not, Tillich claims, imply contempt for or neglect of the types of love which connect us to the world.

In rejecting Nygren's doctrine of a radical conflict between eros and agape, Tillich also opposes the neo-orthodox principle of an unbridgeable separation between divinity and the fallen world. "Being as such is good," Tillich insists, and elements of the essential goodness of creation and of human nature survive even under the reign of estrangement. Transcending the existential split "is a possibility in man's existential situation," although this transcendence must remain

---

[3]Roland Delattre, "Desire," *The Encyclopedia of Religion* (New York: Macmillan, 1987), 4:312.

"fragmentary," "anticipatory" (*ST* 3:243). Under the impact of the Spiritual Presence, the alienation characterizing human existence can be —"fragmentarily"—overcome in reunion through love. In contrast to the radically transcendent concept of agape defended by Nygren, Tillich sees no essential opposition between the "ultimate" forms of love and "preliminary" concerns and relationships, no necessary conflict between agapic love as the spontaneous creation of the Spiritual Presence and the forms of erotic, libidinal, and philial love and involvement which anchor us as embodied creatures in the material world.

In his opposition to Nygren's views, Tillich articulates a bold and sweeping affirmation of human passion and embodied human love relationships. Where Nygren had seen a radical opposition between agape and the "Heavenly Eros," and claimed that between agapic love and sexual desire there is "no relationship at all," Tillich insists that agape, eros, philia, and libido form a "multidimensional unity." At the essential level, "Love is one. Its different qualities belong to each other" (*MB,* 41–42). Espousing the point of view which Nygren had associated with the mystical or "egocentric" principle of eros, Tillich denies that human beings who are the objects of God's love have no value in themselves. He is convinced that in coming to themselves human beings do in fact "come to the divine." In expressing our nature as erotic beings, we come into the power of divine love.

Tillich attaches importance to showing that there is no necessary conflict between human "self-fulfillment" and a whole, healed relationship with the ground of being. Indeed, he argues that the two developments—the human being's self-realization and her or his spiritual fulfillment through reunion with the divine source—are different sides of the same fundamental process. The completion or fulfillment of the human self and a healed relationship between the human and the divine are two ways of naming the same state of being.

Agape does not negate the "normal drive towards vital self-fulfillment" implied in the libidinal and erotic forms of love. Rather, the impact of agape raises the other forms of love out of their "ambiguities" and restores the essential aspect under which there is no contradiction between self-fulfillment and participation in the other being. The New Being as a spiritual "process" drives, Tillich claims, "toward a mature relatedness. The divine Spirit has rightly been described as the power of breaking through the walls of self-seclusion." Yet the type of "relatedness" shaped by the New Being embraces and requires "self-relatedness" at the same time that it opens us to "find the other person"

(*ST* 3:233–35). The ultimate form of self-fulfillment comes in the reunion of the personal self with the God who is the "principle of participation as well as the principle of individualization" (*ST* 1:245).

The false theological assertion of an "irreconcilable conflict between eros and agape," Tillich writes, should not be allowed to mask the fundamental truth that human beings find not the negation, but the completion of their personal being in their relationship to God, and that they long for this fulfillment in an explicitly erotic manner (*ST* 1:281). Thus, Tillich uses the language of eros to shape a description of the religious life that emphasizes the relational character of spiritual fulfillment. Participation in the New Being, expressed through the erotic desire of ultimate concern, brings us into a new relationship with the divine "source and aim" of being. Yet this relation does not swallow up or abolish human personhood. The integrity of the person is an essential part of this healed connection between the human and the divine. Personal "self-relatedness" is maintained and strengthened as the person finds and draws on the empowering force of integration into the New Being.

Tillich's most important claim—and the idea that most clearly marks his radical opposition to Nygren—is that the healed relationship between human beings and God "becomes real" in and through the relationships of concern which connect people to one another and to the world (*ST* 1:13). Participation in the New Being, right relationship to God, cannot be realized in isolation from our human, worldly relationships. The New Being as the manifestation of essential being under the conditions of existence moves us toward a relational maturity that does not limit itself to our spiritual connection to the divine. Tillich explicitly affirms (*ST* 3:233–35) that the New Being necessarily and by its very nature opens us to deepened relationships with other persons. Participation in the New Being is a relational transformation in which a changed relation to God and a healed relationship to the world are inextricably interwoven.

This is the intuition that Tillich articulates in his doctrine of the necessary union of eros and agape. In his rejection of Nygren's views and his insistence that agape without eros risks turning the love of God into a "meaningless word," Tillich's basic concern is clear. Agape represents for Tillich love free from "repulsion and attraction," directly created by the Spiritual Presence. It symbolizes by extension the divine-human relation as theologically conceived in terms of a "spiritual" link qualitatively different from our vital relational connections in ordinary life. Eros, meanwhile, evokes the passion and desire that on the human side link us to one another, to culture, and to the physical world, and that urge us at the same time to seek fulfillment in reunion with the divine. Tillich's claim is that outside of the matrix of erotic connections that give shape to our humanness, the "spiritual" connection to a higher power is indeed a "meaningless word," a fully abstract concept empty of significance for human life. Only when it is integrated into the weave of our erotic connections does spiritual, agapic love "become real" for us.

The abstractness of Tillich's own way of describing the union of agape and eros may undercut somewhat the vitality of the synthesis to which he points. Yet the importance and the radicality of Tillich's fundamental intuition should not be neglected: divine love without human eros is a hollow concept.

Freud: endless libido and the death instinct

A second author whose work left a deep mark on Tillich's theory of the erotic was Sigmund Freud. Tillich's intellectual relationship with Freud was very different from his relationship with Nygren. Where his acerbic criticisms of the anti-erotic doctrines of "theologians who denigrate culture" expressed a sweeping rejection of Nygren's ideas, his attitude toward Freud was fundamentally one of admiration. Tillich viewed many aspects of Freudian theory in an extremely positive light and was convinced that Freud's writings offered anthropological insights of decisive importance for theology.

Nevertheless, Tillich's approach to the teachings of psychoanalysis was not one of total and uncritical acceptance. His affirming view was tempered by criticism of what he perceived as philosophical shortcomings in Freud's work. Tillich took issue with what he saw as unjustified "pessimism" in the Freudian view of the human situation, but he was grateful for the insights into basic desires and personality structures offered by Freud and his followers. Freud's "new insights into the deeper levels of human nature have rediscovered," Tillich argues, the "Biblical realism" in connection with human behavior and motivation. The Bible's realistic grasp of basic psychology had been covered in European theology by "several strata of idealistic and moralistic self-deception about man" (LPJ, 116–17). Freudian investigations open the way for a more lucid theological understanding of human nature in harmony with the wisdom of the biblical authors.

Although limited by Freud's lack of an adequate metaphysical framework for interpreting his own findings, the insights of psychoanalysis can help theology to overcome its tendency toward prudish moralism. Using Freud's ideas, theologians can grasp more fully the authentic significance of the concept of sin. They can recognize the implications of the buried "demonic structures" of the unconscious mind which "determine our consciousness and our decisions." Such a recognition does not, Tillich believes, imply the acceptance of some form of pessimistic determinism. Yet "psychoanalysis and the whole philosophy of the unconscious" have performed a vital service by revealing "the totality of the personality in which not only the conscious elements are decisive." Psychoanalysis, like existentialist philosophy, has expressed ideas of "infinite value for theology" (*TC*, 123–24).

Tillich is convinced that both the positive significance and the limitations of Freud's libido theory can only be fully grasped if Freud's understanding of human nature is interpreted in light of the metaphysical framework developed in the Western philosophical and theological tradition. He writes,

> In the Christian tradition there are three fundamental concepts. First: *Esse qua esse bonum est.* This Latin phrase is a basic dogma of Christianity. It means "Being as being is good," or in the biblical mythological form: God saw everything he had created, and behold, it was good. The second statement is the universal fall—fall meaning the transition from this essential goodness into existential estrangement from oneself, which happens in every living being and in every time. The third statement refers to the possibility of salvation (*TC*, 118–19).

These three aspects of human nature are "present in all genuine theological thinking: essential goodness, existential estrangement, and the possibility of something, a 'third' beyond essence and existence through which the cleavage is overcome and healed." If one fails, Tillich warns, to "distinguish these three elements," one will inevitably "fall into innumerable confusions." The criticisms Tillich raises against Freud's theories are based on this "tripartite view of human nature" and "directed against the confusion of these three fundamental elements" (*TC*, 119). The error at the root of Freud's pessimism is his having taken data concerning one aspect of human being as if these data applied to human nature in all three of its dimensions.

"Estrangement," the intermediate stage between divinely created essence and final salvation, characterizes human existence in the aftermath of the fall, under the domination of sin and ultimate death.

If, Tillich claims, Freud's theories are seen as applying *only* to this dimension of human experience, then they become valuable tools for theologians in their efforts to analyze the existential aspect of the human situation. Read in this manner and against this metaphysical background, Freud's theory of the libido, like Friedrich Nietzsche's doctrine of the "will to power," can contribute to a "rediscovery of the Christian view of man's predicament" (*ST* 2:53).

"Libido in Freud," Tillich states, "is the unlimited desire of man to get rid of his biological, especially his sexual, tensions and to get pleasure from the discharge of these tensions." Freud has demonstrated, furthermore, that "libidinous elements are present" in all forms of human praxis, including the most abstract and "spiritual." Freud's "emphasis on these elements, which cannot be separated from man's sexual instincts, is justified and agrees with the realism of the Christian interpretation" of the human condition. Freud's views "should not be rejected in the name of dishonest pseudo-Christian taboos against sex." Freud "in his honest realism is more Christian than are these taboos" (*ST* 2:53–54).

In interpreting Freud's theory of libido from a theological perspective, Tillich makes use of the classical theological concept of concupiscence (*concupiscentia*), which he defines as "the unlimited desire to draw the whole of reality into one's self." The decisive quality of desire as concupiscence is in effect for Tillich the unlimited quality of that desire, its aim to absorb the "universe" into one individual's "finite particularity." This, Tillich claims, is the fundamental temptation for human beings in their "position between finitude and eternity. Every individual, since he is separated from the whole, desires reunion with the whole" and seeks to draw the world into his personal center. Concupiscence "refers to all aspects of man's relation to himself and his world. It refers to physical hunger as well as to sex, to knowledge as well as to power, to material wealth as well as to spiritual values" (*ST* 2:52).

Tillich asserts that *concupiscentia* is used in Christian theology "exactly as libido is used by Freud" (*TC*, 120). Freud has in fact formulated a precise description of concupiscence, showing the insatiable character of desire under estrangement, while reminding us that the libidinal drives pervade all relationships and all forms of human activity (*ST* 2:53–54).

Tillich finds particular significance in Freud's doctrine of the *Todestrieb*, death instinct, which emerges as a "consequence of concupiscence and of its never satisfied striving." The estranged human being is spurred on by "an infinite libido which can never be satisfied and which therefore produces the desire to get rid of oneself," the desire Freud has "called the death instinct. And this is true not only of the individual." It is also true of human beings' "relation to culture as a whole." Whole nations or civilizations can be seized in the grip of forces driving them toward self-destruction. In analyzing the death instinct, Tillich claims, Freud offers a sobering summary of estranged humanity's predicament: tormented by limitless concupiscence, the "pain of the never satisfied libido," life turns against itself and flies toward the negation of all desire in death.

Freudian libido and "essential eros"

Tillich holds that in laying bare the radical contradictions of the existential situation, Freud "saw more about human nature than all his followers, who, when they lost the existentialist element in Freud, went more to an essentialist and optimistic view of man." Indeed, in several passages, Tillich goes so far as to defend the original Freudian doctrines against a softening revisionism. He criticizes those psychoanalysts and thinkers—he specifically mentions C. G. Jung and Erich Fromm—who have rejected wholly or in part the doctrine of the *Todestrieb* and thus sought to camouflage the full depth of human alienation, suggesting naively that the cause of estrangement can somehow be removed by merely human means (*TC*, 119–21).[4]

In the state of existential estrangement, the perverted libido spins out an endless web of unfulfilled and unfulfillable cravings. Desire becomes a relentless search for pleasure unable to focus on a "definite object." Insofar as Freud's libido theory is taken as describing only this perverted aspect of desire as unlimited and ultimately self-destructive striving, "a theological interpreter of man's estrangement is," Tillich affirms, "well advised to follow Freud's analyses" (*ST* 2:53–54).

The difficulty with the Freudian scheme is that Freud himself failed to distinguish between the libidinal impulses as they express themselves under the conditions of estrangement and libido and eros in their nonalienated, essential state. "Freud in this respect was unclear, namely,

---

[4]Cf. Guyton Hammond, *Man in Estrangement* (Nashville: Vanderbilt University Press, 1955), 119.

he was not able to distinguish" between the human being's "essential and existential nature." This, Tillich asserts, "is a basic theological criticism, not of any special result" of Freud's thought, "but of his doctrine of man and the central intuition he has of man" (*TC,* 119).

Tillich argues that the concept of concupiscence must be understood as applying to human beings only under the aspect of estranged existence. "According to theological doctrine," human beings in their "essential goodness" are not subjected to concupiscence. They are free from the limitless pain of "indefinite libido." Essential love relationships are "directed to a definite special subject, to content, to somebody, to something." They are focused on a particular thing or person with which or with whom the individual is effectively "connected in love." Love can shape such essential connections through all of its forms and qualities: through eros, libido, and philia, as well as agape (*TC,* 120).

The fundamental flaw in Freud's theory, Tillich claims, is the interpretation of libido as motivated in all cases by the "desire for pleasure." Such a reading fails to grasp *epithymia*/libido in its role as one of the creative components of human love. This "hedonistic definition" of libido is, "like hedonism generally, based on a wrong psychology which is itself the consequence of a wrong ontology. Man strives to reunite himself with that to which he belongs and from which he has been separated. And this is true," Tillich affirms, "not only of man but of all living beings."

The fulfillment of fundamental libidinal drives—for example, the "desire" for "food, movement, growth, participation in a group, sexual union, etc."—is accompanied, in human beings as in other life forms, by pleasure. But "it is not the pleasure as such which is desired, but the reunion with that which fulfils the desire." By reducing libido, and with it the whole of human life, to the schema of a "pain-pleasure principle in the sense that life essentially consists of fleeing from pain and striving for pleasure," Freud has, Tillich is convinced, misrepresented the essence of the phenomenon of desire and of human love. "Only perverted life follows the pain-pleasure principle. Unperverted life strives for union with that which is separated from it." This analysis, Tillich believes, "should remove the prejudice toward libido." It provides the foundation for a "partial acceptance, partial rejection of Freud's libido theory" (*LPJ,* 29–30).

In formulating his theories of libido and the death instinct, Freud "omit[s] any reference to man's essential *eros*" (*ST* 2:53). His failure to recognize the essential dimension of human eros, or to distinguish between "libido as love" and "distorted" libidinal impulses is to be accounted for, Tillich suggests, by Freud's "puritanical attitude toward sex" (*ST* 2:54). Indeed, in his pessimistic conclusions about the nature of human sexuality and eros, the father of psychoanalysis "joins many Puritans," including, presumably, Nygren (*LPJ,* 29–30). Freud ultimately emerges, on Tillich's view, as "ascetic in his basic assumption about the nature of man" (*ST* 2:54).

Libido and eros must be considered not only within the horizon of existential estrangement, but also beyond it. Both theologians and psychologists must, Tillich asserts, take into account the essential nature of eros and the libidinal drives, and not simply their twisted expressions under the conditions of alienation. For theological thinking, it is particularly vital to explore the status of the erotic in connection with the "third dimension" in which the cleavage between essence and existence is overcome. This "third" is the "telos, aim, that for which and towards which [human] life drives" (*TC,* 119).

The concept of *essence* and the idea of the human *telos* as the return to an essential state are useful constructs for explaining the "from whence?" and the "where to?" of human being. As such, these ideas have of course been used extensively by Christian theologians and by secular philosophers. But Tillich does not understand the essential and telic dimensions of human life merely as useful abstractions that help hold together a metaphysical system. For him, essence and salvation or *telos* are also matters of lived experience. He does not posit a simple linear movement from essence to existence to final telos. While a linear movement within history is one part of his interpretation of these concepts, he also claims that there is a sense in which all three dimensions are present in human life at all times. "New creation," the breakthrough of the telic dimension, occurs here and now, "within the world of estrangement" (*LPJ,* 115–16). Transforming "revelation" is not, for Tillich, restricted to a bygone prophetic age or to an eschatological future. He speaks of the manifestation of the ultimate as an experiential reality, "the ecstatic manifestation of the Ground of Being" within real "events, persons, and things" (*ST* 2:166–67). This means that in Tillich's system, the "essence" in which creation is "good in itself" is not irrecoverably lost under the conditions of estranged existence. Nor is the *telos* of human being an intellectually perceived, but unreachable horizon.

All three of the dimensions are present, Tillich affirms, in each human being at every moment. Although the "three elements of human nature" must be carefully distinguished in theory, all three "always are together in all of us" (*TC,* 119). Thus the healed state in which the created goodness of love—including eros—is restored is not a mere theoretical possibility whose fulfilment is reserved for a transformed humanity inhabiting a distant future. On the contrary, Tillich affirms that such nonalienated love is possible for human beings here and now, insofar as under the impact of the Spiritual Presence they have been drawn implicitly into the life of the "Spiritual Community" (*ST* 3:155f.).

In discussing the essential and teleological functions and meanings of eros, a very different vocabulary must be employed from that proposed in Freudian theory. When the qualities of love are considered from the point of view of their essence, or again "in the light of the new creation within the world of estrangement," an image of eros and libido emerges which has very little to do with Freud's pessimistic descriptions. "Libido is good in itself!" Tillich proclaims. "We have defended it against Freud's depreciation of what he described as the infinite libidinous drive with its ensuing dissatisfaction and death instinct. We have accepted this as the description in estrangement, but not of libido in its creative meaning." In the "Spiritual Community," under the impact of transforming agape, libido is once again "elevated" beyond its alienated state. And "the same," Tillich affirms, "is true of eros" (*LPJ*, 116–17).

"The endlessness of libido," Tillich stresses again in the second volume of *Systematic Theology*, "is a mark of man's estrangement. It contradicts his essential or created goodness. In man's essential relationship to himself and his world," desire is not experienced as concupiscence. Essential "love does not exclude desire; it receives libido into itself." But the element of desire which is taken into healed, transformed love relationships (the "third" dimension) "is not infinite. It is directed, as all [authentic] love is, toward a definite subject."

Essential love, Tillich argues, "wants the other being." Concupiscence, on the other hand, seeks only "one's own pleasure through the other being," turning the other into a manipulable object. But in the healed state that represents the *telos* dimension of human love experience, and in which the existential rupture is overcome, love, "whether in the form of libido, eros, philia, or agape," opens affirmatively to the other, draws beings to one another in a manner that does not imply reification and domination. In the telic dimension, through the restoration of human beings' "essential nature, the desire to be united with the object of one's love for its own sake is effective. And this desire is not infinite, but definite. It is not concupiscence but love" (*ST* 2:54).

Agape as a form of "unambiguous love," which is "impossible for the human spirit by itself," is the central term Tillich employs in describing the breakthrough of the Spiritual Presence in human existence. Love is more than a "consequence" of the transformation and regeneration of the person through faith. Agape is rather "one side of the ecstatic state of being of which faith is the other." Whereas faith "is the state of being grasped by the Spiritual Presence," agapic "love is the state of being taken by the Spiritual Presence into the transcendent unity of unambiguous life" (*ST* 3:134–35).

Yet Tillich insists that agape does not abolish the structures associated with human life, human emotion and reason, human relationality. Even in its most sublime manifestations, the love that overcomes the existential split embraces and heals human reality, rather than seeking to negate it. Agape affirms the emotions, the volitional component of the personality, the intellectual functions, and human beings' embodiment and sexual nature. Authentic love, like faith, "is a state of the whole person" (*ST* 3:137).

The concept of a healed state of being connecting all dimensions of personhood moves Tillich's understanding of love far beyond the fragmented "pessimistic" views of Nygren and Freud. Tillich explicitly stresses eros's important integrating function in bringing such wholeness into being. In union with the "unambiguous love" created by the Spiritual Presence, eros connects body, mind, and spirit. Tillich writes of eros as the animating principle in the "relation of love and the intellectual function of the mind." He reminds readers that in Greek thought, eros is a driving force linking spirit to all domains of life. "In Aristotle the eros of everything moves the universe toward the pure form." In the concept of gnosis, the language of early Christianity retains traces of the idea of a unity between erotic love and the highest forms of knowledge and religious experience. In a similar way, "the German word *erkennen,* which means 'to know,' is also used for sexual union" (*ST* 3:136–37). These linguistic traces reflect, Tillich suggests, an ancient and deep-seated intuition concerning the fundamental connection between the transforming power of divine love and the erotic and sexual forces at work in human existence. The language of eros in ancient philosophy and the mystical language of the early church point to the power of eros in its union with agape, and to the underlying unity of mind, soul, and body.

As an "ecstatic manifestation of the Spiritual Presence," agape remains in a sense "independent of the other qualities of love." It is able to "judge them" and to recognize aspects of those qualities which reflect the distortions of existential estrangement. At the same time agape is destined not to abolish but to "unite with" and to "transform" the erotic dimensions of human being. Restored to its essential goodness through the transforming power of the Spirit, eros enters into "participation in unambiguous life" (*ST* 3:137).

Exactly how decisive the relation is in Tillich's writings, between eros and those moments of transformation in which existential estrangement is overcome will be shown in the next chapter. In the passages just cited, Tillich is simply concerned with arguing that the breakthrough of divine agape into the human world does not negate, suspend, or render superfluous the erotic relationships through which we are anchored in material reality. It is true that from the point of view of traditional Protestant theology, this affirmation already seems fairly daring. But in other passages that focus in greater detail on the specific functions of eros in human life, Tillich suggests still more radical perspectives.

Rediscovering the "classical meaning of eros"

Predictably, Paul Tillich's writings about the nature of the erotic and about the intimate connection between eros and agape were not received with unmitigated enthusiasm by all of his theological contemporaries. The importance Tillich attributed to the "lower forms" of love disturbed even some theologians who deeply admired him.

One such admiring colleague was Walter Leibrecht. In his essay "The Life and Mind of Paul Tillich," which opened a volume of writings in Tillich's honor, Leibrecht presents an affirming overview of the principal themes and theses of Tillich's theology. But in the closing paragraphs of his essay, Leibrecht raises the question of Tillich's unconventional handling of the concept of eros: "Does Tillich not inadvertently elevate the eros concept" over the other qualities of love? "Does he not incorporate the other aspects of love into the eros aspect?" Is it not in fact "Plato's eros," Leibrecht pursues, "which seeks fulfillment through the self-realization of the individual (strengthened through the romantic ideal of the individual personality), which determines the temper and structure of Tillich's thought?"[5]

---

[5]Walter Leibrecht, "The Life and Mind of Paul Tillich," in Walter Leibrecht, ed., *Religion and Culture: Essays in Honor of Paul Tillich* (New York: Harper & Row, 1959), 26.

Leibrecht perceives clearly the full importance of the erotic in forming the character of Tillich's theology. He correctly sees that eros is
no peripheral detail in Tillich's system, but that the erotic pervades
the entirety of the system, shaping its "temper and structure" at every
level. At the same time, Leibrecht accurately identifies Plato as the
major source of Tillich's ideas on eros.

Over against the fragmented vision of love presented by Nygren
and the negative judgments on the nature of human love implied in
Freudian libido theory, Tillich holds up what he calls "the classical
meaning of eros" (*PE*, 158; *MB*, 93). This classical interpretation of
the erotic is, as Leibrecht understood, principally derived from the
concept of eros developed in Greek philosophy.

Tillich's discussions of love include frequent references to the eros
doctrines of classical philosophers: Plotinus, Aristotle, and, above all,
Plato. In *Systematic Theology*, Tillich cites all three of these thinkers in
discussing the relationship between love and reason (*ST* 1:72). He
refers to Aristotelian and Platonic concepts of eros in exploring the
mystical or affective dimension of knowledge (*ST* 1:95; *ST* 3:136–
37). In *Biblical Religion and the Search for Ultimate Reality*, Tillich attempts to bridge the perceived gap between Plato's doctrine of the
philosophical "eros toward truth" and biblical conceptions of love,
faith, and knowledge (*BR*, 50ff.). In *Love, Power, and Justice*, he cites
Aristotle and Empedocles on love as a cosmic force and "follows Plato"
in his definition of the erotic (*LPJ*, 21–22, 117). The idea of eros
developed in Greek, particularly in Platonic and Neo-Platonic thought,
and designated by Nygren as the "born rival" of the authentic Christian
love concept, was one of the most powerful influences shaping Tillich's
own view of love's nature.

The most celebrated discussion of eros in the literature of classical
philosophy is presented in Plato's *Symposium*. Tillich referred frequently to this text, both through explicit citations and informal allusions (such as *BR*, 50–51; *MB*, 59–60; *NB*, 129; *ST* 1:72, 94–95).
The image of eros offered in the *Symposium* by Socrates' teacher, the
wise prophetess Diotima, became the single most important intellectual influence on Tillich's doctrine of the erotic.

The demi-god Eros as described by Diotima is not by any means
an unambiguous figure. Indeed, ambiguity belongs to the deepest
nature of the erotic. But in Plato's text, Eros is explicitly assigned the
"greatness of a divine-human power." Eros or Love, Diotima claims,
is not a god, as many believe. Rather, he is a " 'great spirit (daimon),' "
who, like all such spirits, is " 'intermediate between the divine and

the mortal.' " Eros is the " 'mediator who spans the chasm' " between human beings and the gods. " 'Therefore by him the universe is bound together.' " Through Eros, " 'all the intercourse and converse of gods with men . . . is carried on.' " The child of Poros (Plenty) and Penia (Poverty), Eros is neither fair nor foul, neither good nor bad, neither wise nor ignorant, but always " 'in a mean between the two.' "[6]

As the longing for the possession of the beautiful, the good, and the true, Eros animates and guides the highest activities of the human mind and spirit, including the quest for philosophical wisdom. For the lovers of wisdom are those who find themselves " 'in a mean' " between knowledge and ignorance. And Eros, Diotima affirms, " 'is one of them. For wisdom is a most beautiful thing, and Love is of the beautiful; and therefore Love is also a philosopher or lover of wisdom' " (*Symposium* 204a–b [535–36]).

The vast powers of Eros, Diotima insists, have often gone unrecognized because different words are used to describe the different areas in which these powers are exercised. Yet in this, " 'there is nothing to wonder at . . . The reason is that one part of love is separated off and receives the name of the whole, while the other parts have other names.' " Thus it may be said that, " 'All desire of good and happiness is only the great and subtle power' " of Eros (*Symposium* 205b–d [537]).

Despite the differentiation in language, Diotima claims, Eros as the " 'love of the everlasting possession of the good' " animates both human beings' sexual drive and their yearning for wisdom and spiritual beauty. For " 'the object which [lovers] have in view is birth in beauty, whether of body or soul.' " Those whose souls are " 'pregnant' " are guided by Eros toward the pursuit of " 'wisdom and virtue in general.' " The noblest among them conceive a love for the " 'greatest and fairest sort of wisdom,' " which is that " 'concerned with the ordering of states and families, and which is called temperance or justice' " (*Symposium* 206a—209b [538–41]).

Beyond these noble concerns, Eros initiates chosen souls into still higher mysteries. Eros guides the soul upward through the ascending stages and degrees of love: from the attachment to beautiful bodies, to the love of the " 'beauty of the soul,' " to the perception of the " 'beauty in institutions and laws,' " to the beauty revealed by the

---

[6]Plato, *Symposium* 201–203e. Further references to the *Symposium* will be cited parenthetically, with bracketed page references to the translation by Bernard Jowett in *The Dialogues of Plato* (Oxford: Clarendon, 1953).

sciences and expressed through " 'fair and noble thoughts and discourses in boundless love of wisdom.' " At last, to the soul moved
by this mystical Eros, " 'the vision is revealed . . . of a single science
of beauty everywhere.' " The soul enters into contemplation of
" 'beauty absolute, separate, simple and everlasting, which is imparted
to the ever growing and perishing beauties of all other beautiful things,
without itself suffering diminution, or increase, or change.' " The soul
raised by Eros to this spiritual height, " 'bringing forth and nourishing
true virtue will properly become the friend of god and be immortal,
if mortal man may' " (*Symposium* 209e—212a [541–43]).

Diotima's description of the vast powers of Eros sums up the "classical meaning" of the erotic which Tillich opposes to the thinking of
Nygren, Freud, and their followers. Plato's famous text portrays the
erotic as a force of unique importance in human life. For Tillich to
have been familiar with this text and to have referred to it occasionally
would not have been unusual. But he does much more than simply
make occasional, casual allusions to Plato's teaching on eros. He takes
over the classical eros and adapts it to serve as one of the central pillars
of his own understanding of love. Nygren's writings show how unconventional this move was for a Protestant theologian in Tillich's
day.

Consciously and systematically, Tillich honors the eros motif that
Nygren had condemned as anti-Christian. For Tillich, the New Being
as the goal of Christian life cannot imply the negation of created nature,
of embodiment, of human eros, all of which are "good in themselves."
Following the vision sketched by Diotima in the *Symposium,* Tillich
theorizes eros as a shaping force in a vast spectrum of human activities
and relationships, including both sexual love between persons and
human love toward God. Among these areas of concern reigns not
radical separation, as Nygren and other theologians had claimed, but,
on Tillich's view, a continuity founded on the "great and subtle power"
of eros.

3

Eros Toward the World
The Faces of the Erotic in Tillich's Thought

Eroticism is an aspect of the inner life, or, if you will, of the religious life of man.

—Georges Bataille

Desire is the primal energy, and that energy is erotic: the attraction of lover to beloved, of planet to star, the lust of electron for proton. Love is the glue that holds the world together.

—Starhawk

"Each person is locked up within himself," Tillich said in a speech during convocation ceremonies at Union Theological Seminary in New York City, "and each desires to transcend himself through the power of eros." Plato tells us, he continued,

> that Eros, half god and half demon, was born from the union of Poverty and Plenty, and that he carries both of these characteristics within himself. He is more than a human being and less than a god. He is a power in every being that strives and yearns for perfection. Eros drives the weaker being to crave a stronger one, the lower to desire a higher, the male to seek the female, and vice versa; it drives the ignorant person to seek the wise one, and all human beings to raise themselves toward God. It is the source of every movement in the world, because every finite being has a desire for infinite reality, and moves toward it.

"This Eros, this daimon," Tillich claimed, is "more than desire," yet less than the totality of love. It is

43

the driving, life-giving force in the highest forms of spirituality, and also in sexual love. It is even the "first foundation" of the intellectual and religious community to which he addressed his convocation talk. Without the animating force of eros, the shared passion of scholarly inquiry and the sustaining bonds of the spiritual community would dissolve (GW 13:353).

In texts such as this one, Tillich expressed in audacious terms the scope and depth of life-giving power he attributed to the erotic. Some of his listeners—especially those who had read Nygren—must have been rather taken aback by Tillich's ideas. The force that neo-orthodox theology denounced unequivocally as the most treacherous enemy of true Christianity was raised by Tillich to the rank of a universal creative power. To stand before an audience of Christian theologians and students of theology and celebrate the erotic as the moving power of the universe was, in the middle decades of the twentieth century, an act of resolute unconventionality, if not of outright defiance.

Tillich was almost always careful, of course, to subordinate eros explicitly to the judging and transforming power of divine agape. In the convocation speech, he stresses that eros is "less than love" in love's most full and perfect form, the unified totality of the qualities of love under the dominance of agape. Yet the powers that Tillich ascribes to eros are still astonishingly vast. In his talk at Union Seminary, Tillich characterizes eros not just as the "driving force" in all culture and all forms of mystical experience, but now quite simply as the force animating "every movement in the world." Eros is active in the shaping of human communal bonds and in biological processes, in intellectual creativity and in the drive for religious self-transcendence.

Painting in broad and vigorous strokes, Tillich makes similar surprising claims in a number of passages about the importance of the erotic. Such statements are interesting and provocative in themselves. One might inquire whether, beyond these suggestive general descriptions of eros, it is possible to find in Tillich's writings more specific information about the areas of human thought and practice in which the erotic functions. And within these particular fields, do his writings in fact furnish precise descriptions of some of the ways eros shows its power and of the effects that it produces? In short, does he have anything to say about the impact of the erotic that develops and adds concrete substance to the sweeping statements he makes in texts like his Union Seminary address?

Fortunately, Tillich's treatment of the erotic is not limited to broad pronouncements. In a large number of passages, he focuses carefully and precisely on questions connected with the specific functions of eros in human existence. In discussions of significant and problematic areas of psychological, social, and religious reality, he presents clear, pointed assertions about the role of the erotic. In fact, in a theological system marked by an intimidating level of abstraction, eros moves Tillich's work in a more concrete and less cerebral direction than some of his other preferred themes. His writing on eros points to areas in which abstract theological ideas can connect effectively with the lived experience of ordinary people.

This chapter examines the specific applications of eros in Tillich's thought under seven headings, most of which are suggested, although not fully delineated, in his convocation speech. Passages drawn from all periods of Tillich's career reflect the persistence of his concern with eros and its impact on human life.

Eros and the "primal powers of existence"

Tillich insists that eros should not be reduced to a synonym for "sex" or "sexual desire." Yet it cannot be separated from libidinal urges. The "libidinous quality of love is always present" in the erotic, even in eros's highest and most spiritualized forms (*MB,* 41). Tillich conceives of eros as intimately and inescapably bound up with the drives and powers that inhabit the creative (but also potentially demonic) depths of human being. Human existence is embodied, sexual existence; thus, eros—the moving force in all life—is of necessity closely connected with sexuality.

Tillich's work on eros provides clues to his understanding of sex. Such clues are important since, in spite of his frequent complaints about puritanical moralism and Christian prudishness, Tillich himself was not always especially frank and direct in his theological writing on sex. His published discussions of sexuality are marked by a distinct taste for euphemisms and circumlocutions. The character of Tillich's private life may have been one reason for the circumspection in his published references to sexual topics. Tillich may have wanted to avoid awakening curiosity about his own sex life. Yet an important reason for his framing discussions of sex in a vocabulary based on eros was Tillich's acute awareness that sex is not, and should not be portrayed as, a simple thing.

Tillich's statement that libido is in all eros and elements of eros are in all expressions of human libido indicates that looking at sex as something more than a physiological phenomenon means entering an area of complex relationships and competing values. Since in human societies, sex is always more than just a physiological phenomenon, a vocabulary that focuses attention primarily on the mechanics of sexual activity is hopelessly inadequate for analyzing the psychological, social, political, and spiritual aspects of sexual relationships. The concept of eros offers Tillich a structure in which physical appetites, psychological drives, and social forces can be brought together and held in tension, rather than split off from one another. True "creative eros" includes sex (*ST* 2:54); but even in situations where sexual activity is a primary focus, psychological, social, and religious factors exert an influence. Such influences can be either nurturing or destructive, but they are always important. The vocabulary of eros provides a means of reflecting the full complexity of sexuality in its connection to other dimensions of human life.

The language of eros in some of Tillich's earlier texts, those written before his exile from Germany, makes these connections especially clear. He uses terms that anchor the erotic in the deep, nonrational life-drives described in the philosophy of Nietzsche and theorized in the literature of psychoanalysis. These early texts point to the ambiguous relationship between the highest intellectual and social values and the nonrational forces that Western culture has struggled to repress. In "The Demonic: A Contribution to the Interpretation of History" (1926), Tillich identifies "impulse for power and impulse for Eros" as the two fundamental, "polar and yet related forces of the subconscious." Tillich claims that the "poetical, metaphysical and psychoanalytic explorations of the soul have equally shown how the vital forces of the subconscious," including the erotic, "support even the finest and most abstract mental acts and instill them with the 'blood' that makes the spirit creative."

The creative power of "subconscious" erotic drives also contains the seeds of potentially destructive "demonry." Eros is not an unambiguous element. Tillich counts it among the "vital original forces" necessary for the expression of artistic creativity and for the attainment of religious depth. Like the "will to power," however, erotic energies can take on demonic qualities and rise to "limit and destroy the spiritual form." The "holy demonries of the sphere of power and Eros" can destroy the individual personality. Likewise, in the realm of politics and community life, the same demonic forces can overwhelm the structures of social order and plunge an entire people or civilization into chaos. With Eros, as with the will to power, Tillich maintains that "creative power" and form-destroying tendencies are tightly interlaced (*IH*, 89–92).

Eros is closely connected with what Tillich calls "powers of origin," elemental forces that shape human existence in its pre-rational connection to the earth, to the cyclical rhythms of the cosmos and the life-death cycle, to the structures of the primal community. These "powers of origin" include "soil," "blood," and the shaping force of the primitive "social group."

"The most widespread and at the same time the most concrete power of origin," Tillich writes, "is *the soil*." The earth "generates life from itself, supports and nourishes it, and then takes it back into itself again. It holds everything under the spell of the cycle of birth and death." Out of the "vegetative form represented by the soil" develops the "animal form of origin," the "*origin of blood*." "Power of being in the animal sense is not brute strength, but rather a fullness of life that has been given form." In addition to "the origin of soil and blood, there is the origin coming from the *social group*," the primitive stage of tribal social organization, with its reverence for the "line of ancestors" expressing the bonds of blood origin and the sacred continuity of the social order (*SD*, 13–15).

The forces of eros are deeply rooted in these primal powers, the energies of what Tillich refers to as "the irrational, the living, the depth dimension, undisturbed nature" (*SD*, 55). Eros seeks "to be in union with the primal power of existence prior to any analysis. The erotic energies, along with "fate" and "death," are counted among the primeval forces that "resist the rationality of the Enlightenment." Eros is rightly "set in opposition, especially by youth, to the ways in which we rationally order the world." Erotic power overwhelms and dissolves the orderly categories through which we attempt to give a fixed, harmonious, predictable structure to existence (*SD*, 25).

Partaking of the immense power of the elemental forces, eros also shares their ambiguities and their dangers. Its demonic, form-destroying potential is great. Yet its creative powers are indispensable in the social, artistic, and religious realms. Eros breaks down the rigid structures of a stultifying bourgeois rationalism and opens the way for renewed creative contact with the powers of origin. Such contact is, Tillich insists, essential to the shaping of political and social structures responsive to the full complexity and richness of human life. "The origin cannot be effaced," he writes, in attempts to bring order to human existence through politics. Rather, the organization of the human community must take into account the "depth dimension" of our rootedness in the world of physicality, affect, and desire. Politics must acknowledge and use the dimensions of human passion and the life-drives. Attempts at political transformation must not be directed toward a sanitizing rationalization of human being. They must aim at "the fulfillment of being" in its richness, at the realization of "being in its true power, with all its particularities, its tensions, and its forces of eros" (*SD*, 107).

Tillich sees the elemental, nonrational dimension of eros as directly connected with the female. He writes of *"the powers of origin possessed by woman by virtue of her resonance with eros and with motherhood"* (*SD*, 152; italicized in original). He suggests that women "resonate with," or are disposed toward eros in a particularly deep and decisive way.[1] A special constellation of attitudes and capacities is associated with women's lives and women's consciousness. Women's experience, through a deep erotic resonance and the dispositions and practices associated with motherhood, includes a strong, organic connection to the powers of origin which affirm and sustain life.[2]

Tillich asserts that this situation has political consequences for women in an exploitative society founded not on life-sustaining values, but instead on the relentless use of manipulative, instrumental reason. For although women have been "emancipated in the liberal sense" within advanced industrial societies, women's basic dispositions are opposed to the types of power relations and modes of production that structure existence in such societies. Women's status within the capitalist order remains correspondingly ambiguous. Although nominally liberated, women by no means "immediately attain to a higher level of fulfillment, as was posited in the bourgeois belief in harmony." Instead, women have been forced into a situation analogous to the class situation of the proletariat under the conditions of bourgeois-democratic rule: "emancipated" in principle, enslaved in fact.

---

[1]The original German reads: "Die mit der Bestimmung zu Eros und zu Mutterschaft gegebenen Ursprungskräfte der Frau" (*GW* 2:356).

[2]Tillich's sexual essentialism can only appear highly problematic from a contemporary point of view. Interestingly, however, some of the same qualities that Tillich views as belonging to the female "essence" have been utilized by feminists in their effort to describe a critical political "standpoint" based on types of women's experience. Tillich never attempts to deal with the social construction of the traits and qualities he thinks of as connected with the feminine. Yet his discussion of the difficulties faced by women in bringing themselves into conformity with the exploitative logic of capitalist free market competition remains suggestive. See also *D*, 287–88: "Die Geistigkeit der Frau ist vom Eros nicht zu trennen"; and cf. Nancy Hartsock, *Money, Sex, and Power* (Boston: Northeastern University Press, 1985), esp. part 2.

The difficulty of women's situation of oppression is compounded by the fact that, "generally speaking, the economic power of women in free competition turns out to be less than that of men, while the psychological power of women is more deeply opposed to the mechanical forms of a rationalized economic system" (SD, 152). Shaped by a "resonance with eros and motherhood," women's consciousness "*cannot easily be incorporated into the extremely one-sided, male-oriented, rationalistic system*" (italicized in original). Women are, Tillich implies, in an ironically privileged position for understanding the conflict between eros and the dehumanizing social and economic structures of a technological and rationalistic society (SD, 152–53).

The "philosophical eros"

Eros includes, Tillich believes, nonrational elements connected with the "primal powers" of existence, that is, with the earth, with sexuality and fertility, with primitive blood ties and social bonds. Yet the erotic in its essence is not an antirational force. The erotic energies can be united with the highest reasoning functions of the human mind. Tillich claims that eros is in fact the animating power in the most elevated of human rational activities, the philosophical pursuit of wisdom.

One of the most significant forms of the erotic is for Tillich the "philosophical eros" that spurs the inquiring intelligence toward the good, the beautiful, and the true. He follows Plato in viewing eros as the power that urges and guides persons in the pursuit not only of physical beauty and the pleasures of sexual communion, but also in their striving after intellectual and spiritual values (ST 1:22, 72; LPJ, 30; GW 13:353; MB, 59–60). "Philosophy from Plato on," Tillich writes, "praises the eros which carries the soul in its search for ultimate reality" (BR, 50). In the quest for philosophical understanding "eros drives the soul through all levels of reality to ultimate reality, to truth itself, which is the good itself" (BR, 72).

Tillich's understanding of philosophical eros is rooted in his somewhat unusual concept of the nature of reason. For him, there is no necessary clash between rational thought and emotion, indeed, human affect includes fundamental rational structures, and reason likewise embraces affective elements. "According to the classical philosophical tradition, reason is the structure of the mind that enables the mind to grasp and to transform reality." "Classical" or "ontological" reason is effective in many different "functions" of the mind, including not only the practical and technical, but also the cognitive and aesthetic areas. Emotional life "is not irrational in itself" (*ST* 1:72). There is no irreducible conflict between eros in its philosophical-rational form and the dimensions of the erotic connected with affect, the primal or libidinal passions, the psychological depths. Tillich's eros concept is vast enough to embrace both of these realms, and daring enough to claim that the two are intimately related.

"An emotional element is present in every rational act" (*ST* 1:77). An element not only of emotion, but of passion is necessary in order for reason to attain its highest form in the philosophical "love of wisdom." This passion is provided by eros. Eros toward truth is what distinguishes a passionate philosophical search for ultimate reality from the technical manipulations and detached calculations of the natural scientist. Animated by eros, philosophy becomes an approach to the world which is guided not by a disinterested, "controlling" rationality, but by the erotic desire to participate in the beautiful, the good, the true, in ultimate meaning. "Ontological passion," the specific form of concern that drives the mind to seek reuniting knowledge of ultimate reality, "has the character of eros" (*BR,* 51).

Philosophy includes, of course, an abstract, theoretical aspect. Basic ontological investigations into truth are performed with "the same strictness, the same logical and methodological rationality, with which a mathematician" might work. "But the philosopher is driven from one step to another, and to the last step, the question of being itself, by something else," something other than a calculating, methodical desire for abstract knowledge. "This 'something else' can be called, with Plato, the eros for the idea." A "driving," erotic force in the depths of his or her being is always what "makes the philosopher a philosopher. The question of ultimate reality is produced not by a theoretical interest in abstraction from the totality of man's being," but instead "by this rare union of passion and rationality" (*BR,* 18–20).

Pedagogical relationships constitute an aspect of the search for wisdom in which Tillich sees the role of the erotic as especially crucial. In praising the teaching gifts of his friend Hermann Schafft, he evokes Schafft's "enormous pedagogical eros," connecting this erotic quality with his friend's contagious passion for the arts and describing Schafft's "way of dealing with people" as a deeply compelling "mixture of eros and agape" (*GW* 13:29–31). Tillich's own inspirational power as a teacher and lecturer also became something of a legend. He showed, in the words of his wife Hannah, a "special eros for his students, anywhere in the world."[3]

In the relationship between teacher and student or in the camaraderie among students sharing a passion for learning, "eros toward the truth" unites with the forces of erotic-libidinal attraction which shape relations among persons. The result is an erotic energy of rare and volatile force. The catalyzing of such energy can have unpredictable and sometimes destructive consequences. But for Tillich, an authentic learning community capable of pursuing wisdom in its highest forms can only be founded upon the basis of this shared erotic passion. Thus, eros is the "first foundation" of the academic and intellectual life (*GW* 13:353).

"If your teachers stand outside the immediate circle of your youth," Tillich tells students in his convocation speech at Union Seminary, "there is nevertheless a way to overcome this difference in age and experience: namely through the same power of Eros which creates your natural community." The traditional symbol of such bonding across lines of age and status is the relationship between Socrates and his pupils. "I am convinced," Tillich affirms, "that without the presence of Eros in the relationship between teacher and student, a fruitful community in teaching and learning is impossible" (*GW* 13:353–54).

The drawing of erotic forces into the pedagogical relationship carries with it serious risks. Eros is not a god, "but rather a demon between god and man. And every demon has two sides. He acts creatively but at the same time destructively." In the erotic, Tillich warns, "destructive forces are at work," and must be carefully guarded against by "those who follow Eros." Without the element of erotic passion, however, no authentic and productive pedagogical relationship, no fruitful search for truth could be undertaken (*GW* 13:354).

The creative union of the rational faculties with the emotions emerges in a palpable and persuasive form in art. Accordingly, Tillich sees art as another extremely important province of the erotic. He praises the power of artworks to "interest us" in the profound, original sense of the word, to draw us erotically into the midst of their being: *inter esse*. By what Tillich calls "their hidden sublimity," such objects "evoke our eros, attract us, draw us into themselves." In "works of art, music, literature, one may easily feel this eros-provoking power" (cf. *GW* 13:474).

As his autobiographical writings prove, Tillich was himself deeply responsive to the erotic force of art, especially visual arts and literature

---

[3]Hannah Tillich, *From Time to Time* (New York: Stein and Day, 1973), 144.

(see *OB,* 22–23, 26–30, 68), but he was also aware that this aesthetic force carries with it risks and ambiguities. There is in the passionate love of art, Tillich believes, the ever-present danger that one may slip into a posture of "aestheticism" in which eros is separated from the criterion of justice and the pleasure of art is pursued for its own sake. "An aesthetic detachment can take hold of our relation to culture" and make the cultural/artistic eros "ambiguous." In philosophy and Christian theology, this phenomenon of superficial aestheticism has been explored most fully by Søren Kierkegaard. The Danish philosopher's "aesthetic stage of man's spiritual development is not," Tillich claims, in fact merely a stage, but rather an ever-present "quality of love exposed to the dangers Kierkegaard describes. The ambiguity of cultural eros is its detachment from the realities that it expresses, and consequently the disappearing of existential participation and ultimate responsibility." In such a situation, "the wings of eros become wings of escape" (*LPJ,* 118).

Kierkegaard's warnings on the risks associated with the aesthetic eros must be taken seriously. Tillich himself writes of having experienced a strong pull in the direction of this type of aesthetic flight from the world.[4] However, he insists, such irresponsible detachment from reality does not belong to the basic nature of aesthetic eros. The attitude of detachment is a perversion of the erotic relation to culture and to artistic creation. Authentic, "essential" eros is a force that works to overcome detachment and loss of participation in aesthetic experience, as in other areas. Rather than isolating us, eros introduces a crucial element of existential passion and participation into human experience. Essential eros connects us to the world, rather than cutting us off from it.

Every authentic creative act, Tillich argues, is oriented and inspired not by a desire for pleasure, but by the "creative eros" that calls human persons beyond themselves and draws them into participation in the universal unfolding of creative processes. Every creative act "fulfils something toward which life is driven by its inner dynamics, the classical name of which is eros" (*ST* 3:56). Thus, Tillich argues that "eros and art" can be used together to help heal the disturbed relationship to the world which is produced by manipulative technical

---

[4]See the quoted material and biographical data furnished in chap. 3 of Wilhelm and Marion Pauck, *Paul Tillich: His Life and Thought,* vol. 1: *Life* (New York: Harper & Row, 1976).

reason. Insofar as it remains under the guidance of agape and connected to the notion of justice—and in this sense true to its own essential nature—eros can help in overcoming, Tillich claims, some of the destructive "ambiguities of culture" (*ST* 3:161).

In *Biblical Religion and the Search for Ultimate Reality,* Tillich argues that eros distinguishes the passionate inquiry of the philosopher from the detached, instrumental procedures of the natural sciences. Yet even the operations and products of scientific research and technology can be approached in a spirit of eros.

To the extent that technology and its products are not regarded as ends in themselves, or again as merely objectified "means without an ultimate end," scientific inquiry and technical processes can be reconciled with and guided by creative eros. "The logician and mathematician," although concerned with apparently abstract and technical forms of knowledge, can themselves be "driven by eros, including desire and passion" (*ST* 2:26). Eros, under the healing impact of the Spiritual Presence, catalyzes a form of union between subject and object which heals the splits generated by the exclusive application of objectifying technical reason.

"The technical transformation of parts of nature into things which are only things, i.e., technical objects" is for Tillich the fundamental tendency of instrumental reason and its technological applications. If one asks "how the split between subject and object can be overcome in this realm of complete objectivation, the answer can only be: by producing objects which can be imbued with subjective qualities," that is, objects that have been touched and transformed by eros. Such a transformation can and does occur, Tillich believes, in a situation in which cultural production is carried on under "theonomous" principles.[5] "The style, the overall form of theonomous works of cultural creation expresses the ultimacy of meaning even in the most limited vehicles of meaning" (*ST* 3:250).

"Under the impact of the Spiritual Presence, even technical processes can become theonomous." A theonomous culture avoids the reduction of natural structures, of objects shaped by human skill and

---

[5]In this context, Tillich defines "theonomy" as "the state of culture under the impact of the Spiritual Presence. The nomos (law) effective" in such a culture "is the directedness of the self-creation of life under the dimension of the Spirit toward the ultimate in being and meaning," i.e., the divine (*ST* 3:249).

of human beings themselves to the status of "mere things." For the Spirit, Tillich claims:

> No thing is merely a thing. It is a bearer of form and meaning, and therefore a possible object of eros. This is true even of tools, from the most primitive hammer to the most delicate computer. As in the earliest periods when they were the bearers of fetish powers, so today they can be considered and artistically valuated as new embodiments of the power of being itself. This eros toward the technical Gestalt is a way in which a theonomous relation to technology can be achieved. (*ST* 3:258–59)

Eros can help heal our relationship to those parts of the natural world, culture, and human selfhood from which the unchecked proliferation of technical reason and technological production have cut us off. One can observe, Tillich believes, the seeds of creative eros "in the relation of children and adults to such technical Gestalten as ships, cars, planes, furniture, impressive machines, factory buildings, and so on" (*ST* 3:259).

There is, in Tillich's view, no "essential conflict" (*ST* 3:259) between technical processes and products as such and the creative eros as it stands under the guidance of the Spiritual Presence. Destructive and alienating splits in the consciousness of human beings as users of technology can in fact be healed through a deepened eros toward technical processes and the forms generated by these processes. Eros mediates a transforming involvement in all aspects of the world, including technical production. Our erotic interest can, Tillich suggests, open up new applications for human ingenuity and technical skill. This also implies that technology and its products need not be rejected wholesale by those who seek to develop a way of life grounded in erotic relatedness. Eros may at first seem to have little to do with the mechanical products of technology, but it is not essentially incompatible with technical reasoning and technological processes.

Tillich acknowledges, however, that despite this basic compatibility, a strong tension is present in practice between eros and the types of thinking and behavior associated with technical reason. He observes that the connection between eros and technology can easily be "corrupted" by "competitive and mercenary interests" (*ST* 3:259). The "problem" with technology, and its conflict with the erotic life-energies, lies not in the nature of technical objects themselves, but in the economic and political structures and practices that determine the ways in which objects are produced, distributed, and used.

In practice, the progress of modern technology has been accompanied by the creation of economic and social systems that are hostile to the integrity of individual human persons and deeply harmful to the natural environment. These systems, encouraging an exclusively instrumental way of thinking in which technical reason is not balanced by other forms of knowledge, have tended to undermine the erotic connections that link people to one another and to their world. While not necessarily opposed to technical reason as such, eros represents a threat to ways of life and to socioeconomic structures in which technical reason is the only form of thought recognized as authoritative. Eros, in its connection to other branches of "classical" or "ontological" reason, opens for human beings ranges of experience and knowledge into which technical reason by itself cannot penetrate. Thus, the classical reason animated by eros represents a protest against the exclusive domination of instrumental reason, and an implicit critique of many of the uses to which human technical capacities are put in modern societies. "This is the meaning of Pascal's sentence about the 'reasons of the heart which reason cannot comprehend,' " Tillich writes. "Here 'reason' is used in a double sense. The 'reasons of the heart' are the structures of aesthetic and communal experience (beauty and love)"; these eros-charged forms of experience and thought stand in opposition to a type of reason that "cannot comprehend them," meaning technical reason (*ST* 1:77).

Erotic knowing: gnosis

Tillich considers eros the animating principle in all forms of "cultural creativity" and in particular in philosophy's quest for the good, the true and the beautiful. In the areas of learning, art, and even technical inventiveness, eros is the driving force that urges the mind toward fresh discoveries and new insights. But the role of the erotic in human knowledge reaches, in Tillich's view, still further. He claims, in fact, that all knowledge exhibits an erotic aspect.

Tillich uses the expression "true knowledge" (*ST* 1:95) to refer to those situations in which "cognitive union" between subject and object is achieved. The "cognitive eros" brings about the uniting of the knower and the thing known on which knowledge depends. Attempts to gain knowledge that eliminate this element of erotic involvement separate us from the truth rather than bringing us closer to it. Yet the elimination of eros from the epistemological process can never be absolute. In all cognitive acts, even the most self-consciously detached and (supposedly) objective, a form of participation of the knower in the known, and thus an element of "cognitive eros," is present. "Knowing is a form of union," Tillich writes. "In every act of knowledge, the knower and that which is known are united; the gap between subject and object is overcome. The subject 'grasps' the object, adapts it to itself, and, at the same time, adapts itself to the object" (*ST* 1:94).

The union between knower and known is of course never total. In every epistemological relation, there is also an element of detachment, of what Tillich calls "controlling knowledge." Such controlling knowledge is "one side of cognitive reason and an essential element in every cognitive act." Yet the understanding of cognitive processes which has dominated much of modern European philosophical and scientific thought, with its "exclusive emphasis on the formal side of every rational function," on "controlling knowledge and the corresponding formalized logic," represents a misreading of the true nature of human knowing. It reduces the dynamic, erotic union between knower and known to a mechanical process whose goal is the exploitation of an object by a subject. It sets up a relationship of alienation between human beings and the world in which they live.

Controlling knowledge "unites subject and object only for the sake of the control of the object by the subject. It transforms the object into a completely conditioned and calculable 'thing.' It deprives it of any subjective qualities" (*ST* 1:97). An overemphasis on this detached, manipulative aspect of knowledge "keeps cognitive reason from digging into the strata of things and events which can only be grasped with *amor intellectualis* ('intellectual love')" (*ST* 1:90). It leads to a shallow and simplistic interpretation of the dynamics of epistemology and to an inadequate understanding of the complex relationships that connect human beings with the world and with their fellow creatures. For this destructive and limiting "formalism in the cognitive realm," Tillich employs the term "intellectualism, the use of the cognitive intellect without eros" (*ST* 1:90).

The full deployment of cognitive eros functions as a dynamic corrective to the detached stance of "controlling knowledge." As it introduces a healing element of concern into technical reason, so eros also balances and sets limits to the type of "objective" cognitive operations with which such reason is associated. Cognitive eros implies involvement of the subject in the object. Where "controlling knowledge 'objectifies,' not only logically (which is unavoidable) but ontologically and ethically," erotic knowledge brings the recognition that "no thing is merely a thing." In the perspective of an eroticized cognitive relation with reality, "union with everything [is] possible. Nothing is absolutely strange." Controlling knowledge "looks upon its object as something which cannot return its look." But an erotic "receiving knowledge" believes that "as we look at things, so things look at us with the expectation of being received and the offer of enriching us in cognitive union. Things indicate that they might be 'interesting' if we enter their deeper levels and experience their special power of being" (*ST* 1:97–98). The spirit of eros moves us beyond the urge to master and control the world. Eros helps us to grasp the need for "a knowledge which not only controls but unites" (*ST* 1:90).

Such uniting knowledge implies not fusion, but the erotic tension of a "union through separation" (*ST* 1:94). When this creative tension is maintained, cognition becomes an act of encounter comparable to the act of love. "The passion of knowing for the sake of knowing" reflects the fact that "a want, a vacuum, is filled by successful cognition." In the act of knowing, something that was once strange, but that nevertheless essentially "belongs to us," becomes "familiar, a part of us." According to the Platonic doctrine, "the cognitive eros is born of poverty and abundance. It drives us toward reunion with that to which we belong and which belongs to us." In every act of knowledge guided by this force, a deep, erotic fulfillment is experienced: "want and estrangement are conquered" (*ST* 1:95).

Yet genuine knowledge, Tillich argues, "is more than fulfilling; it also transforms and heals." To designate "knowledge" in the fullness of the term's intellectual, sexual, moral, and religious meaning, Tillich uses the Greek word *gnosis*. He consciously exploits the ambiguous definition of the term to emphasize the role of the erotic impulse in all forms of cognitive activity, and the interrelatedness of different types of "knowing." Socrates shows, Tillich claims, "that true knowledge includes union and, therefore, openness to receive that with which one unites." This cognitive-erotic receptivity is "the knowledge of which Paul also speaks, the gnosis which in New Testament Greek means cognitive, sexual and mystical union at the same time" (*ST* 1:95–96).

Tillich identifies the unresolved tensions between the "emotional" and "formal" elements in human cognitive processes as one of the factors driving human reason beyond itself toward the transformed, "ecstatic" ways of knowing implied in the concept of revelation (*ST* 1:89f.). In attempting to describe the cognitive character of revelation, Tillich appeals once again to the idea of gnosis, with its mixture of

formal-intellectual, erotic, and religious connotations. Revelation transcends and heals the "split between form and emotion, cognitive detachment and cognitive union." To offer a convincing image of how
this resolution of opposing tendencies works, early Christian theologians "used the concept gnosis, which means cognitive as well as
mystical and sexual union." In the dimension of revelation, there can
be no conflict between gnosis and episteme, or "detached scientific
knowledge." For, as the early Christian thinkers affirmed, "the same
Logos who taught the philosophers and legislators" is itself "the source
of final revelation and teaches the Christian theologians" (ST 1:153–
54). Thus, Tillich describes the resolution of the tensions inherent in
human reason and cognition in a type of knowing which he explicitly
characterizes in terms of erotic dynamics. Eros does more than shape
human knowledge at the routine level of day-to-day cognitive experience. Tillich claims that erotic forces are also present in the revelatory knowledge which is the crowning form of spiritual understanding.

In the third volume of Systematic Theology, Tillich uses the vocabulary of gnosis to explore further the intimate connections between
knowledge and love. He develops the theme of a fundamental unity
between knowledge, sexual love, and the ecstatic union described in
religious mysticism. As eros is the dynamic element in the paradoxical
cognitive union between subject and object, so all forms of love include
a cognitive dimension in which this same variety of erotic knowing
unfolds. "Love," Tillich affirms, "includes the knowledge of the beloved. But it is not the knowledge of analysis and calculating manipulation." Knowledge as an essential part of human love is a form of
involved, erotic cognition. It is the "participating knowledge which
changes both the knower and the known in the very act of knowledge"
(ST 3:137).

The decisive quality of knowing as eros-charged gnosis is the fact
that such knowledge leaves neither the knower nor the known un-
transformed. Erotic knowledge is a relation in which there are no
passive parties: no inert "object," and no uninvolved subject who
merely records abstract information. The erotic knowing that approaches the ideal of gnosis is a dynamic relation that implies interest
and healing care. The term "insight" used in depth psychology has
begun to take on, Tillich argues, the connotations of gnosis, "namely,
of a knowledge which transforms and heals." In the therapeutic context, as in philosophy and religion, it has been recognized that true

insight, genuine cognitive union, brings with it a "radical transformation" of the person(s) involved (*ST* 1:96).

In his sermon on "Knowledge through Love," Tillich asserts that
love in the participatory, erotic, mystical sense is the only means to
"full, direct and total knowledge." Full knowledge "presupposes full
love." Once again, Tillich evokes the concept of gnosis, which he
states, "can designate both knowledge and sensual love. It can designate
both, because both meanings express an act of union, an overcoming
of the cleavage between beings." In the final triumph of the Spirit of
which Paul writes, "knowledge shall be done away with insofar as it
is different from love; knowledge shall become eternal insofar as it is
one with love." For Paul, "the difference between knowledge and
love, between seeing and acting, between theory and practice, exists
only when fragmentary knowledge is our concern." But as knowledge
draws nearer to the ideal of gnosis, it unites with careful and loving
action. It becomes "knowing and doing at the same time" (*SF,* 109–
10).

Erotic knowing in its highest forms becomes one with doing, with
practical moral action. The question of the connection (or lack thereof)
between knowledge and responsible action was a central one for Tillich. Especially in his earlier writings, rooted in the political strife of
Weimar Germany and the anguish that Tillich felt at the rise of Nazism,
he was concerned with exploring links between forms of abstract
thought and concrete social and political engagement. The historical
quality of human knowledge was of crucial importance in these early
works. Tillich attempted to define the metaphysical and psychological
structures that permit intellectual knowledge to respond to and influence the concrete historical situation. In keeping with his understanding
of the central role of the erotic in shaping both cognitive processes
and other aspects of behavior, Tillich identified eros as the factor that
bridges the gap between thought and historical action. The orientation
of our eros determines the responsiveness of our knowledge to the
demands of our historical situation.

In the early text "Kairos and Logos: A Study in the Metaphysics
of Knowledge," Tillich argues that a particular individual's erotic-
cognitive attunement will decide whether her or his way of knowing
is consciously involved in and directed toward the historical context,
or whether she or he strives instead primarily after a form of "timeless"
wisdom. Tillich posits the tension between timeless "logos" and the
historical "kairos" (the "fullness of time," the decisive moment for

transforming action) as a metaphysical polarity underlying and conditioning all human cognitive activity. The tendency of persons' "eros" toward one or the other of these poles will determine, Tillich claims, the responsiveness of their thought to the historical situation. "Eros toward the kairos" will create a type of knowledge attuned to the practical demands of the historical moment, while the opposite attitude of "asceticism toward the kairos" and "eros toward the logos" will lead to attempts to reach a type of knowledge detached from history (*IH*, 130–33).

In "Kairos and Logos," Tillich attacks the exclusive valuation of detached "scientific knowledge" as betraying a hidden "desire to dominate" on the part of those who seek such knowledge (*IH*, 148). Shaped by eros, knowledge must always contain an element of passion and of decision, whether or not this is explicitly recognized (*IH*, 137, 144). The "attitude of knowledge" for which Tillich pleads is not manipulative "strangeness," but rather "intimacy," not "distance, but nearness to life." What he describes as the "community between the knowing and the known" should "be expressed in every scientific work," as well as in less abstract forms of knowledge. Through knowledge we enter into "community in responsibility with the life which touches us" (*IH*, 149).

The knowledge which creates an erotic "community" between knower and known is what Tillich elsewhere calls the "seeing which unites." The English language has a word for such seeing, "intuition":

> This means seeing *into*. It is an intimate seeing, a grasping and being grasped. It is a seeing shaped by love. Plato, the teacher of the centuries, whose words and visions have deeply influenced the Fourth Gospel and the Church, knew about the seeing which unites. He called the love which drives us to a genuine intuition the "child of poverty and abundance." It is love which fills our want with the abundance of our world. But it fills us in such a way that the disrupted multitude is not the last we see—a view which disrupts ourselves. The last we see lies in that which unites, which is eternal *in* and *above* the transitory things. Into this view Plato wanted to initiate his followers. (*NB*, 129)

The erotic is the catalyst of knowing that approaches the horizon of "genuine intuition." Erotic knowing is marked by passion and decision in connection to the demands of the historical context. Such knowing means responsiveness to historical tasks and challenges and active participation in the other beings with whom we are "united" through knowledge. Yet eros also allows us, Tillich affirms, to perceive the "eternal," infinite element present within the finite and historically conditioned. Eros offers a way of knowing which holds the "transitory" and the eternal in tension. In the highest stage of erotic knowledge, we respond to the demands of the historical context in light of an awareness of the divine power that dwells in conditioned forms. Our knowledge is a union rooted in love: love to finite creatures, and to the indwelling divine Spirit. Eros opens our eyes for that "seeing into" through which the separation of the transitory and the timeless, and with it the estrangement between ourselves, our world, and the divine ground of being, can be overcome.

Eros and ethics: the "transmoral motivation"

In Tillich's "ontology of cognition," the cognitive act is not a one-directional relationship in which external objects are taken into the self (empiricist-positivist model) or else internal structures are projected outward (idealist model). Instead, he understands the act of knowing as an erotically charged "encounter."[6]

Within the broad class of cognitive encounters, Tillich sees one type as especially important: the act of knowledge which brings together two human individuals. The encounter in which human beings come to know one another is for Tillich both the highest form of cognitive experience, and the foundation of moral life. Thus, the power of eros, the catalyst of the "cognitive union" between subject and object, also fulfills a first crucial function in the area of ethics.

For the highest stage of intersubjective knowing and of moral relationship, Tillich uses the word "communion." The term is charged—intentionally—with powerful erotic overtones. Communion is described in *Systematic Theology* as the "perfect form" of that participatory knowledge that Tillich understands as "rooted in eros" (*ST* 1:176). "When individualization," Tillich writes, "reaches the perfect form

---

[6]In an article entitled "Participation and Knowledge: Problems of an Ontology of Cognition," Tillich argues that "it is impossible to make forms of encounter like love or knowledge understandable by starting either with pure objectivity or pure subjectivity, or by starting, as Spinoza and Schelling did, with preceding identity." In the structure of knowledge, Tillich claims, "what precedes is not identity but polarity, and in the actual processes of life, encounter." This passage is quoted in Ian Thompson, *Being and Meaning* (Edinburgh: University of Edinburgh Press, 1981), 118.

we call a 'person,' " then the "participation" of one being in another "reaches the perfect form which we call 'communion.' Man participates in all levels of life, but he participates fully only in that level of life which he is himself—he has communion only with persons." For the autonomous human subject, "communion is participation in another completely centered and completely individual self" (*ST* 1:176).

As in the erotic give-and-take of the cognitive encounter, authentic communion is born not through a fusion of two separate entities into one, but in the relational tension between two independent selves. The relation that Tillich describes is a dynamic interplay between two fully autonomous beings, each of whom retains its subject-quality while entering into participation with the other.[7] The individual, moreover, "discovers" her- or himself through the "resistance" offered by the other subject, through the encounter of her or his own desires with the independent will of the other. "In the resistance of the other person, the person is born" (*ST* 1:177).

Tillich does not depict this "resistance" in terms of a natural animosity between persons which must be repressed or sublimated at the cost of psychological self-mutilation. His image of interpersonal communion does not resemble the agonal Freudian model of an uneasy truce between beings who would basically be happier if they could tear each other limb from limb. "Resistance" for Tillich signifies simply the intrinsic moral dignity that belongs to human persons, and that will not allow them to be treated as objects without causing total annihilation of their being. An individual "cannot conquer another person" without destroying the other as a person (*ST* 1:177).

For Tillich, the dynamic of moral communion embraces resistance and generates an erotic "union through separation" based on longing for the other and respect for the other's autonomy. Communion in this sense of mutual recognition is "not something an individual might or might not have." It is only through such interplay that the human self with its specific qualities of will, intelligence, feeling, and responsibility can come to be. "Participation is essential for the individual, not accidental." No individual, Tillich asserts, "exists without participation, and no personal being exists without communal being. The person as the fully developed individual self is impossible without other fully developed selves." Our sense of individual personhood is in all cases shaped in a context of relation to others (*ST* 1:176).

---

[7]Tillich's thinking in this area is clearly indebted to that of Martin Buber, an intellectual affiliation that Tillich himself readily acknowledged. See *TC*, 188–99.

Our personal existence cannot be separated from our ongoing encounter with other selves, and thus from our quality as beings who must act and make choices in a communal setting. This means that we persons are by definition moral beings. Tillich views the personal encounter with another human self as the experience through which we come to recognize the binding force of the moral imperative. " 'Oughtness,' " he affirms, is "basically experienced in the ego-thou relation" (ST 3:40).

In the world of existential estrangement in which a potentially infinite number of objects are offered to human concupiscence, the other self represents a crucial limit: the one "object" that the individual's appetites cannot hope to subjugate and absorb. "Man, facing his world, has the whole universe as the potential content of his centered self." Everything can, at least theoretically, become a "content of the self." This, Tillich argues, "is the structural basis for the endlessness of libido in the state of estrangement; it is the condition for man's desire to 'win the world.' "

There is, however, "one limit to man's attempt to draw all content into himself—the other self. One can subject and absorb another in his organic basis, including his psychological self, but not the other self in the dimension of the spirit." One can destroy the other person "as a self," but one cannot "assimilate" her or him as a "content of one's own centeredness." The other self represents the "unconditional limit to the desire to assimilate one's whole world, and the experience of this limit" is the experience of the "moral imperative" (ST 3:40). The "ought-to-be" emerges through the process of attraction to the other being, the inevitable "resistance" that the other offers to one's own will, and the resolution in erotic communion. In the encounter that shapes the moral relation, Tillich maintains, the urge that at first expressed itself as a desire for possession and mastery can evolve into an erotic connectedness inclusive of difference and individual freedom.[8]

Tillich sees our experience of the founding principles of morality as taking place within a relational context shaped by powerful erotic forces. Genuine "morality" is not a set of laws or abstract precepts handed down by a tradition or by some other form of authority, human or divine. Morality for Tillich is a relation among living human beings

---

[8]Cf. the analysis of the Hegelian master-slave dialectic by feminist psychoanalyst Jessica Benjamin in *The Bonds of Love: Psychoanalysis, Feminism and the Problem of Domination* (New York: Pantheon, 1988).

in a concrete existential context. It is a mode of human being-together which emerges in a matrix of personal encounters. Apart from such matrices, "morality" as a category makes no sense, and specific forms and systems of morals could never develop. "Persons can only grow" as psychological and moral entities, Tillich asserts, "in the communion of personal encounter" (ST 1:177).

Thus, the erotic forces at work in the experience of interpersonal communion take on a decisive shaping function in the evolution of moral consciousness. It is eros that draws us toward the forms of participating knowledge which culminate in our experience of communion with other human beings. Eros animates our search for cognitive union with the structures of the cosmos, and our desire to achieve full participation in that microcosmos whose infinite riches are apparent in every human self (ST 1:176).

At a preliminary stage, linked with estranged libido and "drawn into its ambiguities" (LPJ, 119), eros participates in the unlimited desire that spurs us to try to assimilate and master the whole world. This alienated striving itself represents a vital step on the way to moral understanding, for the erotic or libidinal drive to "win the world" reaches an impasse at the point where concupiscence encounters an object that by definition it can never possess: the other self. Here, Tillich argues, the machinery of estranged craving grinds to a halt. Endless concupiscence meets its match in the irreducible autonomy of the other being. Desire for the other is reconciled with respect for her/ his personal integrity. In this phase of the moral relation, the other being is, Tillich insists, still "wanted," but in terms of communion rather than of domination. The libidinal and erotic impulses effective in this transformed relationship are no longer "infinite," but "definite" in their orientation toward a specific being or beings. These urges now take the form of a "desire to be united with the object of love for its own sake" (ST 2:54).

The connection between moral action and love is by no means accidental for Tillich. Love in its erotic and libidinal qualities guides human beings toward the situation of encounter in which they experience the moral "ought-to-be." And in order for the moral demands implied in the personal encounter to receive their full unfolding, Tillich believes that all aspects of the moral relation must be placed explicitly under the "criterion of love." He is convinced that love animates all authentically moral behavior, all forms of genuine justice-making.

Tillich understands justice informed by love as rooted in the experience of standing face-to-face with another human being and recognizing the moral demand implied in the human presence of the other. "All the implications of the idea of justice," Tillich argues, grow out of the situation of personal encounter. They are "applications of the imperative to acknowledge every potential person as a person." Tillich criticizes legalistic systems that claim to establish justice "without creating a relationship." In order for authentically life-enhancing moral relations to be created among persons, Tillich claims that the idea of "pure detachment," of moral objectivity must be given up in favor of the recognition (and the fostering) of an "element of involvement" (*MB*, 38–39).

The form of personal "involvement" which Tillich sees as foundational for authentic moral action is rooted in love as the "ultimate moral principle." "Justice is taken into love," he writes, "if the acknowledgment of the other person as person is not detached but involved." If morality is essentially a person-to-person relation, then love is the principle that can most adequately structure this relation. Tillich claims, "love is both absolute and relative by its very nature. An unchanging principle, it nevertheless always changes in its concrete application. It 'listens' to the particular situation" (*MB*, 42). Therefore, "love liberates us from the bondage to absolute ethical traditions, to conventional morals, and to authorities who claim to know the right decision perhaps without having listened to the demand of the unique moment." Love under the guidance of the Spirit "breaks the prison of any absolute moral law," even when such laws are "vested with the authority of a sacred tradition. Love can reject as well as utilize every moral tradition" (*MB*, 43).

"Love under the dominance of agape," in Tillich's view, constitutes the "ultimate source of moral demands" (*MB*, 42). But he makes clear that the other qualities of love also contribute decisively to this function of love in the moral realm. Without the "mystical," participatory aspect of eros, agapic love could, he suggests, lose its "involved" quality and become merely "moralistic." The compassion present in eros and philia "prevents agape from becoming a detached act of mere obedience to the 'law of love' " (*MB*, 40). A vital element of sympathy and active participation is introduced by the erotic into the encounter with the other person which forms the basis of our understanding and practice of justice.

In *Morality and Beyond*, having identified love guided by agape as the "religious source of the moral demands," Tillich proceeds to look at the problem of moral motivation. What actually moves us, once we have recognized the moral demands implicit in a particular situation, to go ahead and carry out these demands?

Tillich acknowledges that under the conditions of estranged existence, moral choices are usually based on "systems of compromise" in which factors such as tradition, education, institutional codes, and the fear of punishment play decisive roles. In human social practice, he writes: "The moral law becomes embodied in state law, conventional rules and educational principles" and exercises control through these structures and the "threats and promises" connected with them. "From the point of view of the unconditional moral imperative, and love as the ultimate principle of moral commands, these methods of motivating moral action are compromises, unavoidable in view of the human predicament," but nevertheless "far removed from the true nature of the moral" (*MB*, 55).

Authentic morality, in contrast to such institutionalized constraints, is motivated by factors that transcend the legal realm of statutes and punishments. Paradoxically, Tillich claims, truly moral behavior is inspired, shaped, and guided by a "transmoral motivation." At this point, the erotic asserts once again its creative influence in morals, for Tillich identifies this transmorally motivating force with eros.

The erotic is the power, Tillich argues, that in a situation of moral decision impels us to strive for the concrete realization of a good that, albeit conditioned by and responsive to the demands of the situation, aims at an ideal beyond the particularities of the specific setting. Eros creates the ultimate motivation for wise and consistent moral action by linking our activity in the concrete context to our desire to attain an ideal of justice, to reach the "good itself," that is, the divine. Eros connects the love toward the other individual with the desire for the divine, for ultimate value. It is this first sort of love that causes us to "involve" ourselves as persons in moral relationships with other persons. The second type of love—toward the universal ideals that express themselves in the idea of God—enables us to receive empowerment through a healed relationship to the divine, and to reflect that empowerment in our moral praxis. Our erotic encounter with other human beings leads us to care about them, to want to involve ourselves with them in a psychological and in a moral sense. Our eros toward ideals shows us the goals toward which our practical, personal care must be oriented in order to be effective and useful.

"To be impelled by eros" toward the value-shaping ideals associated with the divine nature can also be described, Tillich states, "as being grasped by that toward which eros drives." Thus, Tillich claims, "we return to the principle of love" as the divine force grasping the individual human being and giving coherence and purpose to her or his moral acts. The eros quality, as the "mystical quality" of love, "drive[s] toward reunion with essential being in everything, ultimately with the good as the principle of being and knowing (in Platonic terms)." Accepting the Platonic affirmation that eros raises the mind toward the divine, we can see that eros acts as a bridge between the religious and moral realms by correlating particular moral goods in specific situations with human beings' desire to participate in the divine life which is the good itself (*MB*, 59–60).

"Eros," for Plato, "is a mediating power elevating the human mind out of existential bondage into the realm of pure essences, and finally to the essence of all essences—the idea of the good that is, at the same time, the idea of the beautiful and the true." In this conception, Tillich observes, the powers of eros create a situation in which "the moral and the cognitive are not separated. Eros provides both insight and moral motivation." And these two factors are connected with a third element: "the aesthetic desire for the beautiful which is implied in the good." The goal defined by these ideals orients and empowers all specific instances of moral choice and action. "This goal," Tillich affirms, "can be attained by eros as a divine-human power that transcends the moral command without denying it" (*MB*, 59).

"It is not the moral imperative in its commanding majesty and strangeness which is morally motivating," but instead the erotic "driving or attracting power of that which is the goal of the moral command—the good." The Greek philosophers who shaped the classical doctrine of eros were, Tillich states, "aware of the fact that the moral realm, in the sense of personal and communal justice, does not furnish moral motivation unless it is understood as a station on the way to something ultimate in being and meaning—the divine." The aim of all finite life, Tillich argues, "is to participate in the life of the divine. The moral stage is a stage on the way, and the motivation for it depends on the motivation for the transmoral aim." This motivation, grounded in the concept of eros as the fundamental moving force of the cosmos, is our erotic desire for "participation in the divine life." In this sense, as the erotic spurs us to try to connect with the divine through our concrete ethical choices, eros reveals itself as "the transmoral motivation for moral action" (*MB*, 59–60).

As attributes assigned to the divine, the ideals of truth, beauty, and goodness express the qualities we understand as evocative of a fully realized human life in which "the split between our essential being and our existence is overcome" (*MB*, 64). As gifts we receive through God's grace, these same principles empower us to enter by anticipation into "participation in the divine life," in which this split is effectively transcended (*MB*, 62f.). The eros that connects us to the universal values does not have the character of blind obedience to an unbending law. In discussions of religious experience, Tillich identifies the erotic as the force that combats just such legalistic understandings of human beings' relation to the divine. Eros is not the disinterested application of rules and regulations, but the passionate love of beauty, truth, and justice which opens us to see the potential for realizing the universal values in each situation of concrete action.

Ultimately, Tillich believes, the only firm foundation for morality is human beings' desire to participate in the life of a community shaped by the divine Spirit. The basis of moral behavior is humans' shared erotic yearning for healed relation to the ground of being. In realizing specific moral acts and tasks, human beings must be open to receive and reflect the love of God, that of the divine life that embraces the highest possible forms of the good, the beautiful, and the true. Turned erotically toward the ideals summed up in the living power of the ground of being, persons are empowered to translate these ideals into ethical action that meets the specific demands of the context.

Eros, as the "transmoral motivation for moral action" is united with the agape-love created by the Spiritual Presence, the "ultimate source of all moral demands." From the union of these two qualities of love, from the coming together of "demand" and "motivation," emerges, Tillich claims, a grace-ful and "involved" form of moral care which is able to "listen" attentively to the particular situation while at the same time orienting itself to the ultimate horizon of humankind's spiritual destiny.

Tillich's effort to use the power of eros to connect the abstract ideals of goodness, truth, and beauty with the concrete situation of moral action represents an original and significant step in Christian theological ethics. Yet Tillich's concept of the transmoral motivation is not without its ambiguities. His acknowledgment of love and in particular of eros as a necessary motivating factor in ethical behavior moves Tillich's moral theory beyond the dualistic, moral concepts of the Kantian tradition. Tillich points convincingly to the need to correlate justice and right action positively with the dynamics of human passion. This need has also been recognized as decisive by recent feminist and womanist authors concerned with the erotic. Like some feminists and womanists, Tillich perceives that ethical action cannot be properly understood as a victory over human feeling. Rather, the roots of moral motivation must be sought in the passions themselves.

However, by describing human morality as a "station on the way to something ultimate—the divine," Tillich's theory resurrects dualistic perspectives on another level. The contempt for human feeling and relationality from which Tillich wishes to liberate ethical action returns again in the form of an orientation toward divinized abstractions. These universal values borrowed from classical philosophy transcend the dimension of embodied human relation. They are presented as abstract, universal ends in relation to which specific human relationships and ethical decisions have the status of mere means. The ambiguous connection between the divine ideals and specific human acts robs Tillich's concept of the erotic "transmoral motivation" of a part of its force.

The "eros of community"

The concept of community is a crucial one for Tillich, in his understanding of morality and in other areas of theological and philosophical thought. "The community," he affirms, "is a phenomenon of life which has analogies in all realms" (ST 3:41). Communal structures and relationships shape human life at all levels.

In ethics, Tillich defines the overriding "moral imperative" in terms of the individual's personal relationship to a community. The fundamental moral task is "the command to become what one potentially is, a *person* within a community of persons" (MB, 19; italics in original). If it were possible, Tillich insists, to imagine a being "with the psychosomatic structure of man," yet existing "completely outside any human community," such a being would be entirely unable to "actualize its potential spirit," that is, to realize itself as a choice-making being, a bearer of creativity and responsibility. Such a creature would be "driven in all directions, limited only by its finitude, but it would not experience the ought-to-be." The moral "self-integration" through which the "person as a person" comes into being occurs only "in a community, within which the continuous mutual encounter of centered self with centered self is possible and actual" (ST 3:40–41). To take away the communal dimension of human life would be, Tillich argues, to take away the potential for personhood; it would mean abolishing human life as such.

In politics, Tillich views the "experience of community within the group" as the real foundation of all social and political power relationships (LPJ, 98). In the area of spirituality and religious practice, as well, the concept of the Spiritual Community is one of the central symbols used by Tillich to characterize the emergence of healed New Being within human existence. In *Love, Power, and Justice,* Tillich sets the term "holy community" quite simply equal to the concept of the "new creation within the world of estrangement" (*LPJ*, 115–16). The theme of Spiritual Community shows that, despite his tendency to focus theologically on the existential situation of the individual, Tillich does not conceive human beings' experience of "ultimate concern" simply as a private affair of intellectual questioning or inward-turning spirituality. Persons' spiritual experiences, like their moral dispositions, are shaped by a matrix of relationships to other human beings. The divine Spirit's healing entry into the human spirit does not, Tillich affirms, "occur in isolated individuals." Rather, this transformation of the human condition takes place "in social groups, since all the functions of the human spirit"—moral, cultural, and religious—are "conditioned by the social context of the ego-thou encounter" (*ST* 3:139).

Tillich's insistence on the importance of community is of course by no means unique or surprising in theological thinking. What is surprising is Tillich's emphasis on the role of eros as the binding force that shapes communal life.

In an early article on "The Youth Movement and Religion," Tillich singles out "the eros of community" as one of the most important creative contributions of the anti-fascist German youth movement to the struggle for social, political, and economic justice in the Weimar era. He sees the elements of communal "mysticism" and "eros" emphasized in the youth movement as introducing a new dynamism into the rigid structures of bourgeois society. Tillich is also insightful enough to perceive the risks and ambiguities associated with such a volatile and passionate approach to political and social problems. Yet he remains convinced that the young are right to take an erotic rather than a detached and formalized attitude toward community-building and action for change.

The youth movement of which he writes combines, Tillich notes, a "mystical" respect for nature with "a second element: the mystical quality of the community. To the struggle against the rationalization of nature corresponds the struggle against the rationalistic destruction of community relationships." The "eros" that animates the youth movement "breaks through," he claims, "the barriers of social fragmentation and with them the hardened forms of bourgeois customs along with their hidden hypocrisy." If in some cases, this "creative eros" degenerates into "subjective, anarchic eroticism," the movement as a whole succeeds in freeing itself from these destructive distortions: "The eros of the community remains pure and gains religious depth."

The "mystical aspect of community," Tillich writes, creates common ground within the youth movement in its struggle against a "vulgar capitalist nationalism of power" and against sectarian deformations of the socialist ideal (the National Socialist party and its allies). "From this mysticism, from this eros of community" which informs the thinking and the struggle of youth, "warming, stimulating currents already flow out to loosen the rigidity" of a rationalistically-ordered society built on conformity to preset schemas rather than on genuine human relationships (*GW* 13:131–32).

In *Love, Power, and Justice,* Tillich develops his ideas on community structures and their erotic roots. He affirms that "every social group is a community, potentially and actually." All types of "organisms," natural, living organisms and collective social entities, are "based on some form of reuniting love." The cells of a living body, the members of a family and the citizens of a nation are all, he claims, examples of communal-organic connectedness. The "communal self-affirmation" that informs such organic structures on the social level is called the "spirit of the group." The sharing within the community of an organic, connecting power—and with it the very existence of the group as an organized entity—is dependent upon this "spirit." And Tillich claims explicitly that this spirit of unity, the force of "community within the group" is founded on "love under guidance of its *eros* and *philia* qualities" (*LPJ,* 98).

In a speech to the prestigious assembly gathered to discuss the papal encyclical "Pacem in Terris" in New York City in February 1965, Tillich continued to insist on the central role of the eros of community in shaping relations within and among social groups, and even between nations. His "Pacem in Terris" address was delivered a decade after the publication of *Love, Power, and Justice;* more than forty years separated it from the appearance of the article on the German youth movement. Yet his identification of eros as the dynamic element in communal and political relations remained confident and unchanging. Near the end of his career, Tillich could speak serenely on this subject to an assembly of some of the most celebrated religious and intellectual figures of his day.

Encouragement of a form of erotic relatedness among large social groups, indeed among whole peoples is essential, Tillich told his audience, for the achievement of a stable global peace. "More than a legal organization is needed," if lasting peace is to be a reality. What is required is a form of "consensus." "This consensus is not, however, something as theoretical as the name suggests"; rather, consensus is simply another name for the " 'eros of community,' that type of love which is not directed towards an individual, but towards a group." It is thought, Tillich states, that one cannot "love a people." In reference to the national state as a political structure, this may indeed be true. But it is not true "for the relationship to the people of the other nation." To the other nation as a people with its unique qualities and virtues, bonds of erotic connectedness can be established. Indeed, Tillich insists, these erotic links must be cultivated, for they represent the only real basis for lasting sympathy and understanding between the peoples and countries of the world. "Without this eros, a world community does not seem to be possible. . . . Every expression of such an eros justifies the hope for peace. Every refusal of such eros reduces the chances of peace" (*GW* 13:443).

The erotic quality Tillich attributes to authentic community implies that healthy communal relations can never be those of disinterested contractual exchange. Eros implies a deeper, committed involvement in the lives of others. An erotic conception of community demands a passionate investment in the shared life and integrity of the group which goes far beyond the impersonal relations implied in a social model based on rational "fair exchange." Eros as active, "interested" care strives, Tillich suggests, to establish harmony not through mere detached "tolerance" of the other, but through a respect for others which includes a passionate participation in their being and in their destiny. Furthermore, as Tillich stresses explicitly in his article on the youth movement, the eros of community is not merely different from the mode of relation which dominates social, economic, and political existence under a rationalistic, technical-manipulative order. Eros actively sets itself in opposition to and seeks to undermine the commodification of relationships encountered in a society founded on economic alienation, class exploitation, and the worship of technology, capital, and progress (see *GW* 13:131–32; *SD,* 31, 150–53).

Communal eros as Tillich understands it has profound implications for politics. In several important texts, Tillich explores the political consequences of a view of human community as founded on erotic connections. In *The Socialist Decision,* he associates eros with the "powers of origin"—soil, blood, the primitive "social group"—which he sees as determining the character and the goals of all forms of "political romanticism." Such "romanticism" can, as in the case of Nazism, take demonically destructive forms. Yet the creative force of the powers of origin in the life of social and political groups cannot be denied. Tillich asserts that authentic socialism—in contrast to the caricature of socialist ideals represented by the National Socialist movement— can only succeed if the proletariat and its leaders are able to recover an erotic connection to the powers of origin. If the struggle for economic justice and for political change is to attain its end, the classes and groups that carry on the struggle must be, Tillich argues, empowered by a connection to the deepest levels of shared desire and communal feeling.

Of primary importance in this process of empowerment is a recovery of the eros relations that found community. An authentic experience of community has been denied the proletariat under the rule of capital and the bourgeois-rational principle (SD, 85f.). A reappropriation of communal eros is, Tillich believes, indispensable to the effort of the proletarian movement to generate support for its project of social transformation.

Tillich describes the ideal of community in terms that once more make explicit the opposition of the communal eros to the rationalistic and exploitative structures of bourgeois society. "The return to the social group," Tillich writes, "is expressed in the appeal for 'community' which is so common to all forms of political romanticism. This appeal reflects an intense longing for a supporting group, in contrast to the spiritual, economic and political autonomy of the individual" which characterizes the "rational system" of capitalism. This longing is "the desire to be supported and made secure," a yearning for forms of communal connectedness that only "increases all the more as the critical social situation makes the individual aware of his or her insecurity." Connected with and spurring on this longing for renewed communal relations are "the powers of eros" which have "erupted" in movements seeking to transform capitalist economic and sociopolitical structures. These expressions of the communal eros are "powers that seek to overcome the liberal competition of all against all in the economic struggle for existence" (SD, 31).

Paradoxically, the socialist movement must, if it is to remain viable, draw on the dynamic, nonrational elements that have been so successfully exploited by political romanticism, true socialism's most dangerous enemy. Tillich is convinced that a harnassing of eros in its community-building force and its link to the powers of origin is crucial for the socialist cause. He laments German socialism's inability to produce leaders capable of generating the "spirit of eros and commitment" without which any social or political enterprise, no matter how noble its motives, is doomed to failure (SD, 74).

Socialism must, Tillich claims, galvanize its members by more fully developing and exploiting a sense of "eros and purpose in the life of the community." He devotes an entire section in the closing chapter of *The Socialist Decision* to a discussion of this theme (*SD*, 150f.). The dynamics of political movements and of interactions on all levels of human society are not, Tillich argues, based exclusively on the setting of rational goals and the implementation of measures to attain them. Rather, politic aims and methods are shaped by passionate, communal feeling. Social and political "purpose" is in all cases connected to an "eros" that binds persons together in a community of feeling and struggle. It is for this reason, Tillich believes, that the "idea of the nation" in which "all the powers of origin are combined" cannot simply be eliminated by socialist thought, but must instead be used in combination with the "overarching concept of humanity as a goal." Political and social structures with which strong elements of communal eros are associated—the nation is one example—form part of the context within which any realistic political movement must work. A theory or a group that chose to ignore the power of these erotic bonds would be unable to produce a significant impact (*SD*, 150–51).

Tillich suggests that women will have an especially decisive role to play in introducing erotic, energizing elements into the political struggle for socialism and into the community which carries on that struggle. "Socialism cannot possibly tolerate," Tillich affirms, the continuation of "male patriarchalism." The socialist movement can "ward off" the dangerous, reactionary tendencies associated with patriarchal thinking "only by relating women's powers of origin to the socialist struggle." This introduction of specifically female perspectives must occur above all, he claims, "precisely at those places where a general awakening of the powers of origin for the sake of the socialist principle is needed, above all in cultural and community life" (*SD*, 152–53).

The unabashed sexual essentialism that marks Tillich's discussions of "women's powers" and the importance of such powers in religion and in the cultural-political sphere make certain passages of his early work highly problematic (cf. *D*, 287f.). Despite its essentialist ambiguities, however, there is merit in Tillich's suggestion that women occupy a biological and social position that sets them in particularly strong critical opposition to the dominant values of the capitalist economic and social order. Similar ideas have been explored by more recent feminist theologians and political theorists.[9] Tillich's insistence on the importance of erotic forces in the success of political movements also has disturbing echoes in light of the devastating exploitation of forms of group eros by the Nazis. Yet the Nazi phenomenon in fact brings a confirmation of Tillich's thesis that nonrational erotic forces play a vital role in politics. The crucial question—for which Tillich gives no systematic answer—is how such energies can be made to serve the cause of political and social justice, rather than that of oppression.

Beyond his engagement with the particular political program of German socialism, Tillich remained firmly convinced throughout his theological career that all political and social power structures, as well as all informal types of community, are founded on relationships of eros.

Tillich writes that the power of the "ruling minority" within any political group is based not only on overt structures of enforcement and coercion, but more decisively on the "silent acknowledgment" extended to the rulers by the other members of the group. And this "silent acknowledgment received by a ruling group from the whole group cannot be understood," Tillich affirms, "without an element which is derived neither from justice nor from power but from love," and in particular from eros and philia. The "silent acknowledgment" on which the exercise of authority depends is shaped by the erotic "experience of community" which unites the individual members of the group among themselves, and which at the same time gives them a sense of erotic connectedness to their leaders. "The power and justice of being in a social group is dependent on the spirit of the community, and this means on the uniting love," the binding and nurturing power of eros and philia, which "creates and sustains the community" (LPJ, 98–99).

In *Systematic Theology*, Tillich gives a similar but even more explicit account of his theory that all political power structures are based on eros relations. "Political power," Tillich argues, "is never independent of the life of the group" within which this power is exercised. "In every power structure, eros relations underlie the organizational

---

[9]See Hartsock, *Money, Sex, and Power,* esp. the concluding chaps. on the concept of a critical feminist *Standpunkt*. Also, Haunani-Kay Trask, *Eros and Power: The Promise of Feminist Theory* (Philadelphia: University of Pennsylvania Press, 1986), Introduction and all of part 2.

form." He claims that support for a ruling figure, group, or class is invariably based

> on an experience of belonging, a form of communal eros which does not exclude struggles for power within the supporting group but which unites it against other groups. This is obvious in all statelike organizations from the family up to the nation. Blood relations, language, traditions, and memories create many forms of eros which make the power structure possible. Preservation by enforcement and increase by conquest follow, but do not produce, the historical power of a group. (*ST* 3:309)

Rather, such historical power is rooted in the eros that shapes the communal spirit of the group, giving the group its identity and determining its goals.

As the foundation of political power, eros is also, Tillich believes, a crucial element in the creation and sustaining of legal structures. "One way among others," Tillich asserts, "in which the eros relations that underlie a power structure express themselves is in the legal principles that determine the laws and their administration by the ruling center." Any sort of legal system within a group or society must ultimately be seen as derived "neither from an abstract concept of justice nor from the will to power" of the ruling group. Both of these factors, of course, "contribute to the concrete structure of justice." They can also, however, destroy concrete justice if one of them gains unchecked power within the social order. "For neither of them is the basis of a statelike structure. The basis of every legal system" is rather "the eros relations of the group in which they appear" (*ST* 3:310).

The cultivation and shaping of the eros of community thus emerges as decisive for the making of justice in a concrete historical and social context. Tillich acknowledges that mere "abstract concepts" of justice can never be enough to bring just relations into existence within a society. Authentic, or as Tillich calls it, "creative" justice is founded not on abstract principles or on elaborate discourses, but on the erotic connections that exist (or fail to exist) among human beings within the relational weave of a community. If these erotic connections are sound and nurturing, then the business of the group will be conducted in a just manner. If the underlying eros relations are twisted by fear, hatred, concupiscence, and the desire for domination, then no amount of legal coercion or sentimental rhetoric can bring justice into being.

Tillich's own theory of justice is limited in important ways. The theory does not seriously attempt to unravel the complexity of the relationship between justice as a quality of human feeling and individual moral action and justice as a structural characteristic of institutions. Specific forms of radical injustice, such as racism, sexism, and class exploitation, are referred to and condemned in general terms. Yet these discussions, especially in Tillich's later writings, are often short on concrete details and practical perspectives. However, Tillich's lucid insight into the insufficiency of a detached concept of just action founded on the liberal model of contractual exchange remains profoundly meaningful. His claim that real justice implies committed, erotic involvement continues to resound compellingly, and today finds echoes in the work of leading feminist and womanist theologians.

The "religious eros"

Tillich does not view eros as the negation of the divinely created agapic love which has traditionally been understood as the foundation of the Christian life. On the contrary, he is convinced that agape, which is a divine gift "pouring down" from God to humankind, must be united with eros. Otherwise, it would be impossible to account for human love to the divine, which by definition, Tillich asserts, involves an erotic "elevation from lower goods to the *summum bonum*." Without an erotic element, such love of the creature for the creator becomes not genuine love, but servile fear or mere formal obedience. Tillich does not simply suggest that eros should be tolerated within the framework of Christianity. He maintains that eros is central to authentic Christian life. Eros plays a vital role in the right ordering of the human being's relation to the divine.

Tillich speaks of this relation in terms of "ultimate concern." Persons' "ultimate concern" with their "being and meaning," and thus with their relationship to God, shows that they are "already in the grasp of the Spiritual Presence." This concern is not chosen or created by the human individual. It is itself a creation of the Spirit entering into the dimension of human experience, human love, human destiny. Yet ultimate concern expresses itself in personal life as an "infinite passion" marked by powerful erotic elements. The concern by which persons feel themselves to be drawn toward reunion with the divine source and ground of all being is "basically of the nature of eros" (*ST* 1:281).

"Love in all its qualities," Tillich writes, "drives toward reunion." The particularity of "eros, as distinct from philia and libido," is that eros "drives toward reunion with things and beings in their essential goodness" and ultimately "with the good itself." For mystical theology, however, "God and the good itself are identical." Thus, what Plato describes as eros toward the good is at the same time "in religious language, love toward God." This erotic love can be represented symbolically in different ways: as a yearning awakened within us, as a force pulling us from without, or as a combination of the two. "In Plato it is the divine-human power of eros that elevates the mind to the divine; and in Aristotle, it is the power of the divine that attracts every finite thing and produces by this attraction the movement of the stars, the universe and the human mind" (MB, 59–60).

Correctly understood, eros is the "source of every movement in the world." For Tillich, this implies that the movement in which humanity returns from estrangement and brokenness to reunion with its divine source is a process animated by the erotic. The "unambiguous" agape of God is at the beginning of this movement of reconciliation and reunion in the sense that God initiates the reconciliation by reaching out in love and compassion to estranged human beings. Yet insofar as this movement toward reunion is experienced by human beings under the conditions of existence, it has the character we associate with love as eros.

Tillich is determined to work out a theoretical description of the relationship of agape and eros which will allow both types of love to be recognized as crucial for religion. While none of his attempts to describe this connection is entirely satisfying, his continuing attention to the problem is in itself significant. Tillich will simply not let go of the religious eros, and of his basic intuition that the erotic is a decisive force in spiritual life. As Anders Nygren's writings show, Tillich's convictions about the religious eros set him radically at odds with the neo-orthodox concepts dominating Protestant theology at mid-century. Tillich's stubborn insistence on the importance of eros in spiritual life is in fact unparalleled even among the more liberal Protestant theologians of his day. Despite the theological eccentricity of his position, he refused to abandon the idea that divine agape cannot be separated in human experience from the power of the erotic.

In *Biblical Religion and the Search for Ultimate Reality*, Tillich experiments with a highly unusual description of the connection between eros and agape. The text shows the reshaping of conventional theological structures that Tillich was willing to undertake in order to affirm the vital role of religious eros. "The desire for God," Tillich states in this passage, "is both the desire for him as love and the desire for him as truth." To avoid the confusions associated with the tendency to give eros an "exclusively sensual meaning," it may be wise to use the term agape to describe "the desire for [God] as love." But the erotic element of "desire for God" must not be allowed to disappear from the vocabulary of theology. Tillich suggests the possibility of using eros to designate "the desire for [God] as truth." This would, he thinks, "correspond with the genuine meaning of *eros* (e.g., in Plato's *Symposium*)" as the force that "drives the soul" toward union with the true, the good, and the beautiful (*BR*, 72).

With this rather surprising suggestion, Tillich attempts to secure a credible and important role for eros in religious experience, while minimizing the ambiguities associated with the word's "sensual meaning." Tillich's proposal is an interesting if in some ways perplexing one. Tillich distinguishes two key aspects of the divine nature ("love" and "truth") and assigns a different form of love to each "part." At first glance, this might seem to imply an unacceptable fragmentation of the divine. Tillich's suggestion might be read as dividing God into a specifically Christian dimension on the one hand (God as love, correlated with agape) and an independent secular philosophical aspect on the other (God as truth, connected with the Platonic eros). Tillich's proposal appears to stand in tension with his own desire to understand the ground of being as a transcendent unity. Yet by acknowledging a separation of these aspects of the divine, Tillich's aim is precisely to clarify their underlying unity. Distinguishing these interconnected aspects of the divine nature is a crucial step in the attempt to reconcile the "personalism" of biblical religion with the secular philosophical quest for ultimate reality. God as love and God as truth, the Christian God and the ultimate object of philosophy are to be understood as unified on a higher plane. At this higher level, agape and eros, provisionally separated within human existence, are also reconnected in ontological unity. Divine love and philosophical truth, agapic and erotic connections to ultimate meaning can be honored together. Both demand respect, Tillich argues. In their dynamic complementarity and their ultimate unity, they illuminate the differentiation within human experience of a reality which is, at the highest level, one.

Tillich is willing to treat conventional theological concepts in surprising ways in order to argue that eros plays, alongside and on an equal footing with agape, a central role in religious life. Whether ordinary Christians can correlate Tillich's description of agape and eros with their own lived experiences of connection to the divine is uncertain. It is clear, at the very least, that the proposal offered in *Biblical*

Religion gives a rather unorthodox turn to the traditional Protestant image of God and of human beings' relationship to the ultimate. Since this particular model of the relationship between eros and agape in religious experience is never taken up again in the same form, there is reason to think that Tillich himself was not satisfied with it. However, the somewhat forced quality of the proposal is actually one of its most interesting features. This quality is significant in two ways. First, because it reveals how important it was for Tillich to secure the role of eros in religious experience. In order to present eros and agape as love qualities on an equal footing within religious life, Tillich was willing to experiment with a description of the nature of God that appears highly unconventional in the context of modern Protestant theology. Second, because in forcing his theological vocabulary beyond the usual limits, Tillich makes some very interesting choices of words. These word-choices in the text of *Biblical Religion* point to the possibility of a far-reaching erasure of the boundaries between agape and eros.

Insofar as it is understood as originating in the divine nature, agapic love is conceived of as disinterested, since traditional theological interpretations of the divinity refuse the attribution of need or desire and hence incompleteness to God. Yet Tillich's dicussion in *Biblical Religion* affirms that, within human life, religious agape, like eros, is experienced as a form of "desire" for the ultimate. The characterization of agape in terms of desire narrows the gap between agapic love and eros. But this characterization stands in sharp tension as well to the understanding of agape as in essence free from "passion and sympathy" (*ST* 1:280). If, within the sphere of possible human experience, agape is desire, then the experiential fondation for the distinction between agape and the other love qualities becomes doubtful. Agape as it originates in God may be posited as pure, disinterested, and "unambiguous." Yet this metaphysical hypothesis does not solve the problem of the relevance of pure agape for human experience. The realm in which agape exists as pure, divine love—unambiguous and free from attraction and repulsion—falls entirely outside the realm of possible human experience and understanding. The distinction between agape and eros reveals itself as much more a piece of metaphysical speculation than an experientially verifiable fact with practical consequences for human life.

Reflection on the practical incomprehensibility of pure, divine agape within the framework of human knowledge and feeling awakens the idea that the relational dynamic of love between creator and creature could be described in a very different manner. It is not necessary to accept the hypothesis that, beyond our experience of all forms of authentic love as passionate desire, a superior level exists at which agape as divine love is free of desire, longing, passion. Rather, the highest form of God's love can itself be imaged as already and essentially informed by passionate, erotic elements. Outside of such a model, it may indeed be structurally impossible for us, on the basis of our human capacities, to connect any meaningful sort of content at all with the notion of divine agape. Tillich's observation on the necessity of erotic metaphors to make the divine love "concrete" (*ST* 1:281) reflects his sensitivity to this problem.

Tillich's discussion of agape as "desire" and his consistent mingling of agape with the religious eros bring him to the threshold of a radically new conception of the relationship between God and human beings. Tillich's discussion suggests the vision of a human–divine relation which is not characterized by dependence and helpless passivity on one side, disinterested benevolence on the other. His determination to reconcile agape with eros in religious life points toward the possibility of theorizing the connection between human beings and the divine in terms of a dynamic *interdependence* in which erotic passion is present on both sides of the relation between God and humans. It is only in the work of contemporary feminist and womanist authors that this concept has been systematically developed and explored. Yet Tillich's treatment of the religious eros moves toward a comparable perspective.[10]

Tillich never developed the line of thought opened in *Biblical Religion*. The text remains an anomaly. Here, Tillich's doctrine of the reconciliation of eros and agape is pushed further than in other, better known passages. Reconciliation moves, indeed, close to fusion. The experiential distinction between the two terms weakens almost to the point of disappearance. It is admitted that, even if agape enters the realm of human existence "from another dimension," in terms of actual human experience this fact has little importance. Both agape and eros are and must be experienced by human beings as forms of passionate desire. Thus, the terrain on which the two types of love meet and are united is the ground of eros, the passionate movement of the lower

---

[10]On the concept of divine–human interdependence, see esp. Isabel Carter Heyward, *The Redemption of God: A Theology of Mutual Relation* (Washington, D.C.: University Press of America, 1982). Compare as well the chapter "Eros in God?" in Paul Avis, *Eros and the Sacred* (Wilton, CT: Morehouse Publishing, 1990).

toward the higher. "Certainly," Tillich claims, "agape adds a decisive element to the ancient idea of love." Yet despite its origin in the divine, agape must not be seen as denying or opposing the erotic drive for "union with ultimate reality." Agape "reaches down," Tillich writes, borrowing a term from the vocabulary of Nygren and his followers. "But agape does not contradict the desire for the highest; and part of this desire is cognitive eros" (BR, 72).

The least radical conclusion that can be drawn from Tillich's discussion of agape and eros in Biblical Religion—and more generally from all of his work on the religious eros—is that divinely created agape is not the unique "active ingredient" in the relation between human beings and the divine. Eros does not appear in religious experience as a secondary accompaniment or contingent side effect. Stating the case even more strongly, whatever the metaphysical "dimensions" in which they arise, agape and eros emerge together in human life. They are inextricably interwoven in our lived experience of desire for the absolute. Without erotic passion firing our longing for universal value and informing our "ultimate concern," there would be no human experience of a relationship between God and humankind. The saving intervention of God in the realm of human existence makes itself known to us, Tillich claims, only through the "infinite passion" that the Spirit awakens. God's concern for human beings is revealed in our own "desire for God" as love and as truth. Thus, erotic desire reveals itself as the paradigmatic religious emotion.

The paradigmatic quality of religious eros is confirmed in Tillich's treatment of the mystical dimension of all religious faith. Eros is the "mystical quality of love," the animating element in all types of mystical experience. But the mystical is not, in Tillich's view, an isolated province of spiritual experience reserved for a few persons driven by special aspirations or blessed with exceptional gifts. He claims that all faith contains a mystical element. This confirms once again from a different angle the idea that emerged in the discussion of "ultimate concern": all faith is decisively informed by eros.

Despite the "anti-mystical tendencies in Protestantism," Tillich argues, "there is no faith (but only belief) without the Spirit's grasping the personal center of him who is in the state of faith." This "grasping of the personal center" is "a mystical experience, an experience of the presence of the infinite in the finite." Faith does not necessarily "produce mysticism as a religious type." Nevertheless, all faith does "include the mystical as a category, that is, the experience of the Spiritual

Presence" (*ST* 3:243). As in Tillich's analysis of faith as ultimate concern, the description of faith as mystical experience throws into sharp relief the erotic quality of the religious dimension of human experience.

Tillich argues that even a condition of full and perfect union with God does not abolish erotic and libidinal desire. "The word 'desire' is the expression of unfulfilment." However, Adam and the Christ—human beings in a state of nonalienation from God—are depicted in the Bible as "tempted on the basis of their desire for finite fulfilment." This leads to the conclusion that "desire and unity with God cannot contradict each other (this would include the statement that *eros* and *agape* cannot contradict each other)." Unity with God, Tillich asserts, "is not the negation of the desire for reunion of the finite with the finite. But where there is unity with God, there the finite is not desired alongside this unity but within it" (*ST* 2:129).

Eros inspires our spiritual longing for reunion with the divine ground, our desire to be set free from estrangement and to enter into a healed relationship with God. Yet for those who experience the most perfect forms of this healed oneness with the divine, eros does not simply disappear, giving way to some type of passionless beatitude. Rather, an erotic relationship to the finite world continues to flourish within the framework of unity with God. Implied in this assertion is the claim that an erotic relatedness to the world is the state that best corresponds to a life lived in unity with the divine will.

"Eros toward the world"

In discussing God's love for created reality, Tillich claims that eros can only be used as a poetic description. For divine love, "agape is the basic and only adequate symbol" (*ST* 1:281). However, the concept of eros furnishes the best name for the relationship to the created world which is characteristic of human beings living under the impact of the Spirit. Indeed, Tillich suggests that the possibility of having a relationship of "eros toward the world" is the defining quality of human being as such. The potential for such an erotic connection to reality is in a profound sense the capacity that marks us as human.

Among created beings, the human person is the most fully "individualized," thus the most fully "centered" within herself or himself. Yet as a centered being, the person is not and cannot be static. Tillich believes the structures of a centered and self-contained personhood are

precisely what enable human beings to open themselves toward encounter and change. The "self-integration" characteristic of the fully
individualized human permits him or her to participate in the "movement from centeredness through alteration back to centeredness," the
fundamental dynamic of all truly personal existence (*ST* 3:30–32).

Because she or he is centered, individualized, the person can also
participate in relationships with her or his world. "In this sense, . . .
centeredness exists as a process of outgoing and returning. For where
there is a center, there is a periphery that includes an amount of space."
And this "space," Tillich suggests, corresponds to the dimension of
"participation, with which individualization forms a polarity." Individualization separates one being from all others. Thus, the most
individualized being "would appear to be the most unapproachable
and lonely one." At the same time, however, this individualized being
"has the greatest potentiality for universal participation" (*ST* 3:33).

Turning outside of themselves, centered persons encounter not simply, like animals, a neutral "environment," but instead a "world" with
which they can enter into passionate and creative relationship. " 'Total
centeredness,' " Tillich states, "is the situation of having, face to face
with one's self, a world to which one, at the same time, belongs as a
part." This situation "liberates the self from the bondage to the environment" which is the fate of other life forms. Like these other
creatures, "man lives in an environment." Unlike them, however, the
human being "has a world," that is to say, that she or he is in relation
with a "structured whole of infinite potentialities and actualities." In
the person's "encounter with his environment (this home, this tree,
this person), he experiences both environment and world" (*ST* 3:39).

The human being "transcends [the] merely environmental quality"
of objects, places, beings by connecting with them from the position
of a "centered self" capable of sustaining the tensions of full relation.
This capacity for communion with and participation in the world, a
participation which Tillich explicitly qualifies as erotic, distinguishes
the human being from other life forms. The capacity for eros characterizes, for Tillich, a specifically human mode of relatedness. The
human is capable of "universal participation. He can have communion
with his world and eros toward it." The potential for passionate and
creative engagement with reality and the responsibility that such a
potential implies distinguish human beings from other creatures whose
ability to understand, transform, and possibly destroy their environment is more limited. The capacity for experiencing "eros toward the
world" is the quality that defines a fully human life. It is a fundamental

drive to reach outward beyond the boundaries of the self toward communion with other persons, toward encounter with the world, ultimately toward the ground of being whose creative love shapes and sustains the world. Through eros, which can be "theoretical as well as practical," the human being participates "in the universe in all its dimensions" (ST 3:33). In the absence of such a life-force drawing us into a constantly renewed encounter with the world, human existence could not continue. Eros toward the world identifies the gift and the challenge of human being.

Tillich believes that eros, as he understands the concept, could and should embrace the whole complex of persons, things, creatures, and ideas which constitutes the "world" of human experience. Nothing lies outside the bounds of possible erotic involvement. From the simplest natural forms to the most subtle works of art to the endlessly fascinating microcosmic complexity of the human person, each thing and being can touch us in a way that awakens our erotic response. "No thing is merely a thing." Every object, being, and concept offers itself to the person touched by the Spirit as a "possible object of eros" (ST 3:258).

If we are capable of experiencing a sense of caring connectedness with any part of the world around us, Tillich claims, eros is the basis of that connection. In an address on "Creative Listening," he identifies eros as the first and most important foundation for creativity and a relationship of responsive interaction with the world (GW 13:475). Eros is the power of love which enables us to involve ourselves in existences that touch our own, which moves us beyond the stage of mere observation into participation, passionate interest. "Eros is the love," Tillich states, "which drives toward the sublime quality in all things and all events. And there is sublimity in everything," in the natural world and in the human realm. "One may easily feel" erotic power in works of art, literature, and music. Yet the same power also dwells "in the mysterious rationality of numbers and equations, in the inexhaustible depths of the microcosmic and macrocosmic structures of our universe."

The "eros-provoking power" also shows itself "in the movements of history and in the greatness and tragedy of historical personalities and nations." We can trace the developments of eros in the "changing structures of social groups," the unfolding destinies of collective entities. Yet erotic power is also present in each individual human life, in the "dynamics of consciousness" and in each person's "unconscious depths." In every dimension in which it expresses itself, Tillich claims, life is a phenomenon of fascinating, erotic complexity: simultaneously "mysterious and open, profound and superficial, great and tragic, sublime and profane in each of its manifestations." Moreover, the same is true of us, who as human beings are life's most "inclusive manifestation," representing life in all its fullness and diversity. "Since the equal seeks for its equal," we as microcosmic representations of the full spectrum of cosmic possibilities are drawn outward toward all aspects of the world around us. "Every part and every dimension of the universe can become an object of eros," awakening our desire for participation.

"Poetically speaking," Tillich affirms, "we can say that things wait to be discovered and to be united with us." The "things" of the material world themselves desire to be "loved by us." "They call to us to listen to them." A relationship of mutual care and interest can link us to apparently inanimate objects that "speak to us" as their hidden powers are disclosed by eros. "The eros to the things which speak to us is the first condition of creative listening." Such listening means for Tillich a relationship to the created world and to other people in which participation and care, rather than objectification and control, are central (GW 13:474–75).

Tillich affirms that he does not know "any man or woman of superior creative ability in any realm of life" in whose work one cannot find traces of an erotic "openness to what things [have] to tell them" (GW 13:475). The eros toward the world which characterizes the lives of creative individuals implies a communicative openness that embraces not only persons with whom they can engage in verbal dialogue but also creatures and "things" with whom different modes of communication must be found.

The situation of erotic communication Tillich describes connects us both with nature and with the products of the cultural sphere. In the "Spiritual Community," the "aestheticism" or "lack of seriousness" which is one of the characteristic expressions of an alienated relationship to culture is overcome by an authentic "eros toward the [cultural] creation itself." This connection brings out, Tillich claims, the moral dimension in all forms of cultural production and heals the separation between aesthetic and creative pleasure and the moral concern with justice. "In the Spiritual Community, there is no aestheticist detachment; there is the seriouness of those who seek to experience the ultimate in being and meaning through every cultural form and task. The seriousness of moral self-integration and the richness of moral self-creation are united in the Spiritual Presence" (ST 3:161).

Tillich associates the healing cultural eros with an attitude of "seriousness" which unites the concerns of morality and aesthetic creativity. Yet the seriousness of the life transformed by the Spiritual Presence and by the healing impact of eros is neither self-important nor morose. This seriousness includes a vital element of play. The aestheticism that is combatted by an authentic "eros toward the creation" is not "to be confused with the element of play in cultural creation and reception." This element of playfulness is not opposed to creative eros; on the contrary, it is a vital part of a life lived in the spirit of eros and creative freedom. Tillich maintains that "play is one of the most characteristic expressions of the freedom of the spirit, and there is a seriousness in free playing not to be surpassed by the seriousness of necessary work" (ST 3:161).

The relationship of "eros toward the world" which Tillich describes expresses itself in an attitude of "serious playfulness" and ultimately of joy, the manifestation of a healed connection to the created world and to the divine. The side of Tillich's writings and personality which has been focused on most often is connected with "existential seriousness," anxiety (barely) overcome by the heroic "courage to be." Yet there is also in Tillich's thought a powerful emphasis on joy as the state in which we attain true spiritual fulfillment. Joy reflects not a deluded vision of the world and our place within it, but instead a condition of right relation to the world. "Joy is born out of union with reality itself" (NB, 146). It is the expression of genuine spiritual understanding, of an authentic "seeing into."

Joy is, Tillich observes, an experience that has been maligned and mistrusted in many Christian communities. Yet a passionately loving and joyful relationship to the world is a sign that one's life has truly been touched and transformed by the Spiritual Presence. "The lack of joy" is to be understood biblically, Tillich writes, as a "consequence of man's separation from God." The "presence of joy," on the other hand, reflects, the "reunion" with the divine (NB, 142).

Christians' "inner conflicts about accepting or rejecting joy" result, Tillich argues, from an attitude of "suspicion" toward nature and the created world, a refusal to accept the biblical affirmation, " 'Behold, it was very good.' " The encounter with the "suppression of joy and guilt about joy in Christian groups almost drove me," Tillich states, "to a break with Christianity." For "what passes for joy in these groups is an emaciated, intentionally childish, unexciting, unecstatic thing, without color and danger, without heights and depths" (NB, 143–44). The attitude of eros toward the world generates a joy from which these elements of color, passion, and intensity are not missing. Under the impact of the Spiritual Presence, the individual dares to affirm and to enjoy life: to enjoy it, moreover, erotically, while maintaining the connection to the religious and moral values summoned forth by the transforming power of the Spirit. Whereas God is "infinitely more" than any particular "life process," "He works through all of them. Therefore no conflict is necessary between the joy in God and the joy of life" (NB, 144). The "blessedness" associated with agape-love and the erotic "joy of life" complement and fulfill one another (NB, 150–51).

Once again, Tillich insists that the joy derived from a healed relation to the world is not to be equated with pleasure in the narrow sense. "Love relations," Tillich points out, "most conspicuously relations between the sexes remain without joy if we use the other one as a means for pleasure or as a means to escape pain." Such distortions of the energy of relational connection are "a threat to all human relations" (NB, 145–46).

Yet joy and pleasure must by no means be seen as excluding one another. In *Systematic Theology*, Tillich suggests a criterion for distinguishing positive, healing pleasure from abusive, alienating types. Authentic pleasure can be defined as the "awareness of one's self . . . as the bearer of creative eros" (ST 3:92). The connection to the eros which establishes and maintains a balanced, nurturing relatedness to other persons and to the world is the hallmark of pleasure that is creative and life-affirming. Tillich develops the same idea in a sermon text, basing the distinction between "good" and "bad" forms of pleasure on their relation to authentic joy. "Those pleasures are good," he claims, "which go together with joy; those are bad which prevent joy." It is not, he asserts categorically, "more Christian to reject than to accept pleasure. Let us not forget that the rejection implies a rejection of creation, or as the Church Fathers called it, a blasphemy of the Creator-God." Every Christian should understand "a fact of which many non-Christians are keenly aware: the suppression of the joy of life produces hatred of life, hidden or open" (NB, 148–49).

The joy of life which emerges as the natural expression of an attitude of "eros toward the world" draws sustenance, as eros does, from many areas of experience. These range from "eating and drinking" to "playing and dancing, the beauty of nature and the ecstasy of love"; from "the power of knowledge and the fascination of art" to "community" in "family, friendship, and the social group" (NB, 147–48). Deep, fulfilling joy is not reserved for a distant future, or for a life beyond this one. On the contrary, it is to be experienced here and now, in the world in which we live and to which we are connected by the ties of eros.

"Paul asks," Tillich stresses, "the Philippians to have joy *now.*" "Blessed are those" human beings who "participate in this fulfillment here and now." Of course, certain aspects of human and of cosmic fulfillment belong only to the future. But if this fulfillment cannot be seen and felt powerfully in the present, then it cannot be seen or believed at all. It is present in those moments of our lives in which we feel the joy that springs from a deep, sustaining connection to the world around us. It is present when we experience the erotic "seeing into" that breaks down the barriers between selves. "Where there is joy," there is the type of erotic "fulfillment" of which Tillich speaks. "In fulfillment and joy, the inner aim of life, the meaning of creation, and the end of salvation are attained" (*NB*, 150–51).

Erotic connection-making: the transcendence of estrangement

Eros as Tillich describes it is an energy of connection-making. This is the common denominator that underlies the many different areas in which the erotic finds expression. Eros opens us, draws us out, moves us beyond ourselves into sustaining relationship with things, ideas, and beings. Eros is the force that pulls us as centered beings outward into the surrounding "space," as Tillich calls it, the region of encounter and participation.

Tillich understands love in all its qualities as expressing an onto-logical "drive toward the reunion of the separated." Thus, each of the love qualities within its particular sphere calls us toward reunion with some aspect of "that which belongs to us and from which we have been separated." Yet none of the other aspects of love plays a role comparable to that of eros in shaping at many different levels a passionate, sustaining connection between self and world.

Agape remains the nominally dominant quality in Tillich's discussions of the relations among the types of love. Yet as love entering human existence "from another dimension," agape is a force whose basic nature and practical influence within human life remain difficult to grasp. Unconditional agape, as it springs from the divine, totally unrelated to the "contingent characteristics" of its object, is much more a necessary piece in a metaphysical construct than it is a recognizable factor in human experience. Tillich's insistence on the presence of erotic elements in all human experience of agape is an attempt to compensate for the basic difficulty of relating the agape concept to the realities of our experience of love in concrete relational situations. The simplistic interpretation of agape as a pure and unambiguous "will to self-sur-render for the sake of the other being" (*DF,* 114) does not, Tillich acknowledges, correspond to any recognizable form of human ex-perience. In order to embrace the complexity of human relationality, a more complex understanding of love is required. Agapic commit-ment to the other being and erotic desire for self-fulfillment through and with the other do not exist as "alternatives." The two are inevitably intertwined. "No love is real without a unity of eros and agape," Tillich states categorically. "Agape without eros is obedience to a moral law, without warmth, without longing, without reunion" (*DF,* 114–15).

Tillich's treatments of eros, although surprising in many respects, stick close to the lived and felt realities of human life. Eros remains the connection-shaping form of love whose impact Tillich describes most convincingly. And for none of the other qualities does Tillich analyze specific applications in so many different areas of human ex-istence.

Eros links us, Tillich claims, to the earth, to nature, to the "primal powers" of being. Erotic forces maintain our ties to the deepest, pre-rational levels of our biological origins and to the fundamental struc-tures of our primary relationships in family and the primitive "social group." Yet though it has nonrational aspects, eros is not an irrational force. The erotic is the animating principle in the philosophical quest for wisdom and in all forms of artistic creativity. Even the types of rational practice associated with technology can be touched by the erotic. Indeed, these activities and products must be approached in a spirit of eros if they are not to become dehumanizing and ultimately destructive. Genuine eros toward "technical Gestalten" can help, Til-lich believes, to overcome the alienation from creative work and its products which is characteristic of a technologically advanced society.

In this way, Tillich suggests, eros toward the natural world does not necessarily lead to a sweeping denial of the benefits of technology and scientific learning. Eros can accept the positive aspects of technical progress, transforming where necessary without rejecting out of hand the idea that practical advances that respond to real needs are in them-selves good. Eros is not simply the expression of a romantic nostalgia for a mythical condition of pre-industrial harmony with nature. The eros described by Tillich affirms human cultural creativity in balance with the requirements of a healed relationship to the "powers of or-igin," the earth, the natural world.

Not just philosophical wisdom, but all knowledge includes an erotic aspect. In every act of knowledge, the "cognitive eros" catalyzes a dynamic union between the knower and the known. As this union reaches its most perfect forms, the subject enters into the being of the perceived object while taking it into her- or himself. The knower "participates" in the known, transforming, but also allowing her- or himself to be transformed. In ethics, too, eros plays a vital role. The erotic draws the individual toward the encounter with another self in which the moral imperative emerges from the tension between desire for the other and acknowledgment of the other's autonomy. At the same time, eros connects moral practice to the religious realm. It motivates and guides individual moral acts by orienting moral agents toward the "transmoral" goal of participation in the universal values which express the divine.

Erotic connections underlie all forms of human communal relat-edness, from the clan or tribal group to the most complex and ramified types of political organization. The "eros of community" is the bond-ing force that lends strength and coherence to group structures. The erotic, Tillich maintains, aims at values that transcend the identity of the individual. The power of eros binds individual persons together in the organic unity of the community. Erotic relations represent the basis of all formal political structures and legal systems.

Human beings' yearning for religious communion, for participation in the ground of all being is also, Tillich claims, an expression of the erotic. Without the catalytic force of the erotic, human beings' relation to God remains at the level of mechanical obedience or a purely formal, intellectual "belief" powerless to touch the roots of human feeling and behavior. All faith, Tillich argues, includes a mystical element. Thus, all authentic religious experience is informed by eros, the mystical quality of love.

The erotic and mystical elevation of the spirit toward God does not, however, imply a rejection of the created world. Human con-nectedness with nature and culture, with all of created reality is charged with erotic power. The possibility of a relationship of eros toward the world is the potential that defines human being as such. Under the healing impact of the Spirit, this erotic way of being yields a "joy of life" within the created world which is in no sense at odds with delight in God. In the experience of this erotic joy, "the meaning of creation and the end of salvation" are realized.

At all of these levels, eros establishes connections: among human persons, between human beings and the world, between humanity and the divine. Tillich's claim that eros has the "greatness of a divine-human power" is not a casually tossed-off phrase, poetic exaggeration, or sloppy use of language. Tillich's descriptions of the different roles played by eros in human life add up to a systematic and thorough defense of the idea presented by Diotima in the *Symposium:* eros mediates decisively between the human and the divine. Love animated by eros is the medium through which human beings experience reunion with their divine source. This love shaped by the force of the erotic is the "power in the ground of everything that is," of which Tillich writes that it drives every creature "beyond itself toward reunion with the other one and ultimately with the ground itself from which it is separated" (*DF,* 114).

This is the guiding thread running through all of Tillich's discussions of the erotic. Eros shapes human thought, feeling, and action in those situations in which, within the framework of embodied existence, "want and estrangement are conquered," the gap that separates us from each other and from our divine source is bridged. Eros is experienced in human life as the catalyst of those movements of the mind, body, and spirit in which the split between essence and existence is "fragmentarily" overcome. The faces of the erotic in Tillich's thought correspond to those areas of human life in which what he calls the "telic" dimension—the "third" beyond essence and existence, and in which the two are reconciled—emerges in human experience.

The claim that the estrangement and disharmony that mark unredeemed human life can be transcended in experiences within the framework of embodied being in the world is one of the most radical (and one of the most infrequently discussed) notions in Tillich's theology. This claim is of central importance for a reading of Tillich's theology as one which, by appealing to the power of eros, attempts to break down the dualistic structures associated with the traditional Christian understanding of the human situation. The healing power of the Spiritual Presence enters directly into the matrix of our embodied lives. "The multidimensional unity of life means that the impact of the Spiritual Presence on the human spirit is *at the same time,* an impact on the psyche, the cells, and the physical elements which constitute man" (*ST* 3:276; italics in original). "Fragmentarily," but in a nonetheless decisive way, the power of the divine enters into and works through the forms of human physical embodiment, and of religion, culture, and morality. Through the natural world and the cultural forms shaped by the human spirit, the divine Spirit offers us reuniting participation "by anticipation" in the "transcendent union of unambiguous life" (ST 3:140). "We experience the eternal," Tillich affirms in a sermon text, "in the unconditional moral command, and in the ecstasy of love."[11] Ecstatic love provides a direct experience of the eternal within the framework of our temporal nature. It bridges the split opened between essence and fallen existence. It brings the anticipatory realization of union with the New Being.

The idea of the healing of human estrangement through transformative experiences within material existence is the key to Tillich's attempt to overcome the tradition of Christian matter-spirit dualism. Two common elements connect the most significant forms of such transcendent experience. First, by definition, they represent moments in which the gulf between essence and existence is bridged. In such moments—"fragmentarily" and by "anticipation"—we can know the divine, the ultimate, the loving, healing source of all being. Second, in Tillich's work, the most important of these types of experience are informed by the erotic.

Fragmentary transcendence occurs in those events and practices that open us to the "joy of life" (NB, 147), including the ecstasy of sexual love and feelings of communion with the primal powers of existence. It occurs in moments of philosophical insight, and in the contemplation of works of art, nature, and the incomparable beauty of the human person. This is the uniting "contemplation" of which Tillich writes, "Con-templation means going into the temple, into the sphere of the holy, into the deep roots of things, into their creative ground." Looking into a natural form or a human face, we "see the mysterious powers which we call beauty and truth and goodness." We see the divine "with and through the shape of a rose and the movements of the stars and the image of a friend" (NB, 130). Anticipatory transcendence of the existential split can take place in technical creativity, and in the shared "eros toward truth" which shapes the relation of teacher and student. Transcendence is achieved in every act of genuine, participating knowledge (ST 1:95) and in the communion with another self which is the

[11]Paul Tillich, "The Right to Hope: Sermon on Romans 4:18," The Paul Tillich Audio Tape Collection (Richmond, Va.: Union Theological Seminary, 1984), sermon no. 135, recorded 1965.

highest form of moral connection between persons. Further, as Tillich suggests in "The Meaning of Joy," human estrangement can be transcended, broken through in the whole spectrum of erotically charged familial, romantic, and communal relations shaped under the guidance of the Spirit (NB, 145–46). Eros guides and empowers our ultimate experience of the overcoming of estrangement in love toward and reunion with God (ST 1:281).

The fragmentary conquest of estrangement is ultimately the act of the divine itself and is grounded in divine love, agape. Yet through vital, passionate eros human beings experience ecstatic reunion with one another, with created reality, and with the ultimate source of all values, all love, all life. In human experience, Tillich acknowledges, agape needs the warming, compassionate force of eros to avoid becoming a "moralistic turning away from the creative potentials in nature and in man" (MB, 40–41). If agapic love is not to be interpreted as an other worldly force demanding rejection of created reality, rather than the healing of it, then passionate, life-affirming eros must be placed at the center of an understanding of the religious transformation of human existence.

"Ultimate concern" and agapic love are not opposed or negated by the interwoven "preliminary concerns" that constitute the fabric of our relationship of "eros toward the world." Rather, it is "in and through" the preliminary concerns, the erotic connections we experience to persons, places, things, and ideas, that ultimate concern "becomes real" for us (ST 1:13). We come to know the joy of reunion with God not in inflexible obedience to religious and moral codes, or in an act of abstract, disembodied contemplation. We experience this joy, Tillich argues, within the matrix of our erotic connections with the world: in sex, in aesthetic pleasure, in communion with nature, in human communal life, and in the struggle to realize justice. The joy that springs from these erotic relations is the sign and "consequence of [our] reunion with God" (NB, 142).

In Morality and Beyond, Tillich explicitly assigns to eros the quality of "grace," of that which "create[s] a state of reunion in which the cleavage between our true and our actual being is fragmentarily overcome, and the rule of the commanding law is broken." Eros, he repeats, "is a divine-human power. It cannot be produced at will. It has the character of charis, gratia, 'grace'—that which is given without prior merit and makes graceful him to whom it is given." Graces are "divine gifts" that open the way for a transcendence of the brokenness, isolation, and lovelessness that mark life under estrangement. "Where there is grace, there is no command and no struggle to obey the command." The person who "has the grace of loving a thing, a task, a person, or an idea does not need to be asked to love." In such a situation, "a reunion of something separated has already taken place," the fragmentary conquest of existential alienation has already been achieved. Eros possesses the grace-full power to heal the divisions of estrangement (MB, 61).

In Plato's doctrine of eros, the philosopher's ascetic, antimaterial bias emerges powerfully. Guided by eros, the soul moves upward from mere sexual yearning to increasingly more ethereal expressions of love. To reach the higher, more spiritual stages, the soul must disentangle itself from the snares of sensuality by practicing a conscientious and sometimes cruel asceticism.[12] Tillich's understanding of eros, however, contrasts sharply with this aspect of the Platonic model. He borrows Plato's portrayal of eros as the animating force in a wide range of human activities, but vigorously rejects the idea that "lower" forms of love and pleasure must be given up in order to progress toward "higher" spiritual experiences.

Tillich recognizes that forms of self-control are indispensable, especially in the sexual realm; other human beings must never be used as mere objects, tools to gain pleasure. However, his entire eros doctrine is oriented toward arguing that the types of erotic relationality which affirm most strongly our sensuous, embodied nature do not need to be renounced in the quest for spiritual liberation. Indeed, Tillich suggests, such "liberation" is meaningless, illusory if it demands that human beings give up their joy in knowledge and in the beautiful creations of culture, their erotic connections to one another as embodied beings, their passionate "interest" in the objects and relationships that compose the natural world. "We may judge asceticism," Tillich writes, on the basis of an understanding of agape as united with, not opposed to the other qualities of love. "Nothing created is bad in itself. Matter is not an antidivine principle from which the 'soul' has to be liberated. The desire for union with material reality through the senses is an expression of love as libido. And in libido, elements of eros, philia, and agape are present, as libido is present in them" (MB, 41). Doctrines requiring the sacrifice of connection to the world through eros and the other, "lower" forms of love are not authentic spiritual teachings, but sterile moralisms.

---

[12]See the ascending stages of love described in *Symposium*, and the equally notable metaphor of the charioteer and horses in *Phaedrus*.

Tillich uses one term—eros—to designate a crucial form of relationship in areas ranging from interaction with the forms and rhythms of the natural world to human sexual love to the philosophical love of wisdom and of values such as truth, beauty, and right action. His use of the same word in very different contexts is not due to limitations in his theological and philosophical vocabulary. Rather, he sees the same force at work in many different areas.

In analyzing "cognitive," "philosophical" and "religious" eros, as well as the "eros of community" and the other forms of the erotic we have examined, Tillich is arguing that there are essential similarities in the way we relate to things, persons, ideas, and beings in diverse domains of experience ranging from sex to the building of a political movement to religion. The way we are drawn to and care for a work of art is not essentially different from the way in which we are drawn to a beautiful landscape, to the persons with whom we live in community, to the divine. In all cases, the force of attraction is the erotic: the transpersonal energy that calls us beyond the boundaries of our selves, opens us, challenges us, and changes us. The experience of eros is an experience of communication and transformation. It opens to something beyond ourselves which helps us to become more fully ourselves: "persons within a community of persons," as Tillich suggests in his definition of the moral imperative. This dynamic of communication and change is an expression of the connection-making impulse that underlies the different forms of eros explored in Tillich's writings. From the primal powers turned toward earth and the origin to the religious eros oriented toward the ground of all being, the erotic is the fundamental energy that catalyzes interaction between the human self and the world. Eros drives and draws the self through the series of transforming encounters that shape and equilibrate the polarities of individuation and involved participation, autonomous personhood and communal connection.

Several important consequences follow from the assertion that the eros that connects to the earth and the powers of origin is fundamentally identical to the erotic longing that urges us to seek the divine, and to the eros of community which binds us to other human persons.

First, the divine is honored in the love that links us to the natural world, to culture, and to one another. This is expressed in Tillich's claim that divine agape is "effective in the libido drives of love," including "the desire for food, drink, sex, and aesthetic enjoyment" (MB, 41), and in his description of the erotic "seeing which unites" as permitting us to perceive within "transitory things" that which is "eternal" (NB, 129). It makes perfect sense, in this context, to affirm that we love and "enjoy" the divine in and through the erotic relationships that connect us to the world and to our fellow human beings. It makes sense to suggest that under the impact of the Spiritual Presence, our erotic links to sources of physical/sexual pleasure and to art, knowledge, and the human community offer us a joy in which "the inner aim of life and the end of salvation are attained" (NB, 151). Under such conditions, it is reasonable and indeed necessary for Tillich to affirm that "where one is grasped by a human face as human, . . . *there* New Creation happens" (NB, 23).

The divine is seen—and loved—in, through, and with the help of the created world in which our lives unfold. As we open to participation in the Spiritual Community, conflicts between different forms of love resolve themselves into a unity marked but not disrupted by creative tension. Such unity allows, Tillich claims, each quality of love to maintain its specificity and its unique value while being reconciled and united with the larger whole. Such unity "is not without tensions, but it is without break." "The Spiritual Community can stand the diversity of the qualities of love. There is no conflict in it between agape and eros." There are "tensions, as there are implicitly in every dynamic process. The dynamics of all life, even the unambiguous life of the transcendent union, implies tensions." But in the Spiritual Community, these tensions among the qualities of love do not lead to irreparable conflicts (ST 3:156–57). As we deepen our participation in the Spiritual Community, our erotic responses harmonize with and open us to the guiding power of agape. In loving the world, in responding to the beauty of a human face, we love and honor the Spirit that created these forms and that dwells within them.

A second important consequence follows from the underlying unity of the distinct applications of eros in Tillich's thought. If the forms of eros which connect us to the earth, to the organic "powers of origin," to moral values, to the human social community, and to the divine are indeed the same love, then blocks, twistings, or refusals in any one of these areas will have immediate repercussions in all the others. If we fail to open ourselves in genuine, healing, erotic care to the earth and to other persons, then our love toward abstract intellectual values or toward God will also be distorted and incomplete.

Tillich's understanding of the ontological unity of love and of the broad powers of the eros principle implies not only that eros can be applied to a wide variety of human concerns and practices—earth-related origins, philosophy, art, knowledge, ethics, communal relations, politics, religion—but that in the context of life lived under the healing impact of the Spirit, eros must be applied to all of these areas. An eros toward beauty which refuses to acknowledge the demands of justice degenerates into aestheticism. A religious passion that tries to eliminate eros toward the created world and the human community becomes an ascetic dualism. Such religious longing is transformed into a flight from the world driven not by love but by fear, fanaticism, and resentment. Meanwhile a community that has lost touch with eros toward the divine may lose, as well, one of the important motivations for just moral action within the group.

Eros is for Tillich the force that calls persons into growth and transforming interaction with other beings, with objects, concepts, value-shaping principles. Through the power of eros we experience participation in the New Being: the fragmentary conquest of estrangement, the paradoxical healing of the split between essence and existence. Eros catalyzes a process of reunion between the human and the divine. But to fulfill this function, the erotic must be whole. It must include all of the elements that Tillich discusses, from the nonrational primal powers to the most subtle rational and religious faculties. It must be an "eros toward the world" in the broadest possible sense: a passionate yearning drawing us toward the forms of the created universe and at the same time toward the divine power that expresses itself through and dwells within created forms. What Tillich implies is that these two drives are in fact expressions of the same basic erotic movement. In loving God, we love the world God has made. In loving and caring for the persons, objects, creatures, ideas encountered in the created world, we love and care for God. Thus, "eros toward the world" is not merely a stage on the way toward a higher, more purified form of love. Our erotic connection to the world is the enduring sign of the impact of the divine Presence in our lives.

4
Chapter

Enchantment and Destruction
Tillich's Erotic Life

> The erotic act is the one that reveals most clearly to human
> beings the ambiguity of their condition.
>
> —Simone de Beauvoir

Paul Tillich's published treatment of eros is thorough
enough that a discussion of the erotic in the theologian's work should not need, perhaps, to be aug-
mented with references to Tillich's private life. Out
of respect for scholarly method, it would appear reasonable to limit a discussion of Tillich's theory of eros
to just that: a discussion of theory, evaluated on purely
intellectual grounds. In such a framework, allusions
to Tillich's personal practice of the erotic would have
no more place than talk about Newton's "practice"
of gravity has for physics. Theories are not proven
true or false on the basis of the personal experiences
of the individuals who shape them. Further, intellectual discipline and simple good taste suggest that we
should avoid airing Tillich's—or anybody else's—private life in public.

For several reasons, however, Tillich's private life
cannot be declared irrelevant to a discussion of his
published thinking about the erotic. Eros, as Tillich
describes it, is not a natural force that functions according to simple, mechanical principles, such as the
law of universal gravitation. Nor is eros primarily an
abstract concept, a component interlocking with other components in an intellectual system. The erotic

is evoked above all as a powerful experiential reality. It constitutes a
dimension of human life that human beings themselves shape in an
active way, either concretely or destructively. Thus, eros is intimately
connnected with issues of personal responsibility. Tillich argues per-
suasively that the erotic is a force which can heal decisive ruptures in
human existence. If and how this force manifested itself in the personal
existence of the one who attempted to describe it is a question of more
than incidental interest. Evidence of Tillich's own practice of the erotic
may reinforce certain aspects of the theologian's theories about eros,
and point to places where those theories are highly problematic.

The public attention that has already been focused on Tillich's sexual
life is another important factor. So much has been written and said
about the details of Tillich's sexual involvements that for many people
the phrase "the erotic in Tillich" inevitably calls up associations with
the theologian's private life, as well as to his published work. During
his lifetime, but even more strongly after the publication of his wife
Hannah Tillich's book *From Time to Time* in 1973, Tillich's erotic life
drew attention and provoked debate. He himself acknowledged this
situation ironically when, shortly before his death, he asked a friend
to help him destroy a mass of love letters from women, with the
comment that this was necessary in order that he be remembered "as
a systematic theologian and not just as a lover."[1] One may regret that
so much attention has been directed toward this side of Tillich's career
and personality. Yet the situation created by this debate cannot simply
be ignored. The fact remains that until the emergence of today's generation of lesbian and gay theologians, and thanks largely to the debate
stirred up by the publication of *From Time to Time,* Tillich was the
modern Christian thinker whose erotic life had attracted the greatest
public scrutiny and generated the widest discussion. It would be naïve
to imagine that the rumors that have circulated on the subject of
Tillich's sex life could simply be ignored by those trying to evaluate
his understanding of the erotic.

Another point to consider concerns the relevance of Tillich's thinking on eros for discussions in contemporary theology. In dialogue with
feminist and womanist theories of the erotic, Tillich's ideas, as will
be shown later, have deep significance for today's theological work.

[1]Quoted in Ann Belford Ulanov, "Between Anxiety and Faith: The Role of the
Feminine in Tillich's Theological Thought," in Jacquelyn Ann K. Kegley, ed., *Paul
Tillich on Creativity* (Lanham, Md.: University Press of America, 1989), 142. Further
references to Ulanov's essay will be cited parenthetically.

Clearly for feminists and womanists, especially for lesbian authors, the question of personal erotic practice cannot be secondary. Radical openness on sexual issues has become, rightfully, a key concern among many feminists, even and indeed especially when such openness appears problematic or threatening. If Tillich's ideas are to enter into today's theological conversation, then the issue of how he worked with the forces of eros in his own life must be considered carefully and honestly. A fair assessment of the value of his theory of the erotic for current theological reflection cannot avoid this issue, despite the difficulties and risks involved.

Tillich's own attitude toward his practice of eros offers another reason for paying attention to details of the theologian's biography that it might appear more tasteful to ignore. That Tillich himself took the issues raised by his personal erotic life very seriously is shown in a letter that he wrote to a female friend in the last years of his life. In the letter, Tillich expresses his powerful emotion at the public revelation of a close friend's "erotic misbehavior." Tillich questions the meaning of his own way of living out the force of eros:

> My soul is hurt because a dear friend's soul is hurt, and I identify myself with him inescapably. . . . [He] is accused . . . of erotic misbehavior. He must and is willing to bear the consequences. When I was told about it, it produced a tremendous earthquake in my whole being. I saw myself as I would be seen by others. Was my way right? I dared much (as you did) internally. Daring includes the possibility, and often the probability, of failure. Was my erotic life a failure, or was it a daring way of opening up new human possibilities? I do not know the answer.[2]

In this passage, Tillich states the question that we must attempt to resolve in weighing the character of his practice of the erotic and trying to assess the significance of that practice for understanding the theologian's writing about eros.

An important change revealed in this text must be pointed out at the beginning of a discussion of Tillich's erotic life. In the preserved traces of Tillich's private speaking and writing about eros, a subtle but significant shift in vocabulary can be noticed. In Tillich's correspondence about his own intimate life, and in accounts of Tillich's relations with women written by some of his close friends, the word

---

[2] Quoted in Rollo May, *Paulus: Reminiscences of Friendship* (New York: Harper & Row, 1973), 65. Further references to May's book on Tillich will be given parenthetically.

"eros" takes on a much more explicitly sexual character than is the case in most of Tillich's published treatments of the eros theme. For Tillich eros never becomes simply a polite synonym for sexual intercourse. Yet when Tillich questions the ultimate significance of his own "erotic life," he very clearly means for sex to be understood as central to that life, and to the whole concept of eros as he uses the term in this context. This connection is rarely so explicit in Tillich's published writings. Thus, one immediate benefit of looking at Tillich's erotic life is that, here, the sexual component of the erotic is brought more clearly into focus than in Tillich's theoretical discussions. The record of Tillich's private life shows that, whatever his hesitations about treating the topic in published form, Tillich valued sex as a central element of life-giving eros. This raises the problem of why Tillich was so hesitant to write clearly about the sexual side of eros in his professional work. But the character of Tillich's personal life will also suggest an answer to that quesion.

It is not necessary here to try to reconstruct the minute details of Tillich's sexual activities. Quite a bit of information on the topic is already available from several sources, some of them more flattering to Tillich, some less.[3] What follows draws both on the work of two of Tillich's friends, Rollo May and Ann Belford Ulanov, and on points of view of some who are looked at as "hostile" critics, including principally Tillich's wife Hannah. A conscious and carefully weighed decision has been made to accord central importance to Hannah Tillich's account of her husband's erotic life and of its impact on her own existence. Hannah Tillich's writings are colored by profound psychological suffering for which her husband was certainly not the only person responsible. Her texts bear the marks of pain, jealously, and an anguished search for understanding. Yet precisely because of the suffering they express, these writings by the person Tillich called "the companion of my life" must be taken with the utmost seriousness.

Its flaws notwithstanding, Hannah Tillich's *From Time to Time* provides essential material for understanding the dynamics of Tillich's

---

[3]Sources of information on Tillich's personal life include the previously mentioned texts by Ulanov and May, the standard biography of Tillich by Wilhelm and Marion Pauck, and Hannah Tillich's memoirs: *From Time to Time* (New York: Stein and Day, 1973), and *From Place to Place: Travels with Paul Tillich, Travels without Paul Tillich* (New York: Stein and Day, 1976). A number of shorter articles also focus on the question. They include Seward Hiltner, "Tillich the Person: A Review Article," *Theology Today* (January 1974): 382–88; and Melvin Vulgamore, "Tillich's 'Erotic Solution,' " *Encounter* 45, no. 3 (Summer 1984): 193–212.

personal eros. When the memoir was first published, it provoked a scandal in the theological community. Its descriptions of Tillich's tireless pursuit of women and his taste for sadistic pornography were so shocking that many readers and critics interpreted the work as an act of pure vengeance. Those who did so neglected the tenderness, compassion, and even deep admiration mixed with the anger in Hannah Tillich's portrayal of her husband. An unwillingness to face the truth about Tillich's erotic conduct was evident in the embarrassment of many conservative theologians. Some even indicated explicitly that they would have preferred not to be informed about Tillich's behavior. Excessive attention to the details of Tillich's biography, they feared, might cloud one's judgment of his intellectual achievement. "How much do we need to know?" asked the editors of one journal.[4]

To a certain extent, such doubts are understandable. The relationship between an author's work and her or his private life is complex: Searching for correlations between biography and artistic or intellectual creation is, at best, a delicate and uncertain enterprise. This may be even more so since biographical sources are themselves never fully neutral or dispassionate. At worst, examination of biographical materials can degenerate into cheap sensation-seeking. By speculating about anecdotal details, it can distract from the central question of the constructive value of the author's ideas for present tasks.

In the case of Tillich's approach to the erotic, however, the risk of correlating private life and published thought cannot be avoided. Public discussion of the theologian's erotic life has created a situation where, precisely in order to free the constructive power of Tillich's vision of eros for contemporary theology, the questions associated with his private life must be considered. The most substantive writings on Tillich's concept of eros (for example those by May and Vulgamore) have given at least as much attention to the theologian's biography as to his published discussions of the topic. Thus, in a real sense, Tillich's personal erotic life has already been given the status of a central text for grasping the theologian's complex vision of the erotic. If Tillich's theology of eros is to enter constructively into today's debates and help illuminate current theological challenges, then this unconventional text must be examined and interpreted. The difficulty and ambiguity

---

[4]E. Pratt Green in *The Expository Times,* quoted in Raymond J. Lawrence, Jr., *The Poisoning of Eros: Sexual Values in Conflict* (New York: Augustine Moore Press, 1989), 228.

of such interpretation do not make the task any less essential. No simple, one-to-one correspondence is assumed between biography and work. Yet the close interweaving of these factors in Tillich's case has been stressed by many sources, including the theologian himself. The text of his erotic life raises questions and suggests perspectives vital for an appropriation of the theory of eros that is part of Tillich's intellectual legacy.

To grasp the strengths and weaknesses of Tillich's teaching on eros, we are not required to probe every detail of the theologian's personal life, but we must gain a clear sense of the general shape of that erotic life and think carefully about the implications of its successes and failures for the theory of eros that Tillich sought to develop. A brief account of the outlines of Tillich's erotic biography will show the ways in which Tillich's practice of eros harmonizes with and reinforces his affirming theory of the erotic. It will also highlight areas in which the destructive aspects of Tillich's eros emerge. The destructive impact of his personal erotic ethics on at least one key relationship points to ways in which Tillich's theological understanding of eros may be seriously flawed.

Biographical background: Tillich's "erotic solution"

In each of its phases, Tillich's erotic development was far from mundane. Tillich's youth was marked by strong intellectual and aesthetic passions, but at the same time by an almost total sublimation of the sexual drives. His father was a Lutheran minister, whom Tillich described as an "angry supporter of the conservative Lutheran point of view."[5] The austere paternal figure injected a note of rigor, discipline, and cold asceticism into a youth and early manhood colored in a very different way by Tillich's warm relationship to his mother and sisters.

One consequence of his family's conservatism, and of Tillich's membership in the strict Wingolfite fraternity during his student years, is that the budding theologian and philosopher kept a vow of chastity until the age of twenty-seven. Tillich was apparently still a virgin

---

[5]Paul Tillich, "Autobiographical Reflections," in Charles W. Kegley and Robert W. Bretall, eds., *The Theology of Paul Tillich* (New York: Macmillan, 1952), 8. Quoted in May, *Paulus*, 77.

when in 1914, before departing to serve as a military chaplain in some of the most harrowing campaigns of World War I, he married Grethi Wever. Grethi, highly unconventional in her thinking and behavior, "scoffed at the idea of monogamy, ridiculing Tillich's wish to be faithful to her."[6] His first marriage ended when Grethi left Tillich for one of his closest friends.

A period of experimentation followed in the permissive, Bohemian atmosphere of post–World War I Berlin. There Tillich rebelled against the repressive attitudes of his youth. In contact with artistic circles and deeply involved in socialist politics, he "began to enrich his emotional and imaginative side with stimuli hitherto only superficially encouraged: the mystical, the demonic (a power he defined as creative and destructive at the same time), and the erotic" (Pauck and Pauck, 81).

A series of sexual liaisons culminated in Tillich's meeting Hannah Werner at a ball at Berlin's Academy of Arts in 1920. The encounter was to be a decisive turning point. As Hannah later wrote, the first meetings were marked by an extraordinary intensity. She herself experienced "a strong sense of shock, that I had fallen into a deep well, not of water, but of raging fire." The consuming passion of the early months of their relationship was not reduced by Hannah's impending marriage to Albert Gottschow, an art teacher. Hannah in fact married Gottschow in July 1920 but continued to see Tillich secretly. Giving in to Tillich's pleading, she obtained a divorce from Gottschow in December 1923, and she and Tillich were married a few months later.

Their once-torrid relationship quickly began to show signs of strain. Tillich refused to adapt himself to the conventional demands of a sexually exclusive marriage relation. The couple had agreed from the start that their marriage was to be an open one, not subject to the usual bourgeois constraints. Their ways of interpreting this openness, however, differed considerably. Along with the freedom he felt was vital, Tillich also wanted to maintain the outward appearances of a committed relationship. Hannah Tillich, meanwhile, affirmed openness in principle, but longed in fact for a more stable, traditional marriage. The result was a situation of ongoing conflict and intense suffering. Tillich himself suffered considerably, but his wife was the principal victim.

---

[6]Wilhelm and Marion Pauck, *Paul Tillich: His Life and Thought* (New York: Harper & Row, 1976), 80. Further references to the Paucks' biography of Tillich will be cited parenthetically in the text.

Narrating the humiliating events of her wedding night—on which Tillich went out for a bachelors' evening with a group of friends, leaving her alone at home—Hannah later wrote that the marriage was marked by ambivalence on both sides from that first night on.

> On our trip home, Paulus told me that he planned to go out the same evening. Dox had arranged a final bachelor's outing for him, and I was not invited. I was stunned, then infuriated. Was I to spend my first legally married night alone in my now legal home? . . . Above all, I was exasperated at Paulus's refusal to recognize that the evening without me was meant to be an orgy. . . . Jealousy had sprung from the catastrophe of my wedding night, jealousy manifesting itself as rage.[7]

In spite of often bitter conflict, and despite their avowed distaste for "bourgeois convention," the couple would cling to the external forms of a traditional marriage for more than forty years. Hannah's account implies that, especially in the later years of their relationship, the marriage was maintained largely at Tillich's insistence (H. Tillich, 240). She states that the cost to her, in humiliation and relentless psychological suffering, was enormous. Yet Tillich was unwilling either to remain faithful to her or to break off their relationship.

What Tillich called his "erotic solution" was worked out in the 1920s, and the pattern of behavior associated with this solution remained virtually unchanged throughout the rest of his life (Pauck and Pauck, 92). The semblance of a traditional monogamous domestic existence was combined with numerous extramarital involvements. Many of Tillich's friendships with women did not include an explicitly sexual component; many others did. All of these relationships, especially in the early years of their marriage, fueled Hannah's bitter jealousy. Violent disputes and passionate reconciliations, suspicion, secrecy, and reciprocal torment marked the couple's relationship in the series of cities in which they lived together in Germany and the United States: Berlin, Frankfurt, New York, Cambridge, and Chicago.

Despite the many crises and conflicts, however, a form of loyalty subsisted between the Tillichs. Unable to be conventionally faithful to Hannah, Tillich also felt, according to the reports of friends and of Hannah herself, a deep devotion toward her that never disappeared. The dedication of the final volume of *Systematic Theology* to "Hannah,

---

[7]Hannah Tillich, *From Time to Time,* 104–5. Further references to Hannah Tillich's book will be cited parenthetically.

the Companion of my Life" was no mere hollow gesture. " 'You were my reality and my necessity,' " he tells his wife in a conversation recalled in *From Time to Time,* "You were my bridge across the seasons, my continuity in past, present and future.' " Yet Hannah's reply is devastating: " 'I served you,' she countered. 'I served you in order that we might celebrate life together, but you turned away from me and followed other women. And when I break down and weep, you pity me' " (H. Tillich, 218).

In the couple's last years together, a new warmth, tolerance, and compassion entered the relationship, which had seen so many days of stormy conflict. In their later days, as Tillich's biographers note, the couple moved into a period of relative calm and stability. "As his dependence on her grew, and her compassion for him deepened, there was often mirrored in their deeply-lined faces a new and tender understanding" (Pauck and Pauck, 89). Hannah describes the days of her husband's last illness, and the partial reconciliation that this period brought:

> "My poor Hannachen," he said at the beginning of his stay at the hospital. He cried, "I was very base to you, forgive me." I could not see him cry. I was glad I had experienced forgiveness as something very rare and precious, and I was glad I could say to him that I had liked his face from the first day to the last, that I never doubted his spiritual power, and that in my heart some sort of benign smile, not cynical laughter had come through for him. (H. Tillich, 223)

The creative impact of Tillich's eros

The ecstatic power that marked Paul Tillich's existence was seen in various ways by different people. For Hannah Tillich, it was a dangerous and ambiguous force that catalyzed creations of beauty and deep meaning and also brought intense suffering. Others, though conscious of the ambiguities connected with Tillich's sexual involvements, saw the effects of his personal eros in a much more positive light. For example, Rollo May, weighing all the factors and circumstances, views Tillich's existence as a testimony to the positive, creative power of eros: "Paulus's life was the clearest demonstration of eros in action that I have ever seen" (May, 52).

By calling Tillich's personal life a "demonstration of eros," May is not, of course, making a statement merely about the quantity of erotic relationships—sexual and nonsexual—in which the theologian was involved. Instead, May wants primarily to say something about the quality of creative passion that characterized Tillich's way of interacting with people, places, things, ideas. Passion and a sometimes overwhelming intensity of personal presence were traits that struck almost all those who came in contact with Tillich, even superficially. This erotic quality colored Tillich's thoughts, actions, and relationships. The force of this personal eros—creative as well as sexual— led Hannah Tillich herself to describe her husband as a "cosmic force," a "magician of the mind" who was able to "call on ecstasy as the tremulous instigator of sacred action" (H. Tillich, 23).

May, Hannah, and others who knew Tillich intimately saw the power of his eros manifested in many ways: in his reverence for the beauty of nature, his lifelong love of art, his intellectual passion and his religious mysticism, as well as in his personal relationships. Tillich's way of living confirmed important aspects of his theoretical understanding of eros as a uniquely powerful creative force active in many different areas of human existence. Thus, seeing Tillich's life as a demonstration of eros, May has no hesitation about stating his own answer to Tillich's question concerning the ultimate value and meaning of his erotic life. Clearly, May asserts, this life was a success, an "opening up of new possibilities." In his living out of eros, Tillich "ventured greatly and was rewarded greatly, despite all the difficulties he so keenly felt in his own heart." Tillich's erotic journey, like the unfolding of his theological thought, was a "courageous pilgrimage on another frontier" (May, 65).

Tillich invested an erotic intensity in the full spectrum of his professional and personal activities. There was an erotic quality in Tillich's intensely romantic love of nature. "All his life, his sense of wonder would be ignited," May writes, "by almost any natural scene." The pounding waves on the shore at East Hampton were a source of endless fascination. Tillich loved to contemplate the ocean at night, especially during or after a storm. The waves crashing against the seawall produced "a seductive and bewitching rhythm, a magnificent daimonic power" by which Tillich was "sent into ecstasy" (May, 47).

Art, especially the visual arts, also offered a source of erotic joy on which Tillich drew throughout his life. He wrote of the revelatory quality of painting which he encountered against the background of the horrors of World War I and which was to transform his approach to theological thinking. The "creative ecstasy" he sensed in the process and in the products of artistic work became for Tillich a criterion by which to measure all areas of experience. He attempted to infuse his own work and his personal life with the same erotic power that manifested itself in the paintings he admired (*OB*, 27–28).

The Paucks rightly connect the erotic with Tillich's mystical tendencies and with his passionate involvement in the Bohemian culture of Berlin in the twenties. Tillich's theoretical view of eros as the "driving force in all cultural creativity and in all mysticism" was rooted in a personal experience of the way in which mystical, aesthetic, and erotic feelings are interlaced with one another on a deep level.

Tillich lived the erotic as a link to the depths of being, the primal, nonrational forces that in his writings he called the "powers of origin." Through erotic experience—which often, although not inevitably, included sex—Tillich sought to move beyond rational, conceptual understanding, to "return to the inexhaustible springs of the subterranean depths" (H. Tillich, 21). Through an erotic relatedness primarily to women, whom he believed to be "closer to being itself than men" (Ulanov, 136), Tillich sought a nonrational, unifying knowledge of the deepest and most secret levels of human existence. He strove to open the " 'doors of the deep' to the monsters of his convulsed wishes and unfulfilled desires. By boldly naming them and showing their faces, he coined a new philosophical-theological language" (H. Tillich, 23).

Tillich believed his own work as a systematic theologian to be bound up with, and dependent on, the nurturing power of eros. In his personal life, as in his theory of the erotic, eros bridged the gap between the rational and the nonrational functions of the mind, spirit, and body. He was profoundly convinced that his work "suffered when he was deprived of the erotic, whether actual or sublimated" (Pauck and Pauck, 83). He tried to combat his own tendencies toward sterile intellectualism by "getting involved in many different forms" of eros-centered "vitality": diverse types of friendships, the Bohemian life, politics, painting, music.[8] "Without such stimulation," without the constant renewal of multifaceted, life-giving ties to eros, "Tillich could not produce" (Pauck and Pauck, 83).

Hannah Tillich, who knew her husband more intimately than any other person, focuses acutely on his need to sustain his abstract intellectual work through the quickening power of the erotic. For Tillich,

---

[8]Tillich in *Blätter für religiösen Sozialismus* (May, 1924), quoted in Pauck and Pauck, *Paul Tillich*, 83.

she believes, "the seduction of women was not a matter of individual attraction. It was an act of submission to the power of the female. He transmuted his personal experience by shaping it into golden words meant for a world audience." Thus, Tillich sought in the experience of erotic love something more than an immediate personal satisfaction. He "dove into" such love, "and then formulated its cosmic aspects with words." By tapping into the deep sources of eros, Tillich felt that he was empowering himself in a necessary way for his public work. Yet the secrecy with which he tried to surround his sexual involvements and the guilt that he felt exacted a high cost. "Paulus lived in fear. His nervous body was tense; his desires many. . . . His solution was to *suffer* the demons, take them into his being and describe them in words. He was the martyr of the mind" (H. Tillich, 24).

The force of eros expressed itself memorably in Tillich's lecturing, teaching, and preaching. His theorization of pedagogical relationships in terms of erotic dynamics was based on a rich personal experience of the movement of erotic currents in teaching and learning. "I have always," he wrote, "walked up to a desk or pulpit with fear and trembling, but the contact with the audience gives me a pervasive sense of joy, the joy of a creative communion, of giving and taking."[9]

For many of those who studied with Tillich or who simply heard him lecture, the experience was unforgettable. Rollo May notes: "When he lectured, each person in the audience felt that Tillich was addressing him directly and individually, no matter how huge the gathering might be" (May, 26). It was "more than the content of his early teaching," the Paucks observe, that impressed Tillich's first classes and lecture audiences in Germany in the years after World War I. The young instructor's "personal presence" also played a central role. "The same traits that ultimately prompted an American colleague to characterize Tillich as a 'genius teacher' were already there at the start of his career." Powerful erotic energies flowed between Tillich and his listeners, fed by the play of passionate emotions expressed in Tillich's voice, gestures, and facial expressions, as well as in his words (Pauck and Pauck, 60–61).

The same captivating intensity informed Tillich's personal relationships. The Paucks write of his "genius for friendship" with both women and men (Pauck and Pauck, 82). May describes the feeling of

---

[9]Paul Tillich, "Autobiographical Reflections," in Kegley and Bretall, eds., *Theology of Paul Tillich*, 15; quoted in May, *Paulus*, 27.

deep communion, of knowing and being known, experienced by those close to Tillich. Knowing and loving drew together in the experience of intimate connection which Tillich was able to share with an extraordinary number of persons. Empowered through eros, friendship took on some of the qualities which, in Tillich's theological writing, he attributed to gnosis:

> Most important was the intensity of his concentration on whoever was with him. I felt absorbed, caught up, completely grasped by the experience. Everyone who knew him remarked on his capacity to attend completely to the other person. It gave one the pleasant sensation of *being known* (here the trite phrase does have a specific meaning) better, for that moment, than one knew oneself. . . . It is a pleasure to be known, listened to, and have one's opinions authentically asked for and valued. A conversation with Paulus opened up qualities in you which you did not know were there, and after talking with him you went away with a new part of yourself discovered. (May, 28)

Unquestionably, Tillich's personal charisma and his prestigious intellectual and social position came into play in his explicitly sexual advances toward women. Sex, in his private life if not in his public writing, was centrally important to Tillich, and he was willing to take considerable risks in order to multiply his opportunities in this area. Yet May and others who knew Tillich well insist that not simply the satisfaction of sexual conquest, but above all the deeper, sustaining joy of an erotic connectedness is what drew Tillich. He shared with many of the women who became his friends and/or sexual partners the mutual discovery of erotic, not simply sexual possibilities. Hannah Tillich writes of the "erotic reality beyond physical satisfaction" of which she had been largely unaware until she met Tillich, and to which she was awakened through her relationship to him (H. Tillich, 105).

"It was eros," May also affirms, that informed Tillich's "intense presence in his relationships with women." The "center of the attraction" that Tillich exerted "was not sex, which can be and generally is a quantitative thing." Rather, the central force in all of Tillich's friendships was eros "in its strict sense," which is not limited in quantity, but grows and expands, nourishing all those whom it touches (May, 29, 51–52).

Tillich's sexual relationships were inscribed within the larger context of an "eros toward the world" which he himself experienced deeply and which he desired passionately to share with others. "His relationships were always a pull toward a higher state, an allure of new forms, new potentialities, new nuances of meaning" (May, 52). Tillich introduced many of his friends and sexual partners to this powerful erotic reality. The joy that Tillich himself found in eros toward the world of nature and the spontaneous creations of the imagination communicated itself to those around him. He could draw people into his life through the insistent force of his libido or the sheer power of his intellect. But he could also do so through his gift for play, his "extraordinary capacity for fantasy." When Tillich was present, May writes, it was difficult for anything or anyone to appear "mundane or boring." Everything was a potential source of interest. Through this awakening of an erotic relationship to many aspects of the world, Tillich's charismatic presence regularly catalyzed a "kind of joy, a mild ecstasy" for which "the sexual analogy is not out of place" (May, 50, 29).

In many cases, of course, it was more than an analogy. Tillich used the force of erotic attraction to move relationships onto the directly sexual plane. This does not necessarily mean that May's insistence on the centrality of eros "in its strict sense" in Tillich's involvements with women and men is "naïve," as some critics have suggested.[10] In his relationships with his women friends and lovers, Tillich asked for (and gave) more than sexual satisfaction. The power of his eros to mediate a changed relationship to the person's whole world is a theme sounded again and again by those who were familiar with the details of Tillich's private life.

In the context of their conventional relationships with others, especially with other men, Ann Ulanov argues, the women who became Tillich's friends and lovers were often "pushed into the background by social custom, by patriarchal marriage styles, or religious institutions and attitudes that define women as helpers only, never prophets or priests." Through their relationships with Tillich, many of these women found themselves able to perceive and actively to develop facets of themselves—intellectual, creative, erotic in the broad sense— which they had previously been forced to repress. Tillich tried to "bring them out," to help them in "stepping forward to claim their own large selfhood." He sought relationship with them as "partners, not as mothers or daughters, but as persons with clear presence and imagination, with their own authority." He desired more than a simple sexual liaison with the women whose lives he touched. He "succeeded

---

[10]See Lawrence, *The Poisoning of Eros*, 228.

in remaining friends with most of those with whom he was involved
erotically." Many were—and remained—deeply grateful for the experiences of authentic communion, learning, and growth which their
relationships with Tillich had opened up (Ulanov, 141–42).

The destructive side of eros: broken
promises, broken lives

The bitter irony is that the person who had the least reason to feel
gratitude toward Tillich may have been precisely the one who would
normally have expected to benefit most from his affection and interest:
his wife. It was his family, according to Hannah Tillich, which bore
the principal psychological costs of Tillich's hunger for fame and recognition and of his sexual affairs. The frustration of seeing her husband
lavish such prodigious quantities of passionate interest on everyone
and everything but her was clearly and understandably devastating
for Hannah Tillich.

She describes how her husband "wrote poems for our guests,"
celebrating, flattering, comforting each and every person—everyone
but those closest to him and most in need of his attention. She records
the ambiguity for herself and her children of being transformed into
abstract entities, passages in a book, while their own lives as flesh-
and-blood human beings were neglected. Examining Tillich's papers,
letters, and manuscripts after his death, she notes: "I could have found
the sermon he wrote while his daughter was very ill." Tillich "had
not taken her in his arms and healed her with love." He had had,
instead, to "transform her into the magic of words for all the world
to hear" (H. Tillich, 17–18; 241–42). Such descriptions are highly
subjective. Yet the pain, anger, and sense of exploitation they express
are significant and disturbing.

Slowly, over the years, Hannah Tillich saw her own life "broken
into pieces by the relentless assault of the many women": broken, that
is, by the effects of that same erotic power that was the driving force
in Tillich's creative work, and that transformed and enriched the lives
of many of those who entered into friendship with him. This creative,
ecstatic force also had a destructive side that victimized the person
who appeared to stand closest to Tillich.

"I had tried to get away," Hannah writes. She took steps to secure
economic independence from her husband. But the bonds created by
her own feelings, and by Tillich's ability to manipulate them, were

too powerful to break. "How could I get away from the man whose life I had lived, whose children I had borne, whose thoughts I could guess, who was as close to me as my own heartbeat?" Hannah Tillich found herself "exhausted by my own inability to love this man right," and "disgusted . . . by his childish attempts to pretend he loved only me." Yet she was unable to break free from him (From H. Tillich, 240).

Pursuing his interests in other women at every opportunity, Tillich allowed his marriage to Hannah to degenerate into a bitter caricature of an intimate relationship, an exploitative "double game" held together by hollow promises.

> "I remember," she said, "how you pretended you did not know you were caressing a woman friend who was sitting on one side of you, while I sat on the other."
>
> "What is wrong with that?"
>
> "Nothing, except that later you insisted with great intensity that you would never do such a thing in my presence. But I think you did it, knowing you did not want to know . . . pretending you were ignorant of what you did. You were like the Nazis, who pretended innocence, and at the same time enjoyed the terror caused by their double game. You had played on my naïveté so many times." (H. Tillich, 20)

Deep pain mingled with Hannah Tillich's memory of her husband's spiritual and erotic power. That richly creative power had also had a demonic element, the impact of which she had been forced to bear throughout forty years of marriage, while others reaped the benefits of the vitality and joy. Her life with Tillich had been a battle to "survive the onslaught of the greedy male," who was constantly "seeking shelter, deserting shelter, coming back to shelter, embracing, torturing, making suffer, giving happiness" (H. Tillich, 242).

After her husband's death, Hannah Tillich returned to the home the couple had shared on Long Island. Questions, ambiguities, and the unfinished business with Tillich plagued her as, unavoidably, they would continue to do. "Where did I come in?" she asks in the closing pages of *From Time to Time*. "I had shared it, hated it, loved it, rebuked it. I had fought for survival, being submerged, serving him, being aware when I was pressed between the leaves of a folder, cursing him for turning me into an abstraction."

Sorting through Tillich's love letters, manuscripts, and books, she felt a confirmation of the intimate connection between her husband's private erotic passions and the work that had made him famous. She sensed the way in which these two spheres—the published "lifework" and the chaotic "real life" her husband had led—were joined. She saw, too, how her own existence had been drawn into, absorbed by the uncontrolled force of Tillich's "ecstatic power," his "ever-hungry desire to be worshiped."

> I unlocked the drawers. All the girls' photos fell out, letters and poems, passionate appeal and disgust. Beside the drawers, which were supposed to contain his spiritual harvest, the books he had written and the unpublished manuscripts all lay in unprotected confusion. I was tempted to place between the sacred pages of his highly-esteemed lifework those obscene signs of the real life that he had transformed into the gold of abstraction. (H. Tillich, 241–42)

Tillich's practice of the erotic confirms and reinforces important aspects of his theory of eros. Yet the destructive side of his erotic life— in particular the suffering caused to his wife—points to grave inadequacies in his understanding of erotic dynamics. How could a thinker whose words celebrated so movingly the creative and life-affirming power of eros allow his own erotic practices to inflict such deep pain on a person he claimed to love? Highly destructive blindspots marked Tillich's way of living out the power of eros in his most important and intimate relationships.

Previous commentators have suggested that the details of Tillich's erotic life raise questions about his theological understanding of love and ethics.[11] However, the attempt here to trace flaws in Tillich's eros theory on the basis of his personal practice of the erotic takes a different perspective from that of most writers who have tried to assess the consequences of Tillich's irregular sexual career for the interpretation of his theology. The most problematic details of Tillich's erotic and sexual existence are not those that have until now tended to provoke the greatest shock within the liberal theological community. Both the multiplicity of involvements and sadistic character of some of Tillich's sexual impulses certainly raise significant ethical issues. Yet neither of these themes poses the deepest difficulties from the perspective of a contemporary understanding of erotic ethics.

---

[11]I am thinking particularly of the interpretations presented by Jean Gabus in "L'Attitude de Tillich face à l'amour et à la sexualité," *Revue d'Histoire et de Philosophie Religieuses* 58 (1978): 65–79, and by Vulgamore, " 'Erotic Solution.' "

In theories of erotic ethics being shaped by feminist theologians today, the need to recognize and affirm the capacity for caring involvement with a number of sexual partners has been taken as a central task.[12] At the same time, while the issue of sadomasochistic fantasies and practices has been more controversial, those trying to develop new perspectives in feminist sexual ethics and theology have recognized these forms of sexual interaction as rooted in the constructions of desire which dominate Euro-American culture. Sadomasochistic tendencies are not to be condoned or celebrated. They are impulses to be recognized as part of our social framework and thus inevitably of our individual psychological reality. They are present in each of us, insofar as we have been taught to accept and interiorize the paradigm of sexual pleasure as based on a dynamic of domination and submission. While efforts can (and should) be made to limit the destructive impact of these learned patterns on our own lives and those of others, it is of little value to act as if sadistic or masochistic desires are felt only by a tiny minority of "sick" individuals.[13]

The most problematic aspect of Tillich's personal "erotic solution" is not the coloring of his relation to his female friends and sexual partners by promiscuity and occasional sadistic impulses. While significant, these issues are not primary. Rather, the most damning inadequacy of Tillich's "solution" lies at a more obvious, seemingly mundane level. It is Tillich's failure to deal justly and honestly with the person who had the greatest right to expect kind and caring treatment from him: his wife.

The question of relational justice within the structures of a "bourgeois" marriage may seem like a banal one. Nonetheless, the advantages or drawbacks of the institution of marriage do not represent the central problem here. Tillich's doubts about the traditional marriage structure (see H. Tillich, 17–18) may be well founded. But in that case, Tillich should have acted publicly in accordance with his privately held opinions. He should have freed both his wife and himself from

---

[12]See Carter Heyward, *Touching Our Strength: The Erotic as Power and the Love of God* (San Francisco: Harper & Row, 1989), esp. chaps. 6 and 7.

[13]See in particular the discussion of lesbian sadomasochism in Heyward's *Touching Our Strength*, 105–111. And cf. Frigga Haug, *Female Sexualization: A Collective Work of Memory* (London: Verso, 1987); Sarah Lucia Hoagland, *Lesbian Ethics: Toward New Value* (Palo Alto: Institute of Lesbian Studies, 1988); Robin Ruth Linden, Darlene R. Pagano, Diana E. H. Russell, and Susan Leigh Star, eds., *Against Sadomasochism: A Radical Feminist Analysis* (San Francisco: Frog in the Well, 1982); Samois Collective, *Coming to Power: Writings and Graphics on Lesbian S/M* (Boston: Alyson Publications, 1987).

the constraints of a legal relationship that did not reflect the reality of their feelings for one another and that meant years of bitter and unnecessary suffering for Hannah Tillich. The question is not in fact banal or trivial. At issue is the connection (or lack of connection) between the free unfolding of creative eros, and the demands of justice within the setting of a concrete, personal relationship.

While he poured out quantities of erotic attention on others, Tillich allowed a breakdown of honesty, fairness, and respect to invade his relationship to his wife. Unable to remain faithful to Hannah, Tillich was also unwilling to break openly with her, to acknowledge the failure of their marriage and accept his preponderant responsibility for that failure. He thus cut off the possibility of new beginnings for both partners on the basis of a frank, public recognition of their situation. Clearly, Tillich was not solely answerable for the ambiguity and suffering that marked the marriage. Yet it lay within his power to restore a situation of honesty and relational justice by ending the marriage and freeing his wife and himself from the appearance of a commitment they were unable to maintain in fact. The contradiction between appearance and reality was a source of torment for Hannah Tillich. Yet Tillich allowed this contradiction to subsist.

The reasons for Tillich's failure to bring honesty and clarity into the central erotic relationship of his life, and his motives for maintaining this relationship in a form that was deeply damaging to the other person involved, are surely complex. Real tenderness toward Hannah and a desire to spare her pain surely played a role. Yet his biographers pinpoint the main reason for Tillich's unwillingness to bring the public side of his relationship with Hannah into line with the private reality. This motive is not a flattering one. "His overriding fear was that one day his story might be made public and bring ruin upon his work" (Pauck and Pauck, 90). His desire for pleasure and his concern with his own reputation drove Tillich to exploit Hannah by maintaining the semblance of a committed relationship for reasons of professional convenience, and in spite of the suffering inflicted by this cruel "solution."

To a certain extent, of course, Tillich was conscious of the flagrant injustice of this situation. The guilt associated with his double life was by all accounts a source of deep anguish for him, yet it brought no constructive action. Moreover, according to Hannah's account, Tillich developed over the years a frightening capacity to deceive himself about his own behavior and intentions, to keep his right hand from knowing what his left was doing (H. Tillich, 20–21, 240).

Unable to love Hannah in the way she desired, Tillich would also not let go of her. He used her to protect his reputation and professional status, at the cost of extreme suffering to her and of intense pain and humiliating duplicity in his own life. A seemingly mundane problem in comparison to sadism and promiscuity, Tillich's failure to structure the most intimate of his erotic relationships in a just manner has deeper implications for the interpretation of his eros theory than do these more sensational issues.

In and of itself, interaction with a multiplicity of sexual partners is not necessarily destructive. Sadomasochistic desires are an unfortunate but widespread part of our cultural heritage. Having experienced such desires by no means invalidates the opinions a person may express regarding healthy and creative forms of erotic union. In fact, an awareness of the prevalence and power of sadomasochistic dynamics in apparently "normal" sexual relationships may be very useful in shaping an honest and useful theory of eros.

The shape of Tillich's relationship to his wife, on the other hand, calls the moral quality of his understanding of the erotic seriously into question. His relationship to Hannah represents a concrete and central instance in which Tillich's eros functioned as a source of suffering and oppression to those closest to him at the same time that it was a source of joy and liberation for others. It seems clear that an approach to eros that allowed such injustice to invade not simply a peripheral relationship, but the central core of Tillich's own network of erotic connections, must be looked at as deeply flawed. The broken connection between eros and justice in Tillich's private life points to a rupture in the theologian's intellectual vision of the erotic. Tillich failed to give sufficient attention to the concrete connections (or lack thereof) between eros and moral action in actual human relationships.

The gaps that mar Tillich's thinking on the relationship between eros and relational justice will emerge more clearly through an examination of current works on eros by feminist and womanist authors. If Tillich failed to reconcile the power of eros with the demands of justice in his private life, he was also unable to give a satisfying theoretical explanation of the relationship between erotic love and right moral action. Tillich's own private life has pointed to the problem of the link between erotic power and just action. Feminist and womanist theorizations of erotic justice will offer a basis for measuring the full extent of the difficulties with Tillich's approach, and for shaping new visions of eros and "right relation."

Erotic success and failure

We can look again now at the question that Tillich posed in his letter: "Was my erotic life a failure, or was it a daring way of opening up new human possibilities?" It was probably both.

On one hand, Tillich's eros pointed to a new, fuller, more vital and passionate form of engagement with the world than had previously been possible for many of the women and men who came under his influence. As May and Ulanov point out, Tillich's "erotic spell" was experienced by many quite literally as a life-transforming force, an awakening to an entirely new way of being, for which the persons who experienced it remained deeply grateful to Tillich. The eros that Tillich was able to catalyze and to share with so many around him opened for numerous individuals possibilities that the regnant religious and intellectual traditions had taught them to suppress and negate.

The eros toward the world which Tillich demonstrated by example in his teaching and preaching, his passion for creative thought, his love of nature and art, his genius for friendship came to many as a message of liberation. His powerful eros was experienced as a call to share a new and deeper connectedness with life. Writing about the women who had been her husband's lovers, Hannah Tillich observes that undoubtedly Tillich "changed the life-feelings of all these women," helping to open for them the possibility of a new and richer way of being. "Whether they cursed him or loved him, he had pushed the knowledge about the *mysterium tremendum* a little beyond their narrower concept of life, love, and the powers of enchantment and destruction" (H. Tillich, 242).

As Hannah Tillich knew all too well, however, enchantment and destruction were closely woven together in Tillich's practice of eros. And these two qualities of the theologian's eros were portioned out in very different ways to different people. While large numbers of friends, admirers, and lovers saw only the enchantment, Tillich's wife bore the destructive weight of his inability to connect eros with the concrete demands of justice in a specific and undeniably central relationship.

Tillich's practice of eros opened new perspectives for many who knew him as friend and teacher. The record of his erotic life offered by such friends as May and Ulanov confirms important aspects of his theoretical understanding of eros as a life-affirming creative force. Yet the person who had the greatest moral claim on Tillich's attention was well placed to see the destructive incompleteness of this understanding.

The failure of justice in Tillich's erotic life shows clearly the need to move beyond the limited concept of the erotic that he was able to shape. New visions of eros must be sought out and explored. Only in this way can we begin to understand fully both the positive qualities and the flaws in Tillich's view, and to find answers to the questions raised by his ambiguous "erotic solution."

5
Eros and "Power in Right Relation"
The Erotic in Feminist and Womanist Theologies

> We who are feminist theologians find much that is divine—
> work for justice, love, creativity itself, the web of life, joy,
> and beauty. Innumerable states and qualities of acting are
> divine. By naming joy as divine, we affirm that these aspects
> of human life are worthy of worship.
> —Sharon D. Welch

Paul Tillich was one of the first modern Christian
theologians to write extensively and affirmingly on
the topic of eros. Whereas he was hesitant about describing the sexual dimension of the erotic in an open
way, this reticence in connection with sexual topics
has all but disappeared among contemporary theological authors. In fact, what philosopher Michel Foucault termed the irrepressible proliferation of discourse on sexuality has, over the last ten or fifteen
years, received unexpected confirmation from Western theology. Theologians of all backgrounds and political orientations have seemed determined to outbid
each other in their zeal to "extract the truth from sex."
Although the authors express widely different—often
diametrically opposed—opinions on the subjects they
discuss, they are in agreement on one point: issues of
gender, sexuality, and sexual ethics are central to theological thinking and to a religious world view.[1]

---

[1]In the Christian context alone, the plethora of recent books
connecting theology with questions of gender and sexuality in-

Religious feminists and womanists have shaped the most original and challenging of these new theological discourses on sex, gender, and relationality. Among the most conspicuous characteristics of much of their work is a heavy reliance on the concept of eros. As in Tillich's writings, the understanding of eros employed by feminist and womanist authors includes but reaches far beyond the domain usually designated by the term "sexuality." A significant number of feminists and womanists have claimed importance for the eros principle not only in personal relationships, but also in the areas of cognition, creativity, religious experience, social ethics, and politics. It is possible to uncover the main themes of recent feminist and womanist theorizations of the erotic, focusing primarily on Jewish and Christian authors and on those secular writers whose work has been most important for feminist and womanist theology. Women working within neopagan or Goddess traditions have also explored eros in important ways which can be touched on only tangentially in the following discussion.[2]

This chapter must concentrate on a limited number of the themes that have emerged as central in treatments of eros by leading religious feminist and womanist authors. Such a brief exposition can, however, suffice to show the importance that the concept of eros has taken on in feminist theory, and to give a sense of ways in which this concept might influence traditional theological constructs. Womanist and feminist understandings of eros will open up perspectives on erotic dynamics which will help us more effectively to critique and appropriate Paul Tillich's work.

Clearly, the established goal is not to argue that religious feminists have been directly influenced by Tillich in their work on the erotic.

---

cludes an astonishingly wide spectrum of theological points of view, from uncompromisingly radical to rigidly conservative. A sample of such recent work emerging out of a broadly Christian or post-Christian framework: Mary Daly, *Beyond God the Father* (Boston: Beacon Press, 1973); Philip Sherrard, *Christianity and Eros* (London: SPCK, 1976); Margaret Miles, *Fullness of Life: Historical Foundations for a New Asceticism* (Philadelphia: Westminster Press, 1981); James B. Nelson, *Between Two Gardens: Reflections on Sexuality and Religious Experience* (New York: Pilgrim Press, 1983); Rosemary Radford Ruether, *Sexism and God-Talk: Toward a Feminist Theology* (Boston: Beacon Press, 1983); Paula M. Cooey, Sharon A. Farmer, and Mary Ellen Ross, eds., *Embodied Love: Sexuality and Relationship as Feminist Values* (San Francisco: Harper & Row, 1987); James G. Wolf, ed., *Gay Priests* (San Francisco: Harper & Row, 1989); Greg Speck, *Sex: It's Worth Waiting For* (Chicago: Moody Press, 1989).

[2]On eros in neopagan religions, see the work of Starhawk, especially *Dreaming the Dark: Magic, Sex, and Politics* (Boston: Beacon Press, 1988), and Carol Christ's forthcoming volume on eros-thealogy (to appear in 1991). See also the articles in the "Special Section on Neopaganism," *Journal of Feminist Studies in Religion* 5, no. 1 (Spring 1989): 47–100.

In many of the texts to be discussed here, Tillich's name does not even appear. None of the authors discussed in this chapter draws explicitly on his doctrine of eros; and more subtle, implicit influences, if indeed they exist at all, are so faint as to be negligible. Feminist and womanist interpretations of the erotic are not simply an outgrowth of a previous academic and theological tradition. They represent a strikingly original creation, shaped in dialogue and debate among women. For their new insights into the erotic, these women are indebted primarily to one another, and only in the most limited and indirect way to figures from the male theological tradition. On the other hand, as the concluding chapter will show, the parallels between Tillich's understanding of eros and recent work by feminist and womanist theorists confirm the theological importance of the theme of eros. These parallels could also help facilitate conversation between emerging feminist and womanist perspectives and mainstream Christian theology. Such conversation is vitally important if the tradition is to come to terms with new understandings of the erotic and to measure their implications for all areas of theological thinking.

The erotic in feminist and womanist thought: definitions

Womanists and feminists have employed the term *eros* in a variety of contexts, both in theology and secular theory. They have responded to the uses of the term in traditional settings, especially Greek myth,[3] but they have given a new shape to the concept, expanding the sphere of the erotic in unexpected ways. These authors have utilized the creative ambiguity of eros to shape a field of discourse which embraces but does not limit itself to the area traditionally identified under the rubric of sexuality. Eros, in feminist thought as in Tillich's work, is not a poetic synonym for sex.

Lesbian experience and concerns have been central to the elaboration of new understandings of eros. Such writers as Audre Lorde and Carter Heyward have made notable contributions to this effort, arguing that

---

[3]See Audre Lorde, "The Uses of the Erotic: The Erotic as Power" in *Sister Outsider* (Trumansburg, N.Y.: The Crossing Press, 1984); Susan Griffin, *Pornography and Silence: Culture's Revenge against Nature* (New York: Harper & Row, 1981), 255–59; cf. the myths presented by Starhawk in *The Spiral Dance: A Rebirth of the Ancient Religion of the Goddess* (San Francisco: Harper & Row, 1979), esp. 24–27.

one of the primary benefits of adopting an eros vocabulary is precisely that such a vocabulary signals a firm rejection of reductive patriarchal understandings of sexuality. The idea of eros breaks with the "natural" paradigm of heterosexual genital intercourse structured by the dialectic of (male) domination and (female) submission. It has been argued (though in this case not by an author who takes an explicitly lesbian stance) that by "reformulating issues of sexuality in terms of eros," feminist theory can "escape the traps laid by the specifically masculine definition of sexuality that is so widespread in our culture," and move toward developing "a cultural construction of sexuality that does not depend on hostility for its fundamental dynamic."[4]

If it is relatively easy to define feminist and womanist eros nega-tively—as not synonymous with traditional masculinist understand-ings of sex—framing its positive definition is far from simple. The work of black poet Audre Lorde has served as a touchstone for almost all womanist and feminist writing on the erotic. Lorde's concept of eros is complex and many-layered. Exquisite erotic passages are woven into her poetry.[5] Her 1978 essay "The Uses of the Erotic: The Erotic as Power" condenses into its seven suggestive pages more insights into eros than can be found in works many times as long. For Lorde, eros is a fundamental expression of the "lifeforce of women," an empowering creative energy of decisive importance in all areas of life. Rooted "in a deeply female and spiritual plane," the erotic is "the nurturer or nursemaid of all our deepest knowledge," transcending the traditional oppositions between rational knowledge and intuitive feeling, spiritual insight and physical pleasure. The erotic embraces a spectrum of experience from sex to "building a bookcase, writing a poem, examining an idea."[6]

For Haunani-Kay Trask, too, the "new eros" is a life-force that reconciles dualistic oppositions and "integrates the sensual and the rational, the spiritual and the political." It points toward "a release and refashioning of the life instincts from the vantage point of women's

---

[4]Nancy Hartsock, *Money, Sex, and Power* (Boston: Northeastern University Press, 1985), 166.

[5]See esp. "Bridge through My Window," "On a Night of the Full Moon," "The Winds of Orisha," "Progress Report," and "Love Poem" in Audre Lorde, *Chosen Poems Old and New* (New York: Norton, 1982).

[6]Lorde, "Uses of the Erotic," 53–57. Further references to Lorde's essay will be cited parenthetically.

essential experiences. The emphasis is on physical and emotional grat-ifications that connect 'life' and 'work.' "[7] Susan Griffin characterizes eros in similar terms as experience in which "meaning is never separate from feeling," and in which there is at the same time "no feeling which does not ring through our bodies and our souls all at once." The "whole range" of human creative capacities is potentially embraced under this heading.[8]

Feminist psychoanalyst Jessica Benjamin employs a different, seem-ingly more conventional, approach to the language of eros. The erotic in Benjamin's writing refers primarily to sexual activity between adults. Yet Benjamin detects vital erotic components in the bond be-tween mother and infant, and more broadly in all genuinely inter-subjective relationships, that is, all relational connections in which communion is allied with acknowledgment of and respect for the irreducible autonomy of the other. Like the fundamental relationship between mother and child which prefigures it, erotic union constitutes a paradigm of the situation of mutual recognition in which intersub-jective tension is maintained, allowing "both partners to lose them-selves in each other without loss of self."[9]

Still another side of the erotic is illuminated by theologian Elga Sorge. She describes "all-transforming, creative eros" as a genuinely cosmic power, indeed as the "strongest force that exists." Feminist theology is concerned with developing "religion based on unfrag-mented love and healing eros." Viewing creative eros as a sacred force offers a standpoint for "discerning and transforming" those Christian symbols and beliefs which have heretofore been allowed to function in repressive and life-denying ways.[10] Pursuing a similar understanding of eros, Rita Nakashima Brock has sought to shape a life-affirming "christology of erotic power." Brock argues for the rejection of the image of Jesus as a lonely religious hero, and prefers to speak not of the Christ, but of a "Christa/Community" shaped by the unifying force of eros.[11]

---

[7]Haunani-Kay Trask, *Eros and Power: The Promise of Feminist Theory* (Philadelphia: University of Pennsylvania Press, 1986), 92–93, xi.

[8]Griffin, *Pornography and Silence,* 254.

[9]Jessica Benjamin, *The Bonds of Love: Psychoanalysis, Feminism, and the Problem of Domination* (New York: Pantheon, 1989), 29.

[10]Elga Sorge, *Religion und Frau: weibliche Spiritualität im Christentum* (Stuttgart: Kohl-hammer, 1985), 38.

[11]Rita Nakashima Brock, *Journeys by Heart: A Christology of Erotic Power* (New York: Crossroad, 1988), chaps. 3–5. Further references to *Journeys by Heart* will be cited parenthetically.

The image of Christa, the female Christ figure, is an important symbol for authors attempting to introduce new understandings of the erotic into theological discourse. Brock writes:

> As I recall, the first use of the term Christa was in reference to the crucifix in the Cathedral of Saint John the Divine in New York City. The Christ on the crucifix, labeled Christa, was female. In using Christa instead of Christ, I am using a term that points away from the sole identification of Christ with Jesus. . . . Using the term Christa/Community affirms my conviction about the sacredness of community. (Brock, 113–14)

"The Christa/Community of erotic power," Brock states, "is the connectedness among the members of the community who live with heart," in a relational matrix created and maintained by eros (Brock, 70).

Judith Plaskow has used the vocabulary of eros to outline a "new theology of sexuality" from a Jewish perspective. "Our sexuality," she writes, "is a current that flows through all activities that are important to us, in which we invest ourselves." Such activities include "true intellectual exchange, common work," and all forms of "shared experience" which are "laced with sexual energy that animates and enlivens them. The bonds of community," Plaskow insists, "are erotic bonds." While the erotic roots of communal feeling have been recognized implicitly in Judaism, this recognition has usually expressed itself as suspicion and hostility on the part of the (male) shapers of the law. The result has been the elaboration of a complex of statutes and customs whose goal is to restrain the dangerous power of the sexual impulses and to control the bodies and lives of women, who have been seen as bearers of this threatening power. A deep-seated ambivalence toward sexuality "underlies the extensive rabbinic legislation enforcing the separation of the sexes," legislation which attempts to limit and contain the erotic forces it recognizes, "even as it acknowledges the sexual power of community and the continuity of sexuality with other feelings." The status of women as "Other" in Judaism is closely connected with this ambivalence toward sexuality in general and with fears regarding the power of female sexuality in particular.[12]

To date, the most thorough and challenging discussion of eros in the Christian feminist and womanist literature is that found in Carter

---

[12]Judith Plaskow, *Standing Again at Sinai: Judaism from a Feminist Perspective* (San Francisco: Harper & Row, 1990), 201, 171–77. Hereafter cited parenthetically in text.

Heyward's *Touching Our Strength: The Erotic as Power and the Love of God,* a milestone in the development of Christian theological reflection on the subject. Drawing on the work of Lorde, Dorothee Sölle, Brock, and other spiritually oriented authors, as well as on the writings of such secular theorists as Zillah Eisenstein, Heyward constructs a vision of the erotic which synthesizes perspectives developed in many different areas of womanist and feminist thought.

Heyward's approach to defining eros comprehends its breadth and complexity. On the one hand, she identifies the erotic as a desire: a yearning that urges us "to taste and smell and see and hear and touch one another," shaping forms of pleasure and communication which celebrate our embodiment. On the other hand, erotic longing is not simply equivalent to sexual desire. Rather, it is "our yearning to be involved" in each other's bodies, feelings, lives. The essence of eros is, Heyward insists, a relational movement: "the movement of our sensuality," which, as an energy of the whole bodyself, of the sensual/intellectual/emotional/moral person, flows "transpersonally among us" at the same time that it "draws us more fully into ourselves." Eros is the urge toward mutuality, toward rightness in relation.[13] It is "the source of our capacity for transcendence," not in the sense of a spiritual flight from the world, but rather of a " 'crossing over' among ourselves, making connections among ourselves" (Heyward, 99).

Nor does Heyward hesitate to connect the erotic and the divine. Through eros we have "our most fully embodied experience of the love of God." The erotic is "the divine Spirit's yearning, through our bodyselves, toward mutually empowering relation" (Heyward, 99). The name of Christa, symbol of the need for healing power in connectedness, can be thought of, Heyward writes, as "a Christian name for eros" (Heyward, 116).

Once again, as in Tillich's discussion of the erotic, the multivalence, the "thickness" of eros in feminist and womanist writings resists one-dimensional definition. The tension among the elements of the eros

---

[13]Carter Heyward, *Touching Our Strength: The Erotic as Power and the Love of God* (San Francisco: Harper & Row, 1989), 187; cf. 93, 113–14. Further references to *Touching Our Strength* will be cited parenthetically. It is pertinent to note that Heyward explicitly refuses an understanding of "mutuality" as a simple synonym for "reciprocity." She condemns the widespread liberal view of just relationships as founded on a strict economic model of "fair exchange." Mutuality, in her definition, is not a static attribute, but a "relational movement." Mutuality means, *"sharing power in such a way that each participant in the relationship is called forth more fully into becoming who she is—a whole person"* (*Touching Our Strength,* 191, italics in original).

concept is one of its distinctive and most valuable attributes. We can begin, however, to gain a clearer understanding of the precise parallels and divergences between the "new eros" and Tillich's view of the erotic by delineating the principal elements in most womanist and feminist interpretations of eros. Looking at the discussions we have reviewed, five common themes emerge as central strands of such interpretations. These themes do not represent an exhaustive inventory of possible forms of erotic experience. Instead, they reflect the principal areas in which womanists and feminists have assigned a crucial role to eros.

Eros is joy. For feminists and womanists, in contrast to many representatives of the masculine intellectual tradition, pleasure is neither a dirty nor an insignificant word. Carter Heyward writes of the imperative to transform the "body-despising, woman-fearing, sexually-repressive religious tradition" that Christians have inherited. By learning to recognize the creative power of eros, she suggests, we may learn to experience all forms of erotic pleasure, including sex, as "good, morally right, without need of justification." From the standpoint of the Christian tradition, "this perception is scandalous—that our sensual, sexual pleasure is good, in and of itself." Yet this idea is the foundation of a transformed, affirming attitude toward human embodiment, the created world, life itself (Heyward, 46–47). While insisting that eros cannot be reduced to sex, feminist and womanist theologians have broken radically with the hesitation, evident in Tillich's writings, to discuss sexual joy explicitly as a vital dimension of the erotic.

The individual experiences eros, Audre Lorde affirms, as "the open and fearless underlining of [her] capacity for joy." The erotic "is an internal sense of satisfaction to which, once we have experienced it, we know we can aspire" (Lorde, 56, 54). The immediate catalysts of erotic pleasure are diverse. Sex, art, poetry, intellectual activity, communion with nature, all forms of constructive work can yield access to deep and nourishing joy. Lorde claims that, once the empowering pleasure of eros is recognized, "every level upon which I sense opens to the erotically satisfying experience." Eros "flows through and colors my life with a kind of energy that heightens and sensitizes and strengthens all my experience" (Lorde, 56–57). By showing her the ecstatic pleasure she is capable of experiencing, the erotic teaches the individual to demand the most from herself, her relationships, her work. "For having experienced the fullness of this depth of feeling and recognized its power, in honor and self-respect we can require no less of ourselves," and we can measure our lives by no standard lower than the "deep and irreplaceable knowledge of [our] capacity for joy" (Lorde, 54, 57).

Alice Walker identifies an openness to passion and pleasure—"regardless"—as one of the basic attitudes of the womanist. Although she does not use the word eros, Walker describes an approach to life very close to what Lorde speaks of as living "in touch with the erotic." A womanist "[l]oves music. Loves dance. *Loves* the spirit. Loves love and food and roundness. Loves struggle. *Loves* the folk. Loves herself. *Regardless.*"[14]

Eros is a source of knowledge.   Feminists and womanists have also described eros as a mode of cognition, a way of gaining deep and intimate knowledge of persons, things, and ideas. Erotic knowledge, they claim, is a form of wisdom that puts us in touch with the deepest levels of life itself.

For Audre Lorde, the erotic is the force that nourishes the most significant type of knowledge: that which unites rational understanding with intuition rooted in the life-sustaining power of human feeling. Such erotic knowing includes "the physical, emotional and psychic expressions of what is deepest and strongest and richest within each of us." It is a form of knowledge which is closely connected with "the passions of love." The phrase "it feels right to me" represents for Lorde not a superficial assessment, but on the contrary, a recognition that true knowledge is based in erotic intuition prior to rational analysis. This feeling of rightness "is the first and most powerful guiding light toward any understanding." And rational understanding "is a handmaiden which can only wait upon, or clarify, that knowledge, deeply born" (Lorde, 56).

Rita Nakashima Brock criticizes the tendency in Western civilization to view "dispassionate" sensory perception, detached scientific observation, as the only model for reliable cognitive relations with the world. "Through such knowledge," she writes, "things are known externally to us, especially in unilateral causal relationships that are objectifiable." Knowledge gained in this way can certainly be useful. Yet this cognitive model ignores or dismisses "important, subjective

---

[14]Alice Walker, *In Search of Our Mothers' Gardens: Womanist Prose* (San Diego and New York: Harcourt Brace Jovanovich, 1983), xii.

forms of knowing" which are rooted in the uniting power of the erotic. This type of knowledge Brock terms "knowing by heart":

> Erotic power involves inner and outer worlds in a knowing that is multilayered and a causality that is multilateral and intertwined. For example, if I listen to a friend tell the story of a childhood molestation, her pain communicates itself vividly to me. But the pain I experience, triggered by hers, emerges from within me. It is not her pain, though it mirrors hers and enables me to take her pain into me. . . . Our empowerment comes not in her pain or in mine, but in the space where the two meet inside us and between us. In that meeting, in the feelings underneath the speaking and the listening, we are empowered to care and heal. (Brock, 37)

Erotic "knowing by heart" establishes a relationship between knower and known which transcends the simplistic subject-object duality and opens the way for transforming action rooted in "relational power." Such knowledge is not detached and dispassionate but passionately involved.

Erotic knowing, feminists and womanists have claimed, is the basis of all forms of life-affirming creativity and of responsible action in relationships. United with, rather than separated from, deep, intuitional feeling, our sensuous nature can, Carter Heyward writes, "teach us what is good and what is bad, what is real and what is false, for us in relation to one another and to the earth and cosmos." Truly wise moral decisions can only be made in touch with the relational attunement that reveals itself "through our senses and feelings, the basic resources of our intelligence." The moral quality of this intelligence, the rightness of our understanding and of our action in the world is "embedded" in the erotic feelings that connect us to one another (Heyward, 93). True knowledge cannot be gained in abstraction from such shared feeling.

"Our erotic knowledge empowers us," Lorde states. It "becomes a lens through which we scrutinize all aspects of our existence, forcing us to evaluate those aspects honestly in terms of their relative importance in our lives." Erotic knowledge brings with it responsibility: toward others and toward ourselves. Eros demands from us that we not "settle for the convenient, the shoddy, the conventionally expected, nor the merely safe" (Lorde, 57). Yet at the same time, the erotic transforms practices that might to some appear merely mundane. It opens up new areas of creative action within our lives. When our lives have been reshaped on the basis of erotic knowledge, there is still "a difference between painting a back fence and writing a poem, but only one of quantity. And there is, for me, no difference between writing a good poem and moving into sunlight against the body of a woman I love" (Lorde, 58).

Eros is relational.   Although it touches and transforms the individual in her deepest and most intimate dimensions, eros is not a private experience. It is shaped by and in movement toward another person, being, object, idea. The erotic awakens and opens us to the other. It is fundamentally and essentially an energy of relation, of connection-making. Eros, Rita Nakashima Brock suggests, is a life-process "constantly flowing and growing in relationships." Erotic power "is the fundamental power of existence-as-a-relational-process." Eros can be characterized as "the power of our primal interrelatedness" which "creates and connects hearts," involving "the whole person in relationships of self-awareness, vulnerability, openness, and caring." "Eros is a sensuous, transformative, whole-making wisdom that emerges with the subjective engagement of the whole heart in relationships" (Brock, 53, 41, 26).

"In the beginning," Carter Heyward writes, "is the relation, not sameness." Our erotic power calls us into relationships of mutual sustenance and respect, calls us "to touch, not take over, transform, not subsume." Guided by the erotic, we do not seek to blur the contours of difference, but instead to shape relationships in which these differences are respected, in which they become a source of power and of relational pleasure. "Blessed with one another's presence," we develop a sharper sense of and appreciation for difference, a deeper understanding of our own individual identities. Yet learning these lessons "with one another is the only way we can learn them. It is the only way we can experience the love of God, the creative energy of our godding, the erotic as sacred power" (Heyward, 100–01).

The erotic calls us beyond the boundaries of our selves at the same time that it deepens our sense of self. In *The Color Purple,* Alice Walker describes the "feeling of being part of everything, not separate at all," which reveals our profound relational connection to nature, to other people, and to God. This feeling is deeply erotic. It includes a strong element of physical pleasure, yet it flows out toward things and persons with which or with whom "normal" sexual relationships would be excluded: trees, air, birds, friends of the same gender, the divine itself.[15]

---

[15]Alice Walker, *The Color Purple* (New York: Simon & Schuster, 1982), 203.

It awakens Walker's heroines to a sense of the intimate interconnectedness of all life.

Eros is a cosmic force.   As a cosmic force of creativity and love, eros can be imaged in nontheistic ways. In the work of secular poets and theorists, eros is often described as "life-force," a suprapersonal, empowering energy on which individuals can draw, in pleasure and in struggle.[16] As Audre Lorde points out, this life-force manifests itself in a wide variety of different contexts and under many different forms, all of which deserve to be honored for their ability to deepen and enrich our feeling, our wisdom, and our capacity for action (Lorde, 56–57).

The cosmic power of eros can also be conceived theistically, as it is in the work of Heyward, Brock, and Sorge. Heyward identifies God as "our power in mutual relation," and argues that, since we come to know the divine in our experience of human relationality, there is clearly an important sense in which "God is erotic power," a truly Christic—liberating, healing, transformative—energy (Heyward, 188, 91). The value of the Christa symbol may be to "help us envision and embody the sacred/erotic power, which is really our Christic (fully human, fully divine, fully creaturely, fully creative) power" (Heyward, 117). In similar terms, Dorothee Sölle has claimed that, "God is our capacity to love," revealing herself in the matrix of our human relationships. In this relational context, the traditional theological distinction between human eros and divine agape must give way to a unified understanding of love as divine/human power embracing "sexual love, charity and love in the social and political realm."[17]

Brock uses images that strive to bridge the gap between traditional theistic conceptions and a more pantheistic or animistic understanding of eros as a "life-giving force" present in all things. "The presence and revelation of erotic power is the divine dimension of human existence," she writes. "In the beginning is the divine Eros, embodied in all being. As the incarnate, life-giving power of the universe, divine erotic power is the Heart of the Universe" (Brock, 46).

Eros is political.   For Lorde, Heyward, and other womanists and feminists, eros connects deep feeling, wisdom, and responsible action. It

---

[16]See Lorde, "Uses of the Erotic," 55; Trask, *Eros and Power,* 92–96.
[17]Dorothee Sölle, *The Strength of the Weak* (Philadelphia: Westminster, 1984), 138.

shapes the tone and quality of moral behavior. It plays a central role in deciding how (and whether) the individual will act politically. The description of links between eros and political and ethical engagement is one of the most distinctive aspects of the new religious theorizations of eros, both in Jewish and Christian feminisms and in the work of authors connected with Goddess traditions. The claims made in this area by feminist and womanist authors require extended examination.

Eros as a political and ethical force

On its surface, the idea of assigning to the erotic a central place in the theory and the practice of politics may seem surprising, although the notion is not, as Tillich's discussions show, entirely novel.[18] For some, it may appear particularly incongruous that religious feminists and womanists should be among the most active champions of a conscious and systematic integration of eros discourse into politics and ethics. Yet this is indeed the case. Leading Christian and Jewish feminists, among them Heyward, Sölle, Beverly Harrison, and Judith Plaskow, have been in the vanguard of thinkers drawing explicit connections between erotic experience and modes of participation in the moral and political realms.

Of course, the idea that "the personal [including the sexual] is the political" has been something of a stock phrase in feminist circles for many years. Some religious feminist and womanist theorists, however, have gone beyond the vagueness of the formula to make precise and challenging assertions about the political "uses of the erotic," and about the nature of the connection between personal erotic experience and effective political and ethical engagement.

Generally speaking, these discussions of the political and moral dimensions of eros have been organized around three central themes: eros as an analytic concept, as an energy of revolt, and as a source of creative empowerment and positive political and ethical values.

Eros and sexuality as analytic concepts.   Along with their secular counterparts, Christian feminist and womanist authors have insisted that

---

[18]Cf. also Herbert Marcuse, *Eros and Civilization* (Boston: Beacon Press, 1966), Wilhelm Reich, *Sex-Pol: Essays, 1929–1934*, ed. Lee Baxandall (New York: Vintage, 1972).

the concept of eros provides an important intellectual/analytic tool for decoding social power relationships, even those relationships that are (or appear to be) situated outside the domain of the sexual. They base this practice on the feminist insight that the systematic oppression of women by men underlies all forms of social, economic, political, and cultural praxis within patriarchal society. From this perception, feminists have derived the principle that eros could provide a tool for understanding the basic human needs and relational structures on which social and political institutions are founded. Using the criterion of eros as a life-giving creative energy, it would then also be possible to critique those social structures in which the erotic impulses are thwarted and consequently essential human needs are not met. In secular scholarship, Nancy Hartsock has most convincingly defended this use of eros as an analytic category. A broadly defined eros concept is, she claims, vital for exploring "the sexual meanings of issues and institutions which are not explicitly genitally focused." Most significantly, she affirms, grounding one's analysis of social and political forces in an understanding of the erotic can highlight "the genderedness of power," and "the relation of sexuality to issues of power and community."[19]

Christian feminists such as Dorothee Sölle and Shirley Cloyes have also analyzed the oppression of women by men as a crucial aspect of the commodification of human relationships in capitalist society. In a social order structured by class exploitation and frantic consumption, gender roles and the sexual act itself are used as tools of oppression. Alienated sex negates the "eternal eros" that seeks to build authentic, life-enhancing relations among persons. A concept of healthy and nurturing erotic relations can thus be used as a device for revealing the points at which our human needs are frustrated by the socioeconomic order. The concept of eros can measure the depth of alienation and point to areas in which fundamental political change must be effected.[20] Carter Heyward emphasizes the need to utilize categories related to eros in order to create a social history capable of elucidating "the connections between the control of women's bodies for procreation; the suppression of homosexuality; the economic system of a particular place and time." Citing the analyses of sexuality and power relationships by Michel Foucault and Jeffrey Weeks, Heyward argues

---

[19]Hartsock, *Money, Sex, and Power*, 166–68.
[20]Dorothee Sölle and Shirley Cloyes, *To Work and To Love* (Philadelphia: Fortress Press, 1984), 115–25.

for a "historical understanding of sexuality" which breaks free of essentialist categories and looks at the complex interaction between sexuality, religion, and economic and social institutions (Heyward, 38–47).

Eros as an energy of revolt.   The use of eros as a tool in the analysis of social and political relationships is the least unconventional among Christian feminists' applications of the erotic to the political and moral spheres. The other two such applications that I wish to discuss involve claims about the impact, not of the idea, but of the experience of eros in politics and ethics. In this area, feminists and womanists have made assertions that go well beyond what more conservative theorists consider normal or even admissible.

Each of these two radical uses of eros experience in politics exhibits unexpected aspects. The first, however, is in some ways the more surprising. Feminists and womanists have seen in eros an immediate source of the energy of revolt necessary for struggle against oppressive political and social power structures. Although like most feminists, Lorde, Harrison, and Heyward emphasize the positive, nurturing aspects of the erotic, they also describe its combative dimension. They have affirmed that the experience of the erotic and the feelings it awakens sustain the anger that spurs the fight against oppression. Such theorists see an organic and necessary connection between the "work of love" and the "power of anger," both on the level of personal ethics and in political action.

Audre Lorde insists that eros represents the "bridge which connects" the spiritual and the political. The erotic, by the very joy that it affords, empowers and compels us to refuse and combat sex-, race-, and class-based exploitation, to say no to the humiliation, the institutionalized mediocrity, the cheap compromises meted out by patriarchal authorities. "In touch with the power of the erotic within ourselves, . . . we begin to give up, of necessity, being satisfied with suffering and self-negation." Charged with the anger at injustice that belongs to the deepest nature of eros, "our acts against oppression become integral with self, motivated and empowered from within" (Lorde, 56, 58).

In analyzing the connections between sex and political practice, Starhawk suggests that too often, persons have tended to let their sense of what is politically correct dictate their ways of responding erotically. Rather than allowing abstract political ideas to tell us what and how we should feel, perhaps it would be more constructive to ask what we in fact desire at the core of our being, and then to move toward creating a society that would further and enhance our sexuality, deepen our capacity for joy. Needless to say, such ideas are dangerous from the point of view of the currently dominant power structures. Authentic erotic feeling is threatening to patriarchal society, because it attacks "the roots of patriarchal power relationships."[21]

Judith Plaskow notes that when the erotic is understood not simply as sexual feeling but as "our fundamental life energy," the force of eros becomes "threatening to established structures," religious, social, and political. Citing Lorde, she notes that our experience of erotic satisfaction in work well done leads us to refuse types of work that are meaningless and alienating. Likewise, the knowledge of the joy available in authentic, liberated, mutually empowering sexual encounters teaches persons—particularly women—to rebel against a rigid patriarchal system that claims the right to prescribe the channels through which sexual desire can legitimately be expressed. Having begun to gain an experience of their own capacity for creative and joyful action, women and members of other oppressed groups revolt against those hierarchical power relationships that seek to prevent them from bringing the same creative intensity to more and more aspects of their lives.

From a patriarchal perspective, Plaskow writes, "or the perspective of any hierarchical system, erotic power is dangerous. That is why, in Lorde's words, 'We are taught to separate the erotic demand from most vital areas of our lives other than sex.'" For the same reason, women are conditioned to restrain their sexuality, "so that it too fits the parameters of hierarchical control that govern the rest of our lives." From a feminist point of view, however, "the power and danger of the erotic are not reasons to fear and suppress it," but rather grounds on which the erotic should be nurtured "as a profound personal and communal resource in the struggle for change" (Plaskow, 202–3).

The criterion offered by our experience of erotic joy and connectedness requires that we enter into the struggle against those forces and interests that degrade the natural world and reinforce the oppression of marginalized groups within human society. Through eros, the privileged among us learn that we are not "above it all," that if our own capacity for erotic fulfillment is to be realized, we have no choice but to stand actively in solidarity with the threatened natural world and with oppressed communities. To value our own bodies and our own

---

[21]Starhawk, *Dreaming the Dark*, 141.

sexuality means, Plaskow asserts, to value and respect the earth of which our bodies are a part. The feminist revaluation of the erotic entails the active struggle against the destructive misuse of nature which is a "denial of our embodied creatureliness, rejection of our embeddedness in the natural order." At the same time, "the capacity to open ourselves to the world, to allow the power of the erotic to quicken our lives, depends on creating a human world in which this is a possibility." Eros and the knowledge gained through genuine erotic experience demand of us that we take a critical and responsible stance toward "confronting the political questions that shape our total environment—the gentrification of inner cities that is leaving an increasing number of people homeless, the dearth of humane living spaces, the factory closings and relocations that are creating a new group of unemployed and homeless, the structures of racism and class domination." Such issues and the anger they spark are not remote from the area of the erotic. Rather, Plaskow claims, they belong in an intimate way to the "opening of ourselves" that we experience through eros. (Plaskow, 231–32).

Beverly Harrison has focused on the critical and transformative role of love, including the erotic, in ethics and sociopolitical struggle. She stresses the integral connection between the experience of love and the "power of anger" which expresses itself in political struggle for justice. Where anger rises, "there the energy to act is present. In anger, one's bodyself is engaged, and the signal comes that something is amiss." The harmony of a healthy relational attunement has been disrupted. Anger alerts us to the need for change. We must not allow ourselves to "lose sight of the fact that all serious human moral activity, especially action for social change, takes its bearings from the rising power of human anger." To maintain its politically potent character, the anger of which Harrison writes must be intertwined with and rooted in our experience of connection through love. Yet at the same time, honest and authentic love relations depend upon the recognition of anger as a positive transforming force: "Where anger is hidden or goes unattended, masking itself, there the power of love, the power to act, to deepen relation, atrophies and dies."[22]

In many of these analyses, lesbian experience and the discourses fashioned from it move into the center of the picture. Carter Heyward

---

[22]Beverly Wildung Harrison, "The Power of Anger in the Work of Love," in Beverly Wildung Harrison with Carol Robb, *Making the Connections: Essays in Feminist Ethics* (Boston: Beacon Press, 1985), 14–15.

maintains that lesbians and gay men find themselves in an ironically privileged position when it comes to understanding this radical dimension of love. She prefers the term "rage" to that of "anger," underlining with her choice of words the passion and urgency which inform erotic rebellion. Born and nurtured in the face of institutionalized suspicion or outright hostility, lesbian/gay eros will have a thread of rage woven into its very fabric. "Our passion as lovers," Heyward claims, is what fuels "our rage at injustice." Far from being mutually exclusive, rage and compassion, eros and political resistance, "belong together."[23]

"To say that I am a lesbian," Heyward asserts, "is to make a statement at once personal and political." What homosexuals are "perceived to be about (and what some of us are about intentionally) is not simply the right to lead our own private lives, but rather an overhauling of the social structures of our time," a revolutionary transformation of the "economic, religious, educational, business and other structures" which characterize late-twentieth-century capitalist society.[24] The experience of "the erotic as power" becomes in Heyward's work both the final goal of liberatory struggle on the part of the sexually oppressed, and the source of the combative energy necessary to carry on the fight.

"Power in right relation": eros as a source of creative empowerment and positive political and ethical values. Heyward and Sölle in particular stress that the combative political dimension of the erotic ultimately serves the positive side of political eros. Transformed by creative eros, political struggle becomes not merely struggle against, but struggle for: for the broadest possible application of the principles of justice and mutuality to which our erotic experience gives us an indispensable introduction. In other words, eros teaches persons to rebel against oppressive structures and life-denying values; at the same time, the erotic helps them discover new values and modes of relationship to replace the old. Some Christian feminist authors see a close connection between our experience of erotic relatedness and the effectiveness, indeed the very existence of our engagement in the struggle to realize justice on the level of our local community, of the society to which we belong,

---

[23]Carter Heyward, *Our Passion for Justice: Images of Power, Sexuality and Liberation* (New York: Pilgrim Press, 1984), 87.
[24]Ibid., 90–91.

and of the world. Our experience of eros is not the only factor determining our involvement (or lack thereof) in politics. It is, however, these authors claim, an important source of the emotional and spiritual empowerment, of the wisdom, and of the will, all of which we must bring to ethical decision-making and political struggle if our engagement is to be effective.

Eros, including the sexual dimension of the erotic, liberates energies for the physical, emotional, and spiritual effort involved in justice work. Carter Heyward insists that the aspect of eros which we know through sexual pleasure is not irrelevant to the quality of our ethical relations with other individuals, nor to our involvement in political reflection and struggle. Sexual union experienced under conditions of genuine mutuality empowers and galvanizes the participants for effort in other areas: "Sexual orgasm can be literally a high point, a climax in our capacity to know, ecstatically for a moment, the coming together of self and other, sexuality and other dimensions of our lives," including the political (Heyward, 33). Furthermore, through pleasure in shared effort, the tasks involved in political work can themselves become "eroticized," at least in part. The immediate experience of the erotic changes the "color," the emotional tone of the work undertaken, helping us to find pleasure in the effort connected with the pursuit of political change (Lorde, 57–59).

Yet eros does more, according to some feminists' and womanists' understanding, than simply offer a wellspring of vital energy which can be tapped for the purposes of political struggle. The erotic as the experience of both the fulfillment and the endless reawakening of yearning for mutuality in relationship teaches us in an immediate and personal way that right relation between human beings is in fact possible, and that such forms of just relatedness can transform human existence. Rightness in relation, mutually sustaining and empowering attunement is, we learn, a goal toward which human beings can work together, and which, together, they can achieve.

Lorde, Heyward, Sölle, Brock, and other feminist and womanist authors are united in their insistence that the significance of this apprenticeship should not be underestimated. Sharing erotic joy, we are taught how ecstatically beautiful life can be in its highest moments. And we perceive what it is that makes such moments possible. These privileged experiences of fulfillment are born in situations in which justice—dynamic, erotic mutuality—has been called into being among us. There are no oppressors and no victims, no "doers" and no "done-to's," but simply human beings who have come together in what Brock

terms the non-hierarchical "play space" of mutual recognition, co-
creation, healing (Brock, 36–37). In this erotic space, we taste the joy
and the creative energy that justice produces in human life.

The particular types of erotic connectedness that can develop among
women are central to feminist and womanist descriptions of the experience of erotic justice in intimate relationships, and of the carrying-
outward of this justice into the public context of political action.
Starhawk describes the intense erotic power that flows within small
groups of women committed to an "erotic politics" free from hierarchical structures:

> The circles we spin become erotic structures, based on personal contact
> and connection. In small groups, we can share feelings, we can touch
> and stroke each other, cry together or laugh together, as well as do
> business. Circles remain small so we see each other, reflect each other,
> and our unique personalities have an impact on others to whom we feel
> connected.

Within such groups, communal connections are experienced as richly
erotic. And this deeply female eros provides direct knowledge of a
sharing of power which is not hierarchical power-over, but healing
and creative power-with. Within such spaces, "the erotic can confirm
our uniqueness while affirming our deep oneness" with the other
members of the community, and with "all being." Here, "the spiritual,
the political and the personal come together."[25]

Yet the space of eros is not one of saccharine sentiment or of uncritical mutual support. Audre Lorde is grateful for her erotic connections to "those sisters with whom I have danced hard, played, or
even fought" (Lorde, 59). Unqualified affirmation is not a necessary
ingredient of erotic connection. What does belong to the nature of
eros is justice. This means respect for the other, acknowledgment of
her dignity and freedom, above all in those areas in which she differs
from ourselves. It also means honesty: respecting the other enough to
share our convictions with her, and if need be to fight with her, when
we believe she is wrong.

Through the connections woven by eros, womanist and feminist
authors have argued, justice ceases to hover as a vague abstraction and
takes on tangible and cogent meaning *for us*. In the give-and-take of

---

[25]Starhawk, *Dreaming the Dark,* 143, 138.

our erotic lives-in-relation, the abstract idea becomes a sustaining value. In this sense, Carter Heyward writes, our values are "never simply our own private opinions." Our understanding of justice grows in a situation of erotic "relation to those whose lives we trust" (Heyward, 95). Justice as an aim of political effort can become most powerfully credible for us, Heyward believes, through the personal experience of erotic justice, the mutuality that is our "shared experience of power in relation." Through mutuality, "we are called forth more fully into becoming who we are—whole persons with integrity, together. Our shared power is sacred power, and it is erotic" (Heyward, 99).

Going beyond this already daring idea of eros as a morally formative encounter teaching us to understand and value rightness in relation, Christian feminists such as Heyward, Sölle, and Shirley Cloyes have formulated an even more radical hypothesis concerning the connection between erotic experience and justice-making in the political sphere. They believe that the joy and pleasurable attunement experienced through authentic eros express themselves directly and spontaneously as a political impulse: the will to strive for the creation of social and political conditions under which equally intense erotic—that is, sensual and creative, as well as sexual—satisfactions would be available to all members of the society. Sölle and Cloyes assert that "genuine erotic love opens the hearts and minds of lovers to other people." To love deeply is to gain knowledge "not only of our partner," but also of the full community of human beings. "Because we grow into wholeness through love," she claims, "we yearn for reconciliation with the disenfranchised of the earth. In other words, the more I make love, the more I want to make the revolution."[26]

It would be a mistake to minimize the psychological and philosophical radicality of this position. These Christian feminists claim to be identifying a type of committed and effective engagement in the political sphere which springs directly out of what is usually thought of as the intensely private experience of erotic communion. This account involves a fundamental and bold assertion about the relationship between the two areas: the public/political and the intimate/erotic. Sölle, Cloyes, and Heyward join other thinkers in denying the existence of a "private" erotic sphere in the habitual sense of the term. Sexuality is deeply impacted by practices of social construction, and

---

[26]Sölle and Cloyes, *To Work and To Love*, 150–52.

is as such inescapably political. Yet going beyond this fundamental insight, these authors see eros not simply as passively shaped by political and social forces, but as actively shaping life-affirming ethical and political values and generating power for effective justice struggle.

The eros feminists and womanists describe is not an esoteric experience linked to obscure and specialized practices. Rather, it is an unfolding of the fundamental and potentially universal human joy in competent creative activity and in communicative interaction with others. Thus, eros signifies more than an enhancement of personal pleasure. It expresses possibilities for wider cooperation and transformation at the social level. Having tasted—perhaps fleetingly and fragmentarily at first—the joy that eros brings, we can learn to work toward shaping situations of erotic fulfillment in our own lives. And we find that a necessary part of working for our own realization as erotic beings is working for the liberation of others' erotic-creative potential. As Plaskow stresses, eros is only fully realized in community, with the range of political responsibilities that this word implies (Plaskow, 201).

This claim enables us to understand more clearly what feminist and womanist authors mean by authentic, mutual, or nonalienated eros, as opposed to the dehumanizing sex that is the norm in our culture.[27] The erotic in its authentic, liberating form is moral in its essence. Such eros seeks by its very nature to engender the conditions of social justice that would permit its own widest dissemination. Erotic pleasure of this sort demands, like good news, like the tidings of a birth, to be shared. It creates in the person who experiences it a moral need to see it propagated.

This intuition is decisive for much religious womanist and feminist thought on community-building and political struggle. Authentic erotic joy does not isolate the partners in a closed world of private satisfactions, but demands instead to be shared as widely and as generously as possible. Such joy requires and initiates its own translation into the communal-political sphere. This does not occur as an afterthought, but belongs to the essence of the phenomenon of erotic connection as religious feminist authors have described it. To have experienced true joy means to want that joy for others, as well as for oneself. Thus, for Sölle: "Love is not separable from justice. The drive to make love

---

[27]See Sölle and Cloyes, *To Work and To Love*, 150–55; Heyward, *Touching Our Strength*, chaps. 3—6; Brock, *Journeys by Heart*, Introduction and chap. 2.

and to make justice should be one."[28] Carter Heyward asserts that there is direct continuity between authentic erotic passion and our "passion for justice": "To love you is to sing with you, cry with you, pray with you, to act with you to recreate the world. To say 'I love you' means—*Let the revolution begin!*"[29]

The new language of eros

In their current writing on the erotic, feminist and womanist authors are involved in producing a discourse with radically transformative implications for theology, and for many other types of intellectual work and social practice. The work on eros now being done by feminists and womanists has generated a new vocabulary for thinking about human relationships at all levels, from the intimacy of sexual partnerships to the complex interplay among classes, communities, and social groups.

The idea of the centrality of relationship has been seen as one of the cornerstones of feminist theory in its most characteristic and important forms. The feminist and womanist vision of human life as fundamentally relational breaks with the liberal cult of the self as autonomous monad. And the new concept of eros now being explored by women poets, theorists, and theologians has opened the way for an in-depth phenomenological exploration of the way important forms of relatedness "feel" to us. On the basis of their understanding of the primacy of shared feeling, womanist and feminist authors have begun concretely and cogently to show how relationships shape and orient our lives.

Feminists and womanists acknowledge that abstract analysis of the functioning of economic and social structures is necessary in effective action for change. Yet a genuinely probing and useful analysis must not neglect the networks of personal connections—and thus of erotic feeling—which interact with (and which may in fact govern) seemingly impersonal institutions and disembodied politico-economic dynamics. In demanding a "passionate" approach to politics,[30] feminist theorists

---

[28]Sölle and Cloyes, *To Work and To Love*, 152.
[29]Heyward, *Our Passion for Justice*, 93.
[30]See Charlotte Bunch, *Passionate Politics: Feminist Theory in Action* (New York: St. Martin's, 1987).

have affirmed that there is in fact no such thing as genuinely dispassionate politics: no decision making on "purely rational" grounds, no mechanical, disinterested functioning of "pure" economic and political forces (the liberal myth of the quasi-divine "unseen hand" which guides the free market economy). Human feeling is central to all political and economic structures, and to all ethical decisions. Passionate forces of desire and repulsion shape our lives as moral and political agents, whether or not these forces are explicitly acknowledged. The issue is not whether feeling will inform and determine our ethical actions and political choices. It will. The question is only *which* feelings will play the central role in constituting us as moral and political beings, and thus in shaping the character of our life together in community. Will the decisive influence be an authentic, mutually nourishing flow of erotic power and erotic joy, or will it be a twisted eros poisoned by the desire for domination?

With his view of eros as the catalyst of moral interaction, and of eros relations as the basis of all community and of all political structures, Tillich points toward an understanding of the political function of eros which parallels the feminist view in many ways. Tillich—unique among liberal male Christian theologians—perceived and affirmed the formative role of the passions in shaping and maintaining social groups and political entities. Yet Tillich's discussions of the moral and political role of the erotic are for the most part abstract, disappointingly vague, suggestive but short on concrete detail. The conduct of Tillich's personal life shows that his way of constructing connections between life-affirming eros and just action in relationships was destructively flawed.

Feminists and womanists have moved beyond Tillich's position by focusing on the practical dynamics linking erotic feeling to specific patterns of ethical and political behavior, and by making the question of relational justice central to their definition of authentic eros.

Feminist and womanist theorists affirm that our need to engage ourselves politically and ethically, to assume direct responsibility for the choices made in our community and our society, is a function of the quality and intensity of the eros relations that connect us to the world and to other people. Political and moral commitment to justice grows out of our striving to "live with a full sense of our own erotic energy" (Plaskow, 231). Developing this sense of our own erotic potential in an authentic, nonalienated way requires that we also recognize others as erotic beings, and that we take responsibility for fighting against the oppressive structures which thwart our own and others' erotic fulfillment.

The crucial defining quality of authentic eros, as feminists and womanists have begun to discuss it, is that such eros leads us to demand justice, for and from ourselves and others. True eros urges us to embody right relation at all levels of our connection to each other and to the world, from our sexual relationships to our participation in political and economic systems to our too often unacknowledged interdependence with nature. Authentic eros is the quality of feeling that moves us more deeply into right relation with others, by awakening and nurturing within us the passion to see justice done. As the rightness of our relational connections is reinforced, our experience of shared, erotic power grows stronger. Thus, our experience of authentic eros deepens our need for justice, and increases our capacity to work together to realize it.

Defining authentic eros as the creative power we feel in right relationships recognizes, however, the existence of other types of erotic relations: nonmutual, exploitative, life-denying. Our erotic connections can be twisted and distorted, turned in the direction of manipulative power-over, rather than mutually fulfilling power-with. Many feminists and womanists recognize explicitly that under the present socioeconomic conditions, our eros *always* carries within it these abusive and exploitative strains. Our erotic feelings can never be pure, at least as long as the society that shapes us remains structured at every level by dynamics of domination and abuse. Many of our most pervasive cultural patterns are founded on the repression of the life-instincts, the systematic negation of erotic feeling, and the elevation—tacit or explicit—of the domination/submission paradigm to the status of unique model of human relatedness. Our eros inevitably reflects to some degree the alienating constructions of power and pleasure which characterize our society.

Yet feminists and womanists claim that moments of authentic, liberating eros can be experienced even under the conditions of socioeconomic, racial, and sexual alienation which mark contemporary culture and which poison the lives of the oppressed and the minds of their oppressors. Womanist and feminist theologians and poets have affirmed the power of erotic love to break through confining structures and alienating mentalities. Moreover, they argue that once an authentic experience of erotic connectedness has begun to emerge in one area of our lives—be it art or poetry, a sexual relationship, erotic healing experienced in the solidarity of political struggle—the power of eros can and will reach out to color and inform more and more of our existence. Authentic eros is contagious. It flows from one area of an individual's life over into others. It moves between persons, as well, allowing the power of transforming eros to spread through whole communities, entire movements.

Our experience of erotic joy becomes a means by which we can measure the quality and depth of our responses in all areas. As we learn to feel profoundly and to open fully to the knowledge mediated by eros, our erotic feelings reveal clearly to us those parts of our lives in which justice has not been realized. Thus, eros makes available to us a heightened joy, but it also forces us to confront deepened pain. Erotic joy, as Tillich understood and stated eloquently, is not the opposite and negation of suffering. The opposite of joy is not pain, but detachment, lack of feeling: the "emptiness" that springs from our failure to "reach the others and their world in a genuine relation" (*NB*, 146). In a world marked by deep and pervasive injustice, intensified erotic feeling brings with it an increased exposure to pain, to the negative feelings that remind us that "something is amiss in relation."[31]

In some cases, eros opens us to suffering from which we cannot legitimately expect to free ourselves, because this pain is connected to institutionalized forms of violence and injustice which our efforts as individuals cannot impact in a significant way, which can only be "made right" with aching slowness, through shared struggle over long periods of time. The suffering experienced by victims of racial, economic, and sexual oppression and the pain and guilt felt by the perpetrators and beneficiaries of such forms of injustice are often intensified, rather than anaesthetically relieved, by the deepening of erotic sensitivity. These aspects of suffering are ones that we will have to "live with" for as long as our lives continue. And as we seek to live erotically, as we become more fully attuned to the relational patterns in which we are involved, we can indeed expect our experience of such pain to become more acute. Yet insofar as these types of pain and the anger they spark serve as motors of commitment, struggle, and transformation, eros embraces these irreducible forms of pain and uses them to serve the cause of justice.

In other cases, the deepened understanding opened to us by our experience of authentic eros shows us situations of relational disharmony that are in our power to change. Eros increases our sensitivity

---

[31]Harrison, "The Power of Anger," 14.

to the forms of suffering and conflict which, in our personal lives, signal the need for change in relationships. On the level of intimate relational connections, authentic eros spurs and challenges us once again to act out and embody justice.

In contrast to feminists' and womanists' insistence on the direct connection between authentic erotic feeling and concrete justice-making, Tillich fails to focus clearly on the idea that our experience of genuine eros can only be morally significant if it brings with it a heightened sense of ethical and political responsibility, and an increased capacity for just action. The relationship between erotic feeling and right action is referred to but never explored carefully in Tillich's work. This is the most serious flaw in Tillich's portrayal of eros as a creative life-force.

Tillich does make a suggestive distinction between perverted or distorted erotic craving and life-affirming "essential eros." In its general intent, this idea seems to harmonize with feminist efforts to distinguish authentic eros from the exploitative forms of sexuality predominant in Euro-American culture. Tillich even suggests that essential libido and eros may be defined by the fact that they do not "use the other as a tool for gaining pleasure," but instead seek to establish and maintain relationship on a deeper level. Yet the idea that genuinely life-giving eros demands that we "do justice" concretely in politics and in our intimate relationships is only vaguely hinted at. The demand for right action as the criterion of essential eros haunts the pages of Tillich's discussions like a ghost whose presence the theologian does not want fully to acknowledge, but which he also cannot dismiss. Although he approaches the idea in many passages, Tillich avoids affirming unequivocally that the practice of justice in concrete relation is the criterion that separates essential from perverted eros. Tillich was, I believe, afraid of the judgment such a statement would have implied on the conduct of his own erotic life. This anxiety prevented him from framing an explicit definition of essential or authentic eros in terms of the shape of justice in actual relationships.

Feminist and womanist authors have developed their reflections on the erotic in the context of an exploration of concrete forms of relational justice among people. Undoubtedly, the understanding of authentic, life-sustaining eros which has emerged in feminist theory will be a source of controversy. Many will object to the claims that attribute decisive moral and political importance to the erotic. Even relatively conservative thinkers may be willing to accept the use of eros as an analytic category in the critique of social and political power structures.

However, the further claims made by Christian and other womanists and feminists about the direct political impact of personal eros experience will certainly provoke considerable skepticism.

Questions will be raised about the empirical justification for affirming the existence of a direct and empowering connection among the experience of eros, just ethical practice, and effective political engagement. In our society, it might well be claimed, the erotic is omnipresent, yet active political commitment to the struggle for justice is in short supply indeed. To this objection, feminists and womanists supportive of the eros principle will answer that the experience of authentic eros in our culture is not only not universal, but that such experience, even among persons who consider themselves sexually liberated, has been and continues to be exceedingly rare. It is not simply that the alienating, pornographic sex celebrated in our society as the only legitimate paradigm of human erotic interaction does not entirely correspond to the understanding of the erotic developed by feminist and womanist authors. Rather, this common understanding of sexuality—rooted in sadomasochistic fantasies of domination and control—represents the antithesis, the radical negation, of the relational eros described in feminist and womanist discourse.

In fact, the scarcity of genuine erotic mutuality in our culture accounts for the difficulty in tracing the empirical effects of eros in the current political and moral landscape. Violent and depersonalizing sex is indeed ubiquitous; eros as the sharing of power and pleasure in right relation is only beginning to be recognized as a possibility for women and men in Euro-American culture. Feminist and womanist authors suggest that as authentic eros experience becomes available to more and more people, there will in fact be more testimonies such as that of a lesbian student quoted by Carter Heyward: "My love for and commitment with women in relation has come to call me to an ever more radical justice praxis" (Heyward, 119).

A more serious objection to emerging feminist discourses on eros is connected with the problem of race and class relations. It is clear that even what feminists and womanists want to regard as "authentic" erotic joy runs, like other forms of pleasure in a racist and capitalist society, the risk of being denatured and appropriated as a supplementary "life-style enhancement" by those belonging to the already dominant racial and class groups.

Feminist theorists' shaping of a new vocabulary based on the experience of erotic joy and empowering mutuality might well look, to women who are the direct victims of racial and class oppression, suspiciously like an attempt on the part of affluent white women to avoid the harsh and often decidedly unjoyful realities of concrete political struggle. On the subject of such struggle, bell hooks notes with terse irony that it is in fact "rarely safe or pleasurable."[32] Certain members of privileged groups will clearly be only too willing to seize on elements of feminist and womanist discourse on eros as an authorization for pleasure-seeking under the guise of political activism. Such discourse will undoubtedly in some cases reinforce the cherished belief (aggressively criticized by hooks and others) that by "feeling better about ourselves" and our intimate relationships, we are *already* involved in a significant type of political praxis.[33]

The risk is real that authentic eros might, in a caricatured form, become another expression of race and class privilege. However, the decisive role played by black and Asian-American women such as Audre Lorde, Alice Walker, Haunani-Kay Trask, and Rita Nakashima Brock in shaping new discourses on the erotic suggests that the risk can be avoided. The importance of eros in the thought of these women makes clear that the erotic as pleasure, as relational energy, as cosmic power, and as animating force in political struggle can and does have liberating significance for women of color and others in special situations of oppression. Neither poetry nor eros, according to Audre Lorde, should under any circumstances be thought of as a luxury reserved for the leisure class. Eros, like poetry, is a vital tool for the oppressed in their struggle to free themselves from the mental, emotional, and linguistic traps—as well as from the more tangible prisons—into which they have been forced. Lorde's observation on poetic language in general is particularly apt as a characterization of the emerging discourse on the erotic: it "lays the foundation for a future of change"; it functions as "a bridge across our fears of what has never been before."[34]

The new language of eros, then, is both a description of experiences and structures already proven and in place, and a calling into being of "what has never been before." Authors such as Andrea Dworkin are justifiably skeptical about the power of liberal ideas and warm words to combat the institutionalized sexual and economic exploitation that characterizes our society.[35] Yet if there seems at present to be little

---

[32]bell hooks, *Feminist Theory: From Margin to Center* (Boston: South End, 1985), 28.
[33]Ibid., 43–65.
[34]Audre Lorde, "Poetry Is Not a Luxury," in *Sister Outsider*, 38.
[35]See Dworkin's essays in *Letters from a War Zone* (London: Secker and Warburg, 1988), esp. "Violence against Women," "The ACLU: Bait and Switch," "Why So-Called Radical Men Love and Need Pornography," and "Feminism Now."

empirical evidence of the political impact of the new eros, it would nevertheless be wrong to conclude either that eros as described by some womanists and feminists does not exist, or else that it will never be politically significant. Drawing such conclusions would be failing to grasp the extent to which the new language of eros will catalyze and draw out for open recognition the empowering erotic connections that Lorde, Heyward, and others have discussed. It would also be failing to acknowledge and to honor the transformative power that many have felt in moments of erotic communion.

Through eros, through the sharing of creative power in a just relationship, we receive an experience of joy which will not leave our lives unchanged. Like Celie in Walker's *The Color Purple,* as the un-imagined force and depth of authentic erotic connection begin to reveal themselves to us, we find our attitudes toward all areas of our lives transformed. We learn that joy shared and multiplied in mutuality is not a possibility reserved for another world. It is something we are capable of experiencing here and now. And in this assurance we find the power to "talk back" to those who have tried to deny us joy. Such erotic power is not available only to a select group, or dependent upon a knowledge of abstract theories. It is rooted in nothing more obscure than the simple willingness to take seriously basic human experiences of creative pleasure, mutual care, and connectedness, and to acknowledge that these experiences give meaning to our existence.

Such experiences are potentially available to all persons. And the sight of others' suffering becomes an irresistible demand for action when we perceive those others not as broken objects, faceless entities made and shattered by economic forces, but instead as potential bearers of the same creative eros that has brought a new depth of fulfillment to our lives. Eyes opened to the possibility of erotic joy cannot close themselves again conveniently before the daily spectacle of that joy mutilated. Having tasted the power of human creative potential im-plicit in the erotic makes each encounter with a human life twisted by poverty and injustice a call which forces us into action. The pain we feel is a demand for change not out of respect for an abstract concept of justice, but out of the passionate desire to share the eros that gives, strengthens, and transforms life. Anger of the kind that Lorde, Har-rison, and Heyward describe wells up hot against the laying-waste of erotic possibilities, others' and ours. Connection through eros teaches us that our own joy can never be whole as long as others are cut off from joy by force, through racism, sexism, and economic violence.

Over time, I believe, the feminist and womanist discourse on eros as an empowering experience of mutuality will create a conceptual and affective framework within which eros can be thought about, discussed, and experienced in a new way. In its personal dimension and its political consequences, the new eros will become available to increasing numbers of women and men who were previously unable to name and consequently to know it. The new understanding of the erotic will enter into dialogue with theological and philosophical traditions, and reveal sides of those traditions—Tillich's work on eros offers a good example—that have been ignored by conventional interpretations.

Of course, in a context in which sexual violence and abuse pervade all levels of our social existence, it would be foolish to suppose that eros could immediately be accepted as an unambiguous value. In particular for those persons who have themselves been victims of sexual abuse, the idea of a healing eros is deeply problematic, if not positively offensive.[36] However, the understanding of eros as an energy of embodied relation which is not limited to, or even necessarily connected with, genital sexuality—an understanding common to Tillich and to feminist and womanist authors—opens perspectives for healing connections among persons whose lives have been damaged by sexual violence.

Freeing ourselves from the depersonalizing dynamic of violence and exploitation which has governed understandings and experiences of sexuality in patriarchal society means, womanists and feminists claim, inventing a new vocabulary in which to describe and give shape to new forms of sexually erotic relatedness. Such authors as Lorde, Plaskow, Heyward, Brock, and Sölle have taken up this task. Their discourse on eros possesses that poetic power to "give name to those ideas which are . . . nameless and formless, about to be birthed, but already felt."[37]

Especially in the realm of Christian thought—so visibly dominated by a tradition of hostility toward women, human embodiment, sexuality, and the material world in general—creating a new language of

---

[36]This topic was discussed in several sessions of Beverly Harrison's seminar on "Sexuality and Social Order in an Ethical Perspective," Union Theological Seminary, New York City, Oct.–Nov. 1989. I am grateful for the experiences, questions, and criticisms shared by members of the seminar, especially those who are themselves survivors of sexual abuse.

[37]Lorde, "Poetry Is Not a Luxury," in *Sister Outsider*, 36.

eros has radical implications. Indeed, Carter Heyward does not ex-
aggerate in suggesting that eros as she understands the term demands
a transvaluation equivalent to a genuine revolution in Christian moral
and theological thinking (Heyward, 47, 114–18). It is time, she writes,
"to speak the truths of our lives insofar as we can, with one another's
presence and help," while "cultivat[ing] carefully together those truths
we cannot yet speak, truths that may still be very unformed and
young." For in cultivating a new language of the erotic, "we are shaping
history with our words" (Heyward, 47).

6
Chapter

Tillich's Eros and Feminist/Womanist Theologies
Toward the Theological Future

I have become increasingly interested in probing that which is radically good in our commonlife: our power in mutual relation as the basis of our creative and liberating possibilities, literally the only basis of our hope for the world.

—Carter Heyward

Nature has received another meaning; history is transformed, and you and I are no more, and should not be any more, what we were before.

—Paul Tillich

Depending upon which future is envisioned, the past changes.

—Sharon D. Welch

Paul Tillich ascribed to the erotic "the greatness of a divine-human power" (*LPJ,* 117). This remark was no slip of the pen, no momentary oversight on the part of an otherwise staid and intellectually disciplined Protestant theologian. Until now, the theme of eros has been largely neglected by scholars looking at Tillich's work; yet as books, lectures, and sermons from throughout his career reveal, the erotic was central to Tillich's understanding of the nature of human life and of the structure of religious experience. In almost

153

every important sphere of human, and indeed of cosmic, activity, Tillich explicitly assigns a decisive role to the erotic. A full understanding of Tillich's thought cannot be gained, and no fair assessment of his theological achievement made, if his work on eros is left out of account.

Today, the theme of eros, neglected for a time not only in Tillich's work but in the whole of Christian theology, has reemerged powerfully in the writings of Christian and other feminists and womanists. There is good reason to believe that the consequences of the feminist and womanist revisioning of eros for the future of theological thinking will be far-reaching. By entering into dialogue with the interpretations of the erotic developed by feminist and womanist authors, Tillich's thinking on eros can help move the future of Christian theology in a liberative, life-affirming direction. The theme of eros raises questions and opens perspectives that will be decisive for the evolution of Christian religious thought and institutional practice in the coming years.

A new approach to Tillich's theology

Striking similarities, as well as important differences, can be discerned between Tillich's vision of eros and the interpretations of the erotic currently being put forward by such authors as Carter Heyward, Dorothee Sölle, Rita Nakashima Brock, and Judith Plaskow. Yet the appearance in feminist and womanist writings of a subject central to Tillich's theological project does not mean that Tillich's work on eros has exercised a direct influence on Christian feminist and womanist theory, let alone on the thought of women working outside the Christian tradition. Tillich did not help feminists to discover eros. Rather, one might argue that, in a certain sense, it is the other way around.

The work of feminists and womanists has made the concept of eros visible again in Christian theology today. It is thanks to the affirming understanding of the erotic gained by feminist and womanist authors that we can now look back, discern, and retrieve the theorization of eros that Tillich's theology contains. Without the lens provided by recent feminist and womanist writing, the richness and complexity of eros in Tillich would in all likelihood have remained invisible. Thus, rather paradoxically, the thinking on eros developed by feminist and womanist theorists enables us to bring to the surface long-suppressed aspects of the work of a white, male theologian whom Carter Heyward has labeled as the "paradigmatic modern liberal." Yet this effect is consistent with the aims of the best feminist and womanist criticism of patriarchal religious institutions and theologies. At the same time that the feminist critique exposes the destructive aspects of traditional religious constructs, it also liberates and valorizes neglected creative forces within the tradition. In conversation with feminist and womanist ideas, an unexpected side of Tillich's theological project emerges. A new "way in" to Tillich's theological world begins to open up.

An early critic once congratulated Tillich ironically for having achieved a degree of abstraction which "surpasses even Hegel."[1] Yet the themes and issues connected with eros suggest possibilities for engaging Tillich's theology on a more human, less radically cerebral level, and for bringing certain aspects of Tillich's project closer to the lived reality of normal people. Tillich's discussions of the erotic are not always free from a tendency toward broad generalization, but they are less abstract than much of the rest of the theologian's writing. And they raise issues—embodiment, sexuality, the role of emotion, moral interaction with others, community and politics, human beings' relationship to the natural world—that are important in each person's daily practical experience.

Moreover, these issues have often been ignored in scholarly approaches to Tillich. Scholarly work has tended to focus on the vast questions and abstract concepts that are the most obvious hallmarks of his theology: being, nonbeing, existence, finitude, reason, history, the God-beyond-God. His construction of a system based on such massive philosophical concepts is usually considered Tillich's claim to theological greatness.

The theme of eros suggests, however, the possibility of another approach to Tillich's work: one that steers away from overarching systematic considerations and metaphysical language to look carefully at areas of human experience in which erotic power and erotic passion play a central role. These areas include those of aesthetic experience, of the search for a form of knowledge that unites and heals, of moral motivation and the dynamics of community, of the erotic relation between human beings and the divine, of humans' integral link to the rest of the created world. All of these are fields in which further study of Tillich's writings could yield important new insights, and begin to liberate a side of his thought which has, until now, been given little

---

[1]F. Kattenbusch, quoted in Werner Schüßler, *Der philosophische Gottesgedanke im Frühwerk Paul Tillichs (1910–1933)* (Würzburg: Königshausen und Neumann, 1986), 4.

attention. Recent work by a number of Tillichean scholars—especially younger scholars and those based outside the Anglo-Saxon academic world—points toward a growing interest in periods and themes within Tillich's theology which have until now been looked at as marginal. Attention to his understanding of eros could open up new perspectives within many of these fields of inquiry: from Tillich's concept of power to his reading of the communicative power of the symbol.[2]

It is perhaps no coincidence that in many of the areas in which eros plays a crucial role, the large structures of the mature Tillich's metaphysical system begin to show signs of strain. An important characteristic of the erotic is precisely its links to types of human experience that defy easy categorization and ordering within a preestablished metaphysical system (or at least within the system into which Tillich would have liked to fit them). Eros may not be irreconcilable with traditional systematics. Yet looking at Tillich as a theologian of the erotic will mean paying less attention to the harmony and symmetry of a metaphysical architecture, and instead focusing more closely on the concrete experiences of eros in human life to which he points. Future scholarly work and theological reflection on Tillich might seek to explore fully the interconnections of erotic passion, politics, art, and religious experience, or the complex understanding of community explored in some of his less "systematic" writings. New facets of Tillich's achievement as a theologian and philosopher may emerge from a careful consideration of the treatment of eros and human emotion in his sermon texts, and in the books, articles, and lectures produced before his emigration to the United States. In general, as Werner Schüßler points out, while the theologian's better known later writings

---

[2]Suggestive new directions in Tillich scholarship have begun to emerge in Germany and the French-speaking world. See Schüßler's *Der philosophische Gottesgedanke* and his articles "Ontologie der Macht: zur philosophischen Bestimmung der Macht im Denken Paul Tillichs," *Zeitschrift für Katholische Theologie* 111 (1989), and "Theologie muß Angriff sein: das Religions- und Theologieverständnis Paul Tillichs," *Freiburger Zeitschrift für Philosophie und Theologie* 34, no. 3 (1987): 513–29. Schüßler's presentation of the 1925 *Dogmatik* (Düsseldorf: Patmos, 1986) also represents an important new resource for the study of Tillich's early work. For recent approaches to Tillich by French and Canadian scholars, see the essays in *Religion et Culture: Colloque du Centenaire Paul Tillich* (Québec: Presses de l'Université Laval/Editions du Cerf, 1987), esp. Olivier Abel, "La corrélation religion-culture dans la théorie du symbole chez Paul Tillich," and Paul Asselin, "La critique théologique de la société bourgeoise dans l'ouvrage *Die religiöse Lage der Gegenwart* (1926)." Paul Avis makes skillful use of Tillich in his call for a reintegration of eros into the Christian understanding of the sacred; see *Eros and the Sacred* (Wilton, Conn.: Morehouse Publishing, 1990).

have generated an immense critical literature, Tillich's early work has been neglected.[3]

In the early writings in which eros is discussed, Tillich was still "feeling his way" toward an understanding of the full power of the erotic in human life. His early references to eros are allusive, fragmented, at times highly obscure. The complex influences of classical philosophy, psychoanalytic theory, and the thought of Nietzsche are especially evident here. In his later years, Tillich's reading of eros, like practically everything else in his thought, had to be reshaped and regularized to fit the requirements of a rigid theological system. Precisely because of their sketchlike, unfinished, and sometimes contradictory quality, the early discussions of eros may yield further suggestive insights into Tillich's understanding of the importance of human feeling.

Places where the conceptual architecture of Tillich's system begins to appear forced and precarious are in some cases, I believe, the very points at which other types of truth, different, less cerebral and less easily controllable forms of experience are breaking in. Erotic power and the deep force of erotic truth threaten the poise and elegance of a systematic perspective achieved through ontological abstraction. The places in which conflicts emerge in Tillich's work between the requirements of preconceived metaphysical structures and Tillich's own intuition of the power of the erotic are points at which further careful study of Tillich's texts will be highly enriching for contemporary theology. Today's theologians should consider these points of friction closely as they try to reevaluate the usefulness of many aspects of Christianity's metaphysical heritage, of which one of the most important is the relationship between agape and eros (see below, pp. 168–69, 177–78, 184–85).

The theme of eros may function as a key to unlock a dimension of Tillich's work in which feeling and passion are the dominant elements: a dimension in constant tension with—and often hidden by—the philosophical abstraction that rules the surface, the public, readily visible side of Tillich's theology. The sermon texts collected in *The Shaking of the Foundations, The New Being,* and *The Eternal Now,* as well as Tillich's many unpublished sermons and talks, will be helpful in probing the hidden levels of his understanding of erotic power, human feeling, and relationality. In his sermons, Tillich was willing to "let

---

[3]Schüßler, *Der philosophische Gottesgedanke,* 3.

himself go," to express ideas with greater spontaneity and freedom than he allowed himself in his more "serious," academic writings. In his sermons, Tillich generally stayed close to the level of actual feelings and concerns among the people he addressed. Despite their challenging intellectual content, the sermon texts consistently show a sensitivity to the realities of ordinary life that is sometimes missing from Tillich's famous works in systematic theology.

Ultimately, the important place of eros in Tillich's work shows that if he was a highly abstract metaphysical thinker, a theologian of being and nonbeing, of essence and estrangement, he was also deeply concerned with those experiences in which, within human life, these abstract categories are transcended and cease to carry ultimate significance. Although Tillich never abandons traditional metaphysical structures entirely, eros shows that he also focuses on experiences of authentic relationality that relativize the importance of such structures. These are experiences through which metaphysical reflection about the human situation bows before the beauty of shared, embodied life itself; moments in which a healing "rightness," a deep erotic joy connects human beings to each other, the world, and to the divine power active within it.

Of course, Tillich has always been recognized as an "existential" theologian, one who gives central importance to actual human experience as a basic factor in theological work. Yet "existential" has often seemed to mean focused on the negative and painful aspects of the "human predicament" (which translates, in most cases, as the loneliness and anxiety of white, male, middle-class Euro-Americans). However, through the theme of the erotic, a new existential accent can be discerned in Tillich's theology: one that evokes not doubt, alienation, and psychospiritual suffering, but a positive, eroticized existence. This voice speaks of knowledge, morality, and politics shaped by creative passion; of the centrality of community and a deep, nurturing involvement in the world; of erotic passion for the divine.

The eros concept that has been drawn into the center of recent theological thinking by feminists and womanists provides a new reading of parts of the theological tradition. In particular, it offers access to previously unrecognized aspects of Tillich's thought. And through these unexpected aspects, Tillich's theology, in dialogue with feminist work, will have insights to contribute to the shaping of the theological future.

Looked at in isolation and on its own terms, Tillich's understanding of eros possesses interest for the history of theological ideas. It represents a significant and heretofore little explored aspect of the thought of one of the leading shapers of twentieth-century Christian liberal theology. But in dialogue with new feminist and womanist theorizations of eros, Tillich's understanding of the erotic is more than a relic of intellectual history. In conversation with feminist and womanist ideas, Tillich's concept of eros is turned toward the theological future, one in which the central imperatives for theological thinking will be: (1) to shape a concept of the human person capable of reflecting the centrality of relationship and of embracing and affirming all levels of embodied existence; (2) to develop a more sophisticated, justice-centered approach to questions of community, difference, and power; (3) to articulate a convincing understanding of the interconnectedness and interdependence of all life, created and divine; and (4) to foster an effective sense of human co-creativity and co-responsibility in harmony with the divine order.

The aim of this chapter will be to show that important insights connected with these crucial issues can begin to emerge from a conversation between Tillich and feminist and womanist authors on the topic of eros. The volume and quality of current feminist and womanist writing on the erotic suggest that eros will be a key concept, perhaps indeed *the* key concept in Christian feminist and womanist theology in the coming years. Thus, such a conversation will raise questions and open perspectives of significance for a vision of the theological future.

Tillich's work on the erotic may be a point of leverage at which traditional liberal theological thinking can open itself to embrace and affirm the transformative discourses on eros emerging in feminist and womanist theologies. Tillich's work shows that a concept of eros comparable in important ways to that being shaped in feminist thought is neither entirely foreign nor necessarily antithetical to traditional Christian theology. On the other hand, the tensions and contradictions within Tillich's understanding of eros—difficulties that the comparison with feminist and womanist thought can best reveal—point to areas in which the concept of eros enters into sharp conflict with traditional theology, and demands the transformation of certain traditional theological constructs.

The concept of eros as a divine-human, life-shaping, and sustaining power emerges, in Tillich's work, from within the masculinist Christian theological tradition itself. It affirms some aspects of that tradition, while implying the need for radical change in many others. Dialogue between traditional and radical viewpoints on the basis of new understandings of the erotic will serve not only the interests of the liberal

Christian traditions themselves—so visibly and so desperately in need of an influx of fresh and empowering ideas—but also those of feminist and womanist theologians who remain committed to the principle that certain aspects of religious traditions and structures merit salvaging. Those Christian feminists and womanists who believe that traditional religious thought and established institutions should be transformed and healed, rather than simply abandoned, might find in Tillich's work on eros a point on which modern theological liberalism can be engaged in a creative way—critically, but also with the sense that in such conversation are seeds of new possibilities.

Shared understandings of eros

Both in Tillich's work and in the writings of contemporary womanists and feminists, eros is looked at as a creative force mediating vital aspects of human beings' relationship to one another, to the world in which they live, and to the powers that shape, govern, and sustain that world. In Tillich and in feminist and womanist thought, eros designates an attitude toward life, a fundamental mode of relatedness to the world which differs sharply from the world views and models of behavior prevalent in our culture. The generally accepted world views in Western civilization are founded on images of detachment, domination, separation, and control. The human ego stands as a fully independent, isolated monad over against the world, the "other" that it seeks to subjugate, govern, and use. The boundaries of the individual self are rigid and impermeable. That which is "outside" is irreducibly alien, and otherness can only be constructed as a hierarchical relationship of domination and submission, mastery and surrender. Not only is the self as a centered consciousness radically distinct from its environment, but its difference from other selves and from the world at large is interpreted as necessarily implying a relationship of antagonism, fear and mistrust, along with the will to master and control. The alienation of self from self and of self from world—along with the manipulative violence that this alienation generates—is deemed unavoidable.

The eros toward the world which Tillich identifies as human beings' most important capacity, and which—under slightly different names—has reemerged as a central concept in religious feminist and womanist theory, opens the perspective of a new and transformed mode of relation between self and world. In feminist and womanist writings on the erotic, as in Tillich's work, eros is fundamentally identified as an energy of connection-making. Erotic connections take shape among persons, between persons and ideas or abstract values, between humans and the things and beings of the natural environment. Tillich and feminist and womanist authors are in agreement as well—although their vocabularies for describing this relation vary considerably—that eros catalyzes the human experience of connectedness to the divine source of all being, the indwelling, sustaining force of life.

As an energy of connection, eros places the category of relationship at the center of all considerations of human existence. In Tillich's work on participation and community, and still more powerfully in the writing of recent women theologians, the emphasis on the erotic has unfolded within and contributed to an emphasis on the human self as formed and sustained by a relational matrix, that is, by erotic connections to other selves. This does not signify that individual personhood simply disappears. But the self ceases to be conceived as a firm, closed, isolated entity, a thing which may be juxtaposed to, or then again considered in separation from other "things." In Tillich's terms, individualization cannot be separated from the participation in other selves and in the world without which human being as such would be impossible.

For religious feminists such as Brock, Harrison, and Heyward, it is no longer acceptable to discuss "the self" as a discrete entity in isolation from the relational matrix. The feminist concept of community founded on powerful erotic bonds allows a redefinition of the human self which departs from the traditional Western masculinist conception of the detached, autonomous ego. Feminists claim that our experience of communal connectedness nourishes, shapes, and defines our understandings of who we are as individuals. Although Tillich remains committed to a concept of the "centered self" which owes a good deal to traditional models, he, too, consistently emphasizes that the individuated self takes shape within a field of participatory, erotic relationships (see *ST* 1:174–78; *ST* 3:40–41). The development of the individual is only possible in a matrix of encounters with other selves. Tillich's emphasis on eros tempers the ego-centered slant of his anthropology and opens his thought to the perception of human life as fundamentally relational.

Eros conceived of as an energy of creative connection-making points up important similarities in Tillichean and feminist and womanist understandings of the erotic in the areas most central to Tillich's discussion of eros: eros and the powers of origin; the philosophical and cognitive eros; erotic influences on morality, community, and politics; the religious eros; "eros toward the world" as source of joy and catalyst of the healing transcendence of estrangement. The degree of harmony between Tillich's perspective and feminist and womanist views should not be overstated. In decisive areas, radical differences between their positions emerge. Tillich's discussions of eros are consistently more abstract than feminist and womanist treatments, sometimes obscuring common ground even where it does indeed exist. Yet often, beneath the variations in language, similar basic intuitions of the power of eros can be perceived. Shared insights emerge about the ways the eros principle expresses itself in crucial areas of human existence.

We will look now at some of these shared perceptions of eros, before moving on to consider criticisms of Tillich's eros theory suggested by the recent work of womanist and feminist authors. In examining the role of the erotic in morals and politics, we will see that even in areas in which there are strong convergences between the two viewpoints, feminist and womanist writings raise immediate questions about Tillich's handling of important issues connected with the erotic. These questions will point to some of the ways in which Tillich's theory must be critiqued and corrected in dialogue with feminist and womanist work.

Eros, as described by Tillich and by feminist and womanist authors, unites nonrational elements with the "higher" analytical functions of the mind and spirit. Eros embraces the material, embodied structures of existence, as well as abstract intellectual and religious values. The erotic ties persons to what Tillich terms the "powers of origin": the earth, sexuality, embodiment, the primal bonds of family and community (see *SD*, 13–15). This level of nonrational feeling and experience is the plane that Audre Lorde identifies as that of the erotic "lifeforce." It is the channel through which we communicate and are connected with all created things. With the term "powers of origin," Tillich points toward the fundamental level of being at which our lives are enmeshed in and constituted by a weave of tangible, material relationships: to "the soil," that is, to the earth itself; to "blood," that is, to all living creatures; to "the social group," that is, to one another as human beings shaped by and in community. Acknowledging the erotic link to the powers of origin means accepting and affirming our connection to all life, human and nonhuman. It means acknowledging our involvement in the web of relationships that constitute the natural world. It means refusing, as Tillich stresses, all forms of the idea that the human soul is in some way alien to the created world, that there is and must be a relationship of antagonism between "spirit" and "matter" (*MB,* 41). As Carter Heyward also writes, the basic structure of our human being is: "Our sensuality, our shared, embodied participation in forming and sustaining the relational matrix that is our home on this planet." This participatory dimension is the foundation of our spiritual, as well as of our physical existence. Our sensuous, erotic connection to the world is the source of our spiritual wisdom. And this connection can and must "be trusted."[4]

Tillich's view of eros as fundamental to all of our cognitive connections to the world breaks with the traditional Western paradigm in which a purportedly disinterested, dispassionate form of knowledge is regarded as normative. The ideal of dispassionate interaction devoid of feeling and involvement has also been rejected by feminist and womanist authors. Like Tillich, they see in such a concept a dangerous distortion of the true nature of human understanding and relationality. For Tillich and for feminist thought, there is no form of knowledge from which interest and feeling are absent. The attempt to suppress these elements leads to the use of destructive and depersonalizing forms of knowledge based on the impulse for domination and the desire to control. Feeling is always present in our contacts with the world, however "dispassionate" we might wish to make them. Unacknowledged or repressed, feeling takes on demonic forms. The myth of objective knowledge leads directly to an antagonistic, exploitative perception of nature, and ultimately to a view of other human beings, too, as objects to be manipulated and exploited (*ST* 1:89–100).

Tillich and feminist theologians and philosophers assert that all knowledge and all forms of interaction with the world include a passionate element, whether or not this affective quality is recognized explicitly. Grasping eros as the omnipresent energy connecting persons cognitively, psychologically, and spiritually to their world confirms that the basic human attitude is one of passionate involvement in the world and in the lives of others. Understanding this fundamental quality of human being is an essential step in moving toward healing relationships among persons, among human communities, between humankind and the world. Recognizing eros as the basic principle of our knowing can help us open ourselves consciously to erotic involvement in the objects of our knowledge. It can help us draw closer

---

[4]Carter Heyward, *Touching Our Strength: The Erotic as Power and the Love of God* (San Francisco: Harper & Row, 1989), 93. Further references will be cited parenthetically.

to the ideal of gnosis, in which knowing and loving, understanding and acting are no longer separate, but have become a single, unified process.

For Tillich, as well as for feminists and womanists, eros is the force that guides us toward true wisdom (*BR,* 50, 72; *ST* 1:95; *NB,* 129). Eros reconciles the deepest levels of feeling and embodied passion with the human being's most subtle rational faculties. The result is an authentic "love of wisdom" from which the quickening blood has not been drained, but which calls us into passionate engagement with the world we seek to understand. As "ontological passion," it connects rational analysis with desire and intuitive feeling, pointing toward the "knowledge deeply born," the "knowing by heart" of which womanists and feminists also speak.

Eros is the source of artistic creativity, for Tillich as for Audre Lorde. The erotic shapes and flows through all of those creative processes in which we invest ourselves integrally, whether the process involves painting a back fence or writing a poem.[5] We can feel in the products of human creativity—from a symphony to the "technical Gestalt" of an airplane—the power that awakens our eros, that sparks our own creative response. Eros draws us into the ongoing creative exchange that unfolds in human culture at every level (*ST* 3:258–59). Eros allows us to find the satisfaction of involvement in a wide range of activities, including many that might ordinarily be dismissed as mundane. Creative eros is not, as Tillich emphasizes, limited to the domain of art as defined by an elite (*ST* 3:256f.). Both for Tillich and for authors such as Lorde and Heyward, the erotic opens up new and unexpected areas of practice as sources of passionate joy and creativity.

Eros is shared in the pedagogical relationship between teacher and student, and among those who share their quest for wisdom in a less formally organized way. The eros toward truth is deepened and intensified in a community of mutual encouragement and questioning. The interweaving of erotic friendship and deepening knowledge is sketched suggestively in Tillich's convocation speech to the students and faculty of Union Theological Seminary. It is evoked, as well, by Starhawk: "Teaching and learning, too, become erotic endeavors— not sterile exercises in mastery of fact, but journeys together."[6] A

---

[5]Audre Lorde, "The Uses of the Erotic: The Erotic as Power," in *Sister Outsider* (Trumansburg, N.Y.: The Crossing Press, 1984), 54–57. Further references to Lorde's essay in this chapter will be cited parenthetically.

[6]Starhawk, *Dreaming the Dark: Magic, Sex, and Politics* (Boston: Beacon Press, 1988), 145.

similar dynamic is exquisitely illustrated in the interplay among the main female characters in Alice Walker's *The Color Purple*. Celie, Shug, Nettie, Sofia, and Squeak teach and learn from one another. As they do so—and because they are able to do so—a deep love flourishes among them. Sandra Friedman describes the women's relationship as a flowing movement in which teaching, learning, and loving are no longer distinguishable from one another. Through erotic learning and loving, Walker's women nourish one another's minds, bodies, and hearts.[7]

As the catalyst of healing relatedness among human beings, eros does not seek to abolish or efface differences between persons. Here again, important points of agreement emerge between Tillich's views and the positions of feminist authors. Eros, feminists and womanists claim, acknowledges, honors, and uses difference as the dynamic basis of a just relation: the nonhierarchical sharing of power among authentic, autonomous individuals. In such a relation, creative "tension," not "easy peace" is valued. Respecting one another's specific needs and gifts, persons are empowered to "reach through the particularities of who we are toward our common strength" (Heyward, 100). The erotic forms the basis of a relation in which difference ceases to be perceived as menace. "The sharing of joy," Audre Lorde writes, "whether physical, emotional, psychic, or intellectual, forms a bridge between the sharers which can be the basis for understanding much of what is not shared between them, and lessens the threat of their difference" (Lorde, 56).

For Tillich, too, in the moral realm and in all forms of communal interaction, eros functions to draw persons into relationships in which individual identity and integrity are maintained, but within which values that transcend the individual—values connected with participation and community—are also central. Eros constitutes the medium through which the individual is able to experience participation and communal solidarity without a loss of self (see *ST* 1:176; *MB*, 38–41).

---

[7]Sandra R. Friedman, " 'Trying to Please Us Back': Political Effects of Erotic Bonds among Women in *The Color Purple*" (M.A. thesis, Columbia University, 1990). Friedman shows how teaching and learning among Walker's female characters are bound up with the erotic connections between the women, and how a multifaceted type of erotic involvement forms the basis of a reshaping of social and economic power relationships within the community. Friedman emphasizes Walker's portrayal of lesbian erotic experience as a source of transforming knowledge shared among women, a means of learning to see oneself and the world in a new way.

Common ground and conflicts

In Tillich's moral system, eros draws the individual into encounter and communion with a concrete other. Yet at the same time, eros functions as an abstract "transmoral motivation" made effective by the power of divine grace. While it draws us into relation with real, tangible persons, eros orients our moral choices in relation to the universal ideals of truth, beauty, and justice, which transcend the particular situation. These ideals, in Tillich's view, belong to the divine. Thus they possess the motivating power to call the individual beyond her or his own specific wishes in a situation. They are reminders that these wishes, although important in themselves, must ultimately be evaluated in relation to a broader standard and ideal of the good (*MB,* 59–60).

Tillich is convinced that mature moral choices are motivated in large measure by the erotic love for the good that springs from and reflects human beings' desire to participate in the divine life. Such love for the ideal is itself, he states, a gift of divine grace, although human freedom is exercised in the acceptance or rejection of the gift. This seemingly somewhat abstract form of moral motivation is combined with a "listening love" that attends carefully to the demands of the concrete situation. Tillich maintains that love—combining erotic and agapic elements—is a uniquely flexible and powerful principle, on which all authentic morality is based. Love can remain "unchanging" in its fundamental nature, yet change and adapt itself in its applications to each particular situation (*MB,* 43, 88f.).

The erotic yearning toward the values of beauty, truth, and right action which Tillich evokes is, I believe, an attempt not only to ground moral action theoretically, but also to describe the same type of experiential phenomenon that Carter Heyward designates with her phrase "passion for justice." Tillich wishes to argue that there is an ideal of the good—in Heyward's terms, of "rightness in relation"—which can be realized in concrete situations, but which also, as an ideal value, exists apart from any particular context of immediate moral choice. Our attempts to act morally in particular situations, Tillich believes, spring to a considerable extent from the erotic-intellectual passion that we feel toward this idea of just action. Our passion for justice as an ideal (fragmentarily) realizable in human life spurs our efforts to act justly toward those with whom we interact in our day-to-day existence.

Tillich glides very rapidly in his theoretical discussion, however, over the relationship between the erotic passion we feel toward the ideals of goodness, truth, and beauty, and our passion toward other living human beings, the concrete others with whom we are linked in situations of ethical decision making. Tillich's concept of passionate love toward an ideal of the good is suggestive. We can use the word *justice* to designate an ideal quality of "rightness" that we find or do not find present in specific relational settings. Yet where does the content of this ideal concept come from? Can this ideal be thought of as having an independent existence, apart from concrete situations of relational connection among people? We do think and speak of an ideal of justice. Yet the only way we can encounter and grasp its meaning is through our feeling for the rightness or wrongness of specific relationships. Our erotic interest is not primarily oriented toward an abstract moral ideal, but toward the flesh-and-blood people with whom we interact, whose goals and feelings mesh or conflict with ours.

Tillich does not seriously try to make clear how the overarching ideal of right action is connected to our concrete, personal relationships. He strives explicitly to avoid a reified, rigid concept of justice by introducing his idea of the "listening love" which responds flexibly to the demands of each new situation. Yet the suspicion is unavoidable that a sort of Platonic hierarchy is still at work in Tillich's thinking: that "goodness," along with beauty and truth, hovers in an ideal realm to which we can gain (fragmentary) access by intellectual and/or mystical intuition. This intuition of abstract ideals gives only a mediated, secondary importance to the concrete situations of love, struggle, and moral choice in which we are involved as embodied persons.

Like Carter Heyward, Tillich believes that our moral motivation springs from an erotic passion for justice. But the justice he posits as motivating is not experienced and understood primarily in a matrix of concrete human relationships. Instead, the justice that for Tillich awakens our eros is an abstract ideal expressing the nature of the divine life in which we as rational creatures desire to participate. He does not draw explicit connections between the "rightness" we can taste directly in the context of our own relationships and the concepts of truth, beauty, and right action, which seem to float in a higher, abstract sphere. Reading backward from the understanding of eros in ethics that has been gained by womanist and feminist authors, it is possible to see ways in which Tillich's understanding of eros toward the ideal of justice could be reconciled with a primary attentiveness to real human relationships. The eros that draws us toward the ideal is in fact an expression of our desire to participate in the divine. If, as feminist theologians have affirmed, the divine manifests itself most fully in the matrix of tangible relational connections among persons, then our desire for God (and for the justice that is an expression of God's nature) leads us back directly to the framework of our immediate relational connections to other human beings. It is there that we must seek the justice that we long for. It is in our concrete moral and political relationships that we must realize our participation in the divine life, as we act to make justice a reality among God's creatures. This reconciling interpretation can be read back onto Tillich's discussion with little difficulty. Yet this should not mask the fact that Tillich himself makes no move to develop his own reflections in this direction.

Compounding the difficulty of relating the ideal to the real and tangible is Tillich's use of the concept of agape in ethics. He wants, on the one hand, to think of agape as divinely created, unchanging and "unambiguous." According to *Systematic Theology*, such love is free from passionate elements, from "repulsion and attraction" (1:280). On the other hand, Tillich maintains that agape forms the basis of our moral decision making under the guidance of the Spirit. Supposedly disinterested agape commands our choice to struggle for justice and to reject and combat oppression. Tillich's discussions in *Morality and Beyond* show his awareness that our response to moral demands is not in fact dispassionate or abstract (see *MB*, 39: "Justice is taken into love if the acknowledgment of the other person as person is not detached but involved."). Yet Tillich continues to connect his theory of correct ethical action with the influence of agape, which he defines as the "transcendent quality" of love, and in which he explicitly seeks to minimize the affective, passionate element (*MB*, 39–40). The result is that the true nature of moral agape and its role in human beings' ethical life are extremely difficult to grasp.

How does "unambiguous," divine agape interact with eros and the other forms of love in situations of moral choice without either losing its own distinctive qualities, or else abolishing the distinctive aspects of the other love-forms? What does it mean to say (*MB*, 40) that an "unambiguous" love directly called forth by the divine Spirit must be prevented by eros from degenerating into "moralism"? Is agape indeed susceptible to degeneration or perversion? If this is the case, then agape's "unambiguous" status appears problematic. Originating in a higher, spiritual dimension, agape enters the realm of human behavior and moral choice. Yet here, the pure and unambiguous divine love is subject to corruption. A dualistic, "higher versus lower" world view is thus reinstated even as Tillich seeks to free himself from it. In situations of moral decision, Tillich maintains, humans aim at a divinized universal ideal which transcends the realm of actual human relationships. This description tends to reintroduce elements of the matter–spirit dualism inherited from classical philosophy.

Tillich ties his presentation of the role of eros in morals to an abstract concept of justice which has little practical content and is hard to relate to concrete ethical relationships. He adds to this presentation somewhat confusing descriptions of grace and agapic love (*MB*, 39–46; 61–63). While struggling to overcome the dualism of Kantian moral theory, Tillich nevertheless tends to reintroduce dualistic perspectives through his understanding of agape as a dispassionate, divinely inspired, spiritual form of love. Agape as the "transcendent source of the moral imperative" also "transcends the finite limits of human love" (*MB*, 40, 42). Motivating eros is subordinated to the agapic love which exercises its "domination" (*MB*, 46) over all moral demands. This account reconstructs a situation in which disembodied spiritual values take precedence over concrete, embodied relationality. This dualistic slant undermines Tillich's effort to make morals responsive to the "concrete situation." Tillich makes no effort to connect eros in morals with examples of real interaction among human beings. Although he stresses the importance of the person-to-person encounter and of communion shaped by eros, Tillich does not theorize erotic connection, the concrete sharing of erotic joy among persons as in itself morally motivating. This is the central difference between Tillich's view and feminist and womanist understandings.

Feminist and womanist authors claim that the recognition and empowering assimilation of justice as a motivating value occur most effectively through human beings' direct experience of fulfillment in erotic connection to others. We learn, they claim, what justice is and what it can do to heal human life through our own personal experience of mutuality and of the just sharing of power in erotic relationships. Our experience of erotic joy and of the healing power of right relation creates in us a moral need to act directly to bring about conditions under which all other persons could enjoy the same fulfillment. Womanists' and feminists' insistence on grounding their understanding of justice in concrete relational contexts offers a sharp contrast to Tillich's cerebral approach to the problem of erotic justice. The broad theoretical outlines of the two views of eros as a moral principle are not incompatible. Yet deeply significant differences emerge rapidly once we begin to examine the details of the views developed by Tillich and by feminist and womanist authors. We will return to the crucial problem of eros and justice in the next section, in which feminist criticisms of Tillich's eros doctrine are explored.

Tillich prefers to ground important aspects of his theory of moral motivation more strongly in speculative metaphysics than in an analysis of concrete human relationality. Nevertheless, he insists in an extremely firm and convincing way on the importance of community as the matrix in which individual personhood and moral agency come to be. Whatever the source of our motivation for carrying out specific acts, it is only in a communal setting and through the face-to-face confrontation with another individual that we experience the force of the fundamental moral demand to treat the other human being as a person. Tillich recognizes explicitly that outside of the dynamics of a real human community, the idea of morality is meaningless.

Tillich agrees with feminist and womanist writers in assigning to community a decisive role at all levels of human existence, from political dynamics to religious experience. Just as importantly, his writings prefigure feminists' emphasis on eros as the basis of the experience of connectedness within the community. Their common recognition that "the bonds of community are erotic bonds" constitutes one of the most significant and suggestive points of agreement between Tillich's thought and feminist and womanist theorizations of the erotic.

In certain passages, Tillich begins to draw out the political implications of the idea that all community structures and political institutions are founded on erotic relations. He emphasizes the importance of a "spirit of eros" in effective political movements and describes a dynamic of eros among peoples as the only basis upon which a just and lasting global peace could be constructed (GW 13:443). Yet Tillich's discussions of the implications of eros for political action and social change remain in the form of suggestive but incomplete sketches. He never explores in detail the impact of different constructions of eros on the social, economic, and political structures of different societies. He offers no precise treatment of the connections between the individual person's experience of the erotic in intimate relationships and the broader bonds and tensions that shape group relations within a society. He makes no serious effort to connect the communal eros with concrete concepts of social and political justice. Thus, Tillich never works through the full consequences of the fact that forces very similar to the communal eros which he praised in the antifascist youth movement (*GW* 13:130f.) were also utilized and manipulated with considerable success by the Nazis.

While suggesting that an eros that transcends the identity and particular interests of the individual would be a vital element in creating peace among social groups and between nations, Tillich makes no concrete recommendations about how such erotic energies should be catalyzed within a group large or small. He does not explicitly describe the affective and conceptual structures that permit individuals to participate in the eros associated with a collective entity. He does not indicate how and under what circumstances the erotic bonds within a given community can be transformed, nor what the impact of such changes might be in any specific case. Thus, while Tillich's remarks on the fundamental importance of eros to successful political practice are highly suggestive, they leave unexplored essential questions that might help distinguish between creative and destructive forms of political eros and explain the transition from one form to another.

Tillich was painfully familiar with the Nazis' harnassing of communal, political eros to fuel an operation of ruthless tyranny and genocide. He lived through the rise of the Nazi machine and was himself, as an outspoken socialist, one of the early victims of Nazi policies, removed from his teaching responsibilities and forced into exile soon after Hitler's takeover of power. His political experience in Weimar Germany might have equipped Tillich to offer important insights on the subject of political eros and the mechanisms of its preservation or its perversion. Yet he never explicitly analyzed how what he regarded as an essentially constructive and life-affirming force could be transmuted by such groups as the Nazis into an energy of fanaticism and death-dealing hate. He stresses frequently the ambiguity associated with the communal, political eros, as with other forms of the erotic. Simply observing that group eros is ambiguous, however, gives no information about the actual political and social processes through which shifts in the character of shared eros are provoked, nor about how a positive group eros could be more effectively protected against denaturing exploitation. Labeling the erotic as ambiguous represents an important stage in understanding the dynamics of erotic relations among persons and groups. Yet this labeling should be the beginning, not the end, of reflection on the concrete impact of erotic energies in the political sphere. Pointing to communal and political eros as ambiguous simply locates the problem that needs to be addressed. In itself, it offers no insights into how such a complex and powerful force should be used, nor into the mechanisms of its abuse.

In light of this failure to look carefully at the connections and disjunctions between communal eros and concrete political justice, certain disturbing aspects of Tillich's discussion of relations within political and social groups become recognizable as part of a pattern. In fact, Tillich's account of the erotic dynamic between the members of a community and the "ruling group" gives strange echoes of totalitarian rhetoric. The ruling group is always, Tillich believes, "above the law," even if this is not recognized explicitly. This situation is the only "way of making the application of the law possible. The law must be given in a creative act, and it is given by members of the ruling group. It must be applied to the concrete situation in a daring decision, and the decision is made by members of the ruling group." The "silent acknowledgment received by a ruling group from the whole group" is what gives the elite the authority to rule. This acknowledgment is primarily erotic in nature, based on the larger group's ability to see its own "spirit," values and ideals "incarnated" in the "ruling classes" (*LPJ*, 96–99). No convincing criteria or limiting mechanisms are included in Tillich's model which would protect the eros toward the elite from degenerating into a fascist idolatry toward "leaders" invested with unrestricted power.

Questions of the relationship between political and communal eros and the demands of justice are hinted at or raised fleetingly in Tillich's writings on the erotic. Yet his concern with privileging the broad outlines of a system at the expense of coherence and precision in the details prohibits Tillich from addressing these issues in anything more than an extremely superficial manner.[8]

Both Tillich and contemporary feminist and womanist authors have emphasized the role of eros in the area of faith and religious experience. Like many religious feminists and womanists, Tillich describes faith and the relationship of the human being to the divine in terms of passion and erotic desire. Tillich's particular vocabulary harmonizes richly with the writings of authors like Carter Heyward in those passages in which he evokes faith—in opposition to intellectual belief—as an overwhelming passion that touches and transforms all areas of our life, and deepens and intensifies all our experiences. For Tillich as for feminist theologians, the eros toward the divine merges with and

---

[8]Sharon D. Welch offers a suggestive critique of Tillich's theorization of power by linking Tillich's analysis of political power relations to what she sees as liberal theology's idolatrous obsession with the divine as the focus of absolute power. See *A Feminist Ethic of Risk* (Minneapolis: Fortress Press, 1990), 118–20.

flows into the eros toward the world, so that the divine can be revealed in the beauty of a flowering field or a sunset, in a work of art, in a human face suddenly perceived "as human" (see *GW* 13:474–75; *NB,* 23, 127–34, 147).

Sensitive to the logic of Protestant orthodoxy, Tillich insists that the true nature of God is ineffable. The divine as it is in itself lies beyond anything that we can know, beyond any possibility of relationship in the ordinary sense. Yet the divine can and does reveal itself in human experience. Tillich's account of the unfolding of the revelatory encounter anticipates some of the positions presented by feminist and womanist theologians who describe the divine in terms of eros, relational power. While he hesitates to describe the divine itself in terms that attribute need, desire, or relational involvement to God (*ST* 1:271; but cf. *BR,* 29f.), Tillich believes that we experience the presence of God in the framework of erotic yearning, relatedness, and concern which defines our human existence as such. Our experience of the Spiritual Presence and of its "New Creation" occurs in the erotic movements that draw us toward human faces, and into deeper, more fully committed participation in human community. Our love for God is eros, mediated through the myriad connections, the "preliminary concerns" that anchor us in the world, and in which our relation to the ultimate "becomes real."

Moreover, the erotic desire that draws human beings to seek the divine and to affirm and enjoy the created world is not unrelated to, much less the negation of, the agapic love created by the divine Spirit. Religious eros emerges together with agape in human experience, and together the two qualities of love shape our religious lives. Eros, Tillich affirms, has the "character of grace." It complements and completes agape, preventing agape from degenerating into a "moralistic turning away" from creative relationship with and in the created world (*MB,* 59–61, 40–41). Tillich's use of language in describing religious yearning, faith, and communion with the divine makes clear that our experience of God is—and can only be, as long as we are human persons—an experience informed by eros (*ST* 1:281). This is also, of course, the point that the claims of feminist and womanist theologians address: not how the divine may or may not be "in itself," in a metaphysical realm inaccessible to human understanding, but rather, how the divine is revealed to us here and now, in the matrix of our embodied lives-in-relation.

Tillich would no doubt have questioned a simple equation of God with "erotic power." Yet he was not afraid to label eros as a "divine-human" energy. For Tillich as for recent feminist and womanist theologians, the erotic is a cosmic force, the "source of every movement in the world" (*GW* 13:353), above all the movement by which human beings return from estrangement and isolation toward a healed relationship with their divine origin. Eros, in Tillich's understanding, is experienced as the catalyzing energy in those situations in which the split between essence and existence is fragmentarily overcome.

What Tillich in his metaphysical language terms the healing of the existential split, authors such as Heyward and Brock call the experience of mutuality, rightness in relation. Overcoming the split between potentiality and actuality within human being is the experience of a radically transformed "right" relation to the world. By insisting that the transcendence of estrangement can and does occur within the framework of our lives here and now, in the material world, Tillich brings his concept of the transcendence of estrangement close to the erotic wholemaking of which feminist theologians have also written. Carter Heyward also uses the term *transcendence,* not to suggest a flight from the conditions of material existence, but in the sense of a "crossing over among ourselves, making connections among ourselves." *Transcendence* for Heyward—like Tillich's overcoming of the existential split—signifies not the rejection of embodied existence, but rather the process by which we tie into the radical goodness of life through erotic connections.

Salvation, as Tillich likes to recall, means healing (*ST* 3:275f.; *TC,* 119). And he insists that the salvific healing of human brokenness occurs ("by anticipation") here and now, in the moments of our lives in which we are opened to the full, creative power of love. The triumphant force of love "undercuts theological arrogance as well as pious isolation." For "in every moment of genuine love, we are dwelling in God and God in us" (*NB,* 29). Those who are touched by the Christic "healing power" can affirm that "the New Being *has* grasped their bodies and their soul, that they *have* become whole and sane again, that salvation *has* come upon them." The loving power of the New Being is felt in those moments of grace-full rightness in which the "wholeness of God being in all" is anticipated within human life (*NB,* 45).

Tillich's account of healed life remains primarily focused on the individual (white male) psyche. Especially in his later years, he tended to minimize the political and socioeconomic dimensions of the repair of alienation. Yet his "healing of the split between essence and existence" tries to point to the same mode of experience as feminist descriptions of "right relation" to our human community, to the world, and thus to the divine. The moments both of these terms attempt to name are those privileged instants of joy and wonder in which we feel, know, and participate in the fulfillment of our highest capacities as human beings. Such experiences may take the form of mystical rapture, erotic communion with a human friend, aesthetic delight, or joy gained in the midst of struggle for justice. In all these cases the absolute, radical, indubitable goodness of life is revealed to us. This healing "rightness" offers itself not as abstract theoretical knowledge, but rather with the unquestionable force of an immediate experience of joy and fulfillment which rings, in Susan Griffin's words, through our bodies and our souls at the same time.

In such moments, the essential nature, the existential form, and the ultimate *telos* of human existence are united in the power of love and blessedness. We no longer need to ask questions about the ultimate meaning of our lives. We *know:* we experience and participate in that meaning. We experience an ecstatic revelation of the beauty and goodness of life which puts them—for a moment—beyond question, beyond doubt. We are united with and transformed by the healing, loving power of the ground of being. This transformation is not a negation of our nature as human creatures; it represents a deepening, completion, fulfillment thereof. The power that touches us is not something distant, terrible, or abstract; it is our own life-giving source, to which we belong and which belongs to us.

In these moments our full potential as human beings is realized. The Spiritual Presence makes itself known to us with a power that—for a luminous instant—cuts through the confusions and ambiguities of our situation. We know and feel and are the rightness of being. Fragmentarily and "by anticipation," we touch the strength of the divine.

The key to these transformative experiences, both for Tillich and for feminist and womanist authors, is eros. In their different ways, these very different voices say the same thing: that the connection-making, creative power of eros is the catalyst of those moments in which we are most fully human, because most perfectly united with the divine.

Feminist criticisms of Tillich's concept of eros

Although their interpretations of the erotic agree on many points, Tillich and feminist and womanist readings also conflict in significant ways. Some of these conflicts were touched on in the preceding discussion. In four fundamental areas, feminist and womanist perspectives imply particularly serious criticisms of Tillich's treatment of the theme of eros.

First and most broadly, Tillich's approach to the topic is simply too abstract. Tillich makes suggestive references to the power of works of art, natural beauty, and even technical objects to awaken our erotic feelings. Yet he never describes in any detail the feelings evoked in these situations. He affirms that all forms of communal and political relationship are based on eros, yet nowhere does he attempt to explain phenomenologically how these erotic relationships are actually experienced. He is content to draw the theoretical outlines of eros experience in many different areas without ever "filling in" these rapid sketches with details and colors that would make his discussions easier to correlate with concrete, lived reality.

This high degree of abstraction has serious consequences for Tillich's depiction of eros. One obvious negative effect of abstract language applied to erotic relationships is the blindness Tillich shows toward the formative impact of race, gender, and sexual orientation on relational situations. Tillich in fact shares with almost all of his white, male theological contemporaries the tendency to ignore race, gender, and sexual specificities as decisive for human relationships. Tillich demonstrates, especially in his earlier writings, much greater attention to class identity. Yet even class categories find no serious consideration in most of his writing on erotic relationality among people. Even when striving to focus on relational encounter with a concrete other, Tillich neglects to consider the ways in which race, class, and gender contribute to constituting the other as a specific human individual, and thus to shaping the dynamics of her or his relational possibilities.

Another particularly odd consequence of the high level of abstraction in Tillich's writings on eros was mentioned in the beginning of chapter 3: in his published works, Tillich almost never explicitly discusses the erotic dimension of human sexuality. The irregularities in his private life seem to have made him wary of dealing with the topic of sex in a direct way in his theological writings. His allusions to sex are usually couched in euphemistic terms. While affirming that "creative eros includes sex," he fails to develop this perception, explore the ways in which erotic energies are expressed in sexual encounters, or look at how genuine eros can also be thwarted or twisted in non-mutual sexual relationships. His discussion of the rooting of eros in the "powers of origin," which include the sexual energies, is sugges-tive. Yet here again Tillich allows the connection to remain highly abstract, providing only the barest hints about the ways in which this erotic link to the origin is actually felt, known, and used.

If Tillich is often vague about the connections between eros and what have been regarded as "lower" types of love, he also encounters serious difficulties in attempting to work out the relation between the erotic and divinely created agape. This is the second point on which a critique of Tillich's theory of eros in light of feminist and womanist thought is especially illuminating. He fails to make the link that he affirms between agape and eros an entirely credible one.

Tillich attributes, we have seen, a high degree of importance to this problem. On the one hand, he is committed to employing a traditional Christian theological vocabulary in which agape designates a divinely created form of love that surpasses human capacities and can only emerge as a direct gift of the Spirit. On the other hand, he is equally determined to affirm the creative power of love in its erotic, philial, and libidinal qualities. Tillich is convinced that this power is real and immensely significant and that it extends into all areas of life, including religion. He does not want to let go of the intuition, decisive from an existential point of view, that human beings experience religious love as an erotic phenomenon.

Tillich wishes to affirm and legitimate the healing, creative power of eros. Yet the metaphysical structure that he has inherited demands that eros be made secondary and subservient to agape. To retain the Christian concept of agape as divine love without denigrating the other forms of love and slipping toward an antimaterialist dualism, Tillich must claim that agape can be united with eros. Indeed, he goes even further, asserting that agape needs to be completed by the erotic. Without the passionate, vivifying force of eros, agape, though divinely inspired, could degenerate into destructive and life-denying moralism. Yet Tillich is never very precise about just how the union of "un-ambiguous" agape with the lower forms of love is able to occur without the negation of agape's central properties. He acknowledges that, in human life, agape and eros are both experienced as desire. Although agape may be dispassionate in its divine origin, this unambiguous, desire-less quality of pure agape is a metaphysical hypothesis rather than a matter of possible human experience. God's agapic love remains a "mystery for finite understanding" (*ST* 1:280). *For us* as human beings, all real love and religious feeling are marked by a passionate, erotic character (see *DF*, 114–15). Tillich neglects, however, to explore the full implications of his own insight that the agape created by the divine Spirit needs the erotic in order to be complete. This idea seems to imply a far more radical reevaluation of the human-divine relationship than Tillich is willing to develop explicitly.

Tillich tries out several different ways of articulating the relationship that he wants to describe between agape and eros, but none of his solutions is entirely satisfying. Each tends inevitably either to reintroduce some form of hierarchical relation among the qualities of love or to reduce the distance between eros and agape to the point where the distinction seems arbitrary and superfluous. The tension remains, in Tillich's work, unresolved.

Some feminist theologians have resolved the conflict by simply doing away with the distinction between eros and agape. Instead of a hierarchical ordering of types of love, they call for an understanding of love as a unified cosmic power including sexual love, religious yearning, and the passion for justice. Traditional Christian theology, Carter Heyward writes, has held that eros and philia are "at best forms of love derivative from, and less godly than, agape." The distinction among the forms of love is "fastened in classical christian dualisms between spiritual and material/physical reality, between self and other." The reinterpretation of love that Heyward advocates is "not attempting simply to rearrange the traditional christian categories of love." She asserts that the traditional split between agape and the other forms of love represents a "radical misapprehension of love, which is at once divine and human." Heyward proposes to abolish these distinctions as useless and opposed to the crucial theological revaluing of sexual love and erotic relationality (Heyward, 98–99).

In many passages—his definitions of eros as a "divine-human power" not least among them—Tillich seems to move close to a similar perspective. His doctrine of the ontological unity of love posits an underlying connection beneath the different aspects in which love manifests itself. Yet Tillich's commitment to a traditional concept of agapic love as beyond ordinary human capabilities and thus in a decisive way different from the other types of love prevents him from breaking down the final barriers among the qualities of love. Practically speaking, in many of his discussions, Tillich treats love in a way that reduces its various types to poetic labels rather than rigid categories. The qualities of love flow and merge into one another, each present in all the others. But Tillich's attachment to a traditional metaphysical and religious scheme holds him back from the step some feminist theologians have made in asserting unequivocally that the distinction between authentic eros and agape is superfluous.

A third difficulty connected with Tillich's ontological presuppositions has been discussed by Judith Plaskow and others.[9] Founded on a vision of love as an all-embracing cosmic reunion of the separated, Tillich's ontology is basically monist in its structure. Despite his efforts to maintain a balance between opposing poles, his cosmic vision emphasizes fusion at the expense of difference and personhood, participation over individuation. His underlying metaphysics implies that individuality and difference are ephemeral surface phenomena, destined to disappear as human beings (and humankind collectively) move toward reunion with their divine source.

Tillich explicitly stresses the importance of erotic tension as opposed to mystical fusion in many areas, from cognition to the moral encounter to the relationship between human individuals and the divine. He attaches real importance to salvaging the idea of personhood even in speculating on the conditions of the life after death (*ST* 3:406f.). Yet as Plaskow points out, the underlying metaphysical structures in which his theology is grounded conflict with Tillich's claims about the necessity of honoring and strengthening individual personhood. The erotic tension that Tillich struggles to maintain tends to slacken into a mystical vision of all-embracing "reunion" in which differences and particularities dissolve in fusional participation in a "transcendent unity." Thus, on the surface, Tillich's thought bears a highly individualistic stamp. At the same time, at a deeper level, it is haunted by dreams of mystical fusion and obliteration of the isolated self.

In all fairness, it must be said that Tillich is not the only thinker to have encountered difficulties in articulating the tension between individual personhood and communal participation in connection with the erotic. Heyward's and Brock's writings also include passages that seem to weaken significantly—if not to deny outright—the status of the autonomous, self-activated individual. The problem in Tillich's writings, however, is not one of subtle emphasis in a few passages, but rather of the basic metaphysical structures of a theological system.

---

[9] Judith Plaskow, *Sex, Sin, and Grace: Women's Experience and the Theologies of Reinhold Niebuhr and Paul Tillich* (Washington, D.C.: University Press of America, 1980). See also Wayne Proudfoot, "Types of Finite-Infinite Relation and Conceptions of the Self" (Ph.D. diss., Harvard University, 1971).

His metaphysics may weaken his concept of eros by placing excessive emphasis on the idea of love, including the erotic, as a fusional "reunion of the separated." In such a scheme, insistence on the value and integrity of individual personhood and on relationships that construct difference as creative, erotic tension is undermined by the fundamental notion of cosmic reunion in which difference is obliterated. Tillich's difficulties in struggling with this issue reflect the complexity and delicacy of the questions involved, and underscore the need for feminist theorists to pursue further careful work in the area of eros and the constitution of the self.

Feminist and womanist understandings of the erotic signal a fourth difficulty, which is connected with the idea of justice. Tillich views eros as drawing us toward persons, things, ideas, creatures that are "bearers of values." He never seriously takes up the question of where these values come from. Although a historical understanding of values is implied in important passages of his work,[10] Tillich never faces squarely, in his theory of morals, the question of the extent to which values are socially constructed. Despite his concern with historical thinking and the historically conditioned nature of human knowledge, Tillich never frees himself entirely from the tendency to use terms such as beauty, truth, and justice as if these referred to fixed, unchanging entities situated in Plato's ideal realm. Of course, Tillich discusses love, the foundation of all moral demands, as changing according to the requirements of the particular situation of moral choice. He recognizes that the guiding principles of morality do and must undergo alteration in shifting historical and social contexts. Yet the ultimate values toward which we are drawn by erotic forces and which motivate us to act morally remain above and abstracted from concrete situations. The good, the true, and the beautiful are eternal principles rooted in the divine nature itself.

The relationship of these abstract universal values to concrete situations of ethical choice remains problematic in Tillich's work. Tillich fails to make a clear and convincing connection between eros toward the intellectual ideals and the more mundane passions which structure our interactions in daily situations. As a result, the relationship between the ideal of the good and the motivation to behave justly in concrete contexts continues to pose difficulties.

---

[10]On Tillich's grasp of the historically conditioned character of knowledge, see esp. the essays in *The Interpretation of History,* as well as the better known discussion in *ST* 3 of human history in light of divine salvific purpose.

Tillich explicitly recognizes erotic feeling as playing a central role in moral decision making. With this insight, he takes an important step beyond the reason-nature dualism of the Kantian tradition. For Kant, "apathy," the repression of the passions, had been a necessary precondition for proper moral choice.[11] Tillich draws close connections between just action and love, including agape and eros. Yet while stressing the connection between eros and justice, Tillich reintroduces dualistic structures rooted in the Platonic system which serves as the point of departure for his discussion. These dualistic tendencies undermine the link between erotic feeling and the commitment to justice which Tillich had set out to make clear.

On the the one hand, Tillich characterizes justice as the "imperative . . . to recognize every being with personal potential as a person" (*MB,* 46). If this recognition is understood as "not detached but involved," then the dualistic separation of reason from passion and of justice from love appears to be overcome. Yet on the other hand, Tillich sees the underlying motivation of ethical behavior as the human being's desire to participate in the divine. He believes that a system of morals, in order to motivate effectively, must point to values which transcend the sphere of merely human feelings and relationships. Human morality is only possible as a "station on the way to something ultimate—the divine" (*MB,* 59–60). In such a perspective, however, actual human relationships are instrumentalized. They take on the status of mere means to an end: stages on the way to a divine ideal. A dualistic separation establishes itself between the ideal realm and the theater of intersubjective, human feelings and actions.

Eros as a "transmoral motivation" aimed toward participation in a transcendent divine sphere tends to overshoot the level of concrete human relationship, to ignore the passion for justice as an intersubjective phenomenon. In Tillich's framework, justice among persons is not loved erotically for itself and for the interpersonal joy and beauty that it liberates. Rather, Tillich believes that the "moral realm," that is, the context of actual human relatedness and interaction, does not in itself "furnish moral motivation" (*MB,* 60). To find such motivation, the "mind" must be "elevat[ed] . . . out of existential bondage" into a transcendent, intellectual-mystical plane: the "realm of pure essences"

---

[11]Cf. for example Kant, *Metaphysik der Sitten,* 2, XVI: "Zur Tugend wird Apathie (als Staerke betrachtet) notwending vorausgesetzt." In *Werke,* Band IV (Darmstadt: Wissenschaftliche Buchgesellschaft, 1963), 540.

(*MB*, 59). The moral eros must be oriented toward a higher sphere, beyond the level of actual human relationships. Under such conditions, however, the connection between interpersonal eros and just action becomes secondary and contingent. The substitutional of eros toward an abstract ideal for eros as mutual attunement and sympathy among people leaves important questions unresolved.

Unlike feminist and womanist authors, Tillich does not ground his analysis of the moral eros in a phenomenological description of our experience of justice in and through personal relationships. The link between eros and justice on the practical, intersubjective level therefore remains problematic. This is even more so since the content of the ideal of the good toward which the moral eros strives is largely unspecified. The actual role of erotic feeling in concrete ethical decision making thus is hard to describe with clarity. Eros "seeks the noble quality in all things." But since all things offer themselves as possible objects of erotic interest, it becomes difficult to justify the choice of one particular object, course of action, relationship, or situation over another. If everything, as Tillich's concept implies, offers erotic possibilities, then what grounds can be offered for choosing, for example, a structure of political and social equality over one founded on racial, social, and class oppression? In what way would it be necessary or advantageous, from the point of view of eros as a motivating criterion, to choose policies that attempt to conserve certain features of the natural world rather than exploit those features in the interest of procuring immediate utility and pleasure? In the context of a basically undifferentiated erotic relation to the world, it seems impossible to justify revolutionary anger or the desire for change. Tillich's difficulty in establishing a convincing criterion of distinction between the creative political eros of the youth movement and the sadistic eros of Nazism is bound up with this problem. In a world in which eros perceives values in everything and everyone, how can we legitimate struggling for one thing and refusing another?

Feminists and womanists have responded implicitly to this challenge by making concepts of relational justice and mutuality central, rather than peripheral, to their understanding of the erotic. For such authors as Heyward, Sölle, and Brock, justice—defined in terms of concrete human experience as the sharing of power in mutual relation, the "shape of mutuality in our life together"—is the criterion that distinguishes healing, authentic eros from perverted and destructive forms. Justice, for these women, is not simply one value among others toward which eros calls us through a vaguely defined metaphysical attraction.

Instead, justice as concrete, intersubjective relational attunement belongs to the essence of true eros. It defines authentic eros as such. Such eros does not orient itself primarily toward an abstract ideal of the good, but toward justice as a dynamic rightness, a creative mutuality realized and shared in embodied love and friendship among people. Insofar as they are indeed authentic, our erotic interactions with the world are informed by a primary concern with creating just relationships. Thus, an affirming, erotic relation to the whole of the created world does not exclude the anger that rises against oppression. Rather, true eros requires and includes this transforming anger.

Feminists and womanists have founded their restructuring of the concept of eros on the idea of an erotic justice experienced and understood in the tangible dynamic of human relationships. Tillich's failure to explore this connection between personal eros experience and the doing of justice accounts for the ambiguous relation of eros to concrete moral and political values in his discussions. The idea of erotic justice developed by recent feminist and womanist theologians does not conflict with the fundamental structures of Tillich's eros doctrine. But Tillich himself fails to shed full light on the issue of erotic feeling and right action in relationships. Although some of his texts imply such an understanding, Tillich never develops explicitly the idea that justice is the criterion which distinguishes essential or creative eros from distorted, demonic expressions of the erotic.

In Tillich's comparisons of estranged libido and eros with the essential nature of these phenomena, the word *justice* is conspicuously absent. The emphasis in these discussions is largely on private psychological dynamics, the suffering and craving of the individual. Tillich, as Carter Heyward has remarked pointedly, tends to portray estrangement and the pain that accompanies it as radically personal phenomena. In his discussions of estrangement, he often minimizes the communal, political, and economic dimensions of alienation. He fails to explore the connection between personal, psychological suffering and systemic forms of economic, political, racial, and sexual oppression. Tillich is unwilling to look at estrangement primarily as a quality of relationship marked by a breakdown of justice and responsibility. (Heyward, 63–65).[12]

---

[12]Heyward's criticism of Tillich's psychologizing, apolitical interpretation of human alienation corresponds more directly to the work of Tillich's American period than to the writings of his early years in Germany. In many of the books, lectures, and articles written before Tillich's forced departure from Germany, the economic and political

Our consideration of Tillich's erotic life has suggested reasons why it may in fact have been important to Tillich to keep his reflections on eros and justice at the level of rather vague abstractions. At the core of his own intimate life, Tillich maintained for decades an exploitative and unjust relation to his wife. His unwillingness to look carefully at the grave injustice present in his own private life helps to account for Tillich's reluctance to make concrete justice the theoretical criterion for distinguishing authentic from perverted, destructive eros. Tillich may have feared the light in which his own erotic life would have appeared if looked at through the lens of concrete relational justice. Anxious about the consequences for the appraisal of his own eros, he drew back in his published work from a thorough examination of erotic justice as expressed (or denied) in specific relational contexts.

Tillich's personal life also offers an interesting clue to explain his determination to hold fast to the idea of agape as a key dimension of human love experience, despite the conceptual difficulties to which the relationship between agape and eros leads. At first glance, the situation is indeed somewhat puzzling. As is clear from the discussion in *Biblical Religion,* Tillich was prepared to characterize agape in terms that seem to break down all meaningful experiential distinctions between agape and other types of love. But he continued throughout his theological career to use the idea of agape, and to insist on its unique importance. For most other theologians, unquestioning commitment to the language and teachings of the tradition would of course have been a sufficient justification. But Tillich was a thinker of unique courage, willing to take intellectual risks and in particular to modify the traditional theological vocabulary in cases where it no longer appeared adequate to the contemporary situation. Was respect for traditional dogmas Tillich's primary reason for continuing to emphasize the centrality of agape? Was it that the existence of a disinterested, unambiguous form of divine love seemed essential to the architecture of his theological system? Had Tillich himself experienced types of

---

dimensions of suffering and estrangement are given a thorough and explicit treatment. For an interesting example of the tone and focus of these early writings, see Tillich's 1920 essay on "Christianity and Socialism": "Christianity and socialism must develop together and unite in a new ordering of society and of the world, whose basis is an economic structure founded on justice, and whose ethos is the affirmation of each human being, because he or she is a human being [eine Bejahung jedes Menschen um deswillen, daß er Mensch ist]" (*GW* 2:33), quoted in Renate Albrecht and Werner Schüßler, eds., *Paul Tillich: Sein Werk* (Düsseldorf, Patmos, 1986), 52.

love which he felt only the concept of a force entering human life "from another dimension" was sufficient to describe?

Some or all of these considerations probably played a role in Tillich's thinking. His biographers suggest another factor that may have been equally important. Over the years, they report, Tillich developed a rule that helped him to "assuage his feelings of guilt" in connection with his marital infidelities. Tillich was willing to affirm as morally acceptable any relationship (meaning, principally, his own extramarital sexual involvements) from which "agape was not absent."[13] Apart from any judgments about the theological adequacy or inadequacy of the concept of agape, it seems clear that Tillich made use of the concept as a psychological shield against the guilt he felt about his own sex life.

Divinely created agape remains difficult to define or to locate precisely. According to Tillich's theory, it is potentially present in all forms of human relationship, particularly in libidinal and erotic relations (see *LPJ*, 116–18; *MB*, 40–42). Agape offered Tillich a useful protective structure to block both his own guilt and the negative judgments of others on his erotic conduct. The concept of agape is vague enough that traces of such a form of love can probably be discerned in almost any human relationship in which one is determined to find it. Yet precisely because it is by definition mysterious and more-than-human, agape does not necessarily imply the acting out of concrete relational justice that more "mundane" types of love might require. By convincing himself and others that agape was present in some form in his extramarital sexual relationships and in his relations with his wife, Tillich could avoid the painful task of having to focus real moral scrutiny on this web of relationships, and, perhaps, of having to take action to change it.

Tillich's promise for feminist
theologies of eros

In several areas, including notably that of erotic justice, feminist and womanist understandings of the erotic imply fundamental criticisms of Tillich's interpretation of eros. On the other hand, Tillich's treatment

---

[13]Wilhelm and Marion Pauck, *Paul Tillich: His Life and Thought* (New York: Harper & Row, 1976), 90–91.

of the erotic points out issues that will need to be explored more fully as feminist and womanist theologians pursue their work on eros, and deepen their understanding of the importance of the erotic in many different realms of human experience.

Tillich's discussion of the role of eros in cognition, including everything from basic sensory functions to the most highly abstract, intellectual forms of knowledge, highlights an area in which much work remains to be done. As we saw earlier, promising insights have already been suggested by feminists working on the theme of erotic knowledge. Yet until recently the principal task of these women has simply been combatting the tenacious assumptions that feeling is a barrier to true knowledge and that dispassionate, "scientific" cognition represents the ideal and only genuine form of knowing. Explorations of the positive connections between feeling and knowledge and of the precise ways in which feelings shape and condition our experience of different aspects of the world have been held back by an oppressive set of cultural assumptions.

Thus, as the basic idea of the existence of affective or erotic knowledge gains wider acceptance, a broad field for phenomenological description and for theory is opening.[14] Tillich's insight that all cognitive acts are structured by an erotic "union through separation" suggests avenues for exploration in the procesess linking feeling, knowledge, and personality.

Connected with this issue is the function of erotic feeling in teaching and learning. Here, too, some feminist and womanist authors have begun promising reflections, but both theory and the concrete task of transforming institutional structures still have far to go. The power of eros to shape a new relationship to technology and its creations— and perhaps to guide technical creativity itself in life-affirming directions—is an important intuition on which feminist theory could also build. Tillich's vision of technical, productive skill informed by erotic awareness challenges contemporary practice to seek a deeper integration of these modes of being.

---

[14]For interesting recent work on epistemological questions from a feminist perspective, see the essays in Alison M. Jaggar and Susan Bordo, eds., *Gender/Body/Knowledge: Feminist Reconstructions of Being and Knowing* (New Brunswick and London: Rutgers University Press, 1989); also Robin Schott, *Eros and Cognition: A Critique of the Kantian Paradigm* (Boston: Beacon Press, 1988); also important is the discussion of Sandra Harding's concept of an "epistemology of solidarity" in Welch, *A Feminist Ethic of Risk,* 136–40.

The question of the relationship of eros to different forms of work, whether technical or nontechnical, is a crucial area for secular social thought and for theologies committed to grappling with the material and political realities of human life. Few feminists and womanists, however, have as yet turned their attention to this subject. Tillich, like other authors from Herbert Marcuse to Audre Lorde, discusses the possible eroticization of our relationship to the processes and products of socially useful labor. But he insists that this erotic investment in work and its "technical Gestalten" can only take place in a healthy manner under theonomous, that is, just, nonalienating, social conditions. This qualification serves as a useful reminder that the connection of erotic power to the forces of work, production, and the marketplace is a highly ambiguous operation. An erotic passion for justice can color the transforming work of political struggle. On the other hand, the infusion of twisted forms of eros into economic relationships and work processes (through advertising and the manipulation of feeling and opinion through the media) could—and does— function as a tool of domination and social control. In general, foundational investigation still demands to be done on the links between the erotic body and the working body in contemporary society, and on the ways in which distorted erotic forces are used in the exploitative colonization of people's (particularly of women's) bodies.[15]

The personal, social, and political ambiguity of the erotic, its power to destroy and injure as well as to create and nourish, is a theme of which Tillich is keenly aware, and to which he refers frequently. Feminist authors have sometimes tended to celebrate the erotic as an unambiguous good; the identification of justice as the defining characteristic of authentic eros has occasionally led to a relative neglect of the nonauthentic, alienated, and destructive forms that eros can also take on, even among those persons who are consciously trying to extricate themselves from the constraints of hierarchical and exploitative patterns. In writing about the ambiguities of the erotic, feminist authors have occasionally committed the mistake Tillich makes in discussing erotic justice: that is, withdrawing into abstraction. Recent feminist writings on eros have, however, begun to deal with this issue

---

[15]I am grateful to Vivian Lindermeyer for several very enriching conversations on the topic of eros and productive labor, and in particular for her suggestions about the political implications of some of the relationships which can be constructed between these two areas of corporeal experience.

in a more direct manner.[16] On the assumption that authentic eros and relational justice are inseparable from one another, more work needs to be done to analyze the ways in which sustaining, mutual erotic relations are twisted and perverted under conditions of social and political oppression, and to devise concrete strategies for maintaining and expanding networks of nonhierarchical erotic connectedness in the face of hostility from dominant social, political, and economic structures. The conflict between Tillich's eros theory and his failure to practice erotic justice in certain concrete relationships shows how vital it is to maintain the connection between discourses on eros and the doing of justice, and also how easy it can be to let this connection break down.

Tillich's difficulties in reconciling the affirmation of individual personhood with the underlying structures of a mystical metaphysics points to a rather similar unresolved tension in certain versions of feminist and womanist theory of eros. In the framework of an "ontology of relation" (Carter Heyward), the concepts of individual autonomy and of personal moral agency begin to become problematic. While this is by no means a reason to reject such an ontological approach, it is a good reason to dig more deeply into the connections between erotic relationality and personal moral decision making. Tillich's efforts to link erotic interpersonal communion with the experience of the moral imperative offer perspectives that when carefully followed up may be helpful in this work.

Tillich's intuition of an eros toward the world that embraces all aspects of our experience reminds us that while attention to the concrete details of our immediate relationships is indispensable, we must also work not to lose sight of our role in larger global structures that are often, under present political circumstances, structures of oppression and alienation rather than of mutuality, shared power, shared pleasure. Our erotic feelings must also draw us out beyond our immediate experiences into this larger world of complex relationships and responsibilities. At this level of global relationships, sharp analytic skills are necessary to understand the demands of justice. Tillich's emphasis on the intellectual, philosophical dimension of eros warns against interpretations that stress only the subjective, emotional component.

---

[16]Recent works that take up the problem of the ambiguity of eros in a direct and constructive way include: Starhawk, *Dreaming the Dark,* and Judith Plaskow, *Standing Again at Sinai: Judaism from a Feminist Perspective* (San Francisco: Harper & Row, 1990). The discussion of lesbian sadomasochism in Heyward's *Touching Our Strength* also includes some important reflections on this subject.

Implementing erotic justice demands the integration and affirmation of our analytic abilities, as well as our capacity to feel.

Eros and the tasks of theology today

The differences between Tillich's understanding of eros and the interpretations of feminist and womanist authors are profound. They can ultimately function, however, not as reciprocal negation but as a basis for dialogue and further learning about the erotic. And they should not obscure the important points the interpretations have in common. On the basis of what Tillich and feminist and womanist authors share, and of what separates them—on the basis, that is, of a creative erotic tension—these two discourses on eros open a conversation that will be significant for the future of Christian theological thinking.

To enter into this conversation is to take a risk. Tillich states repeatedly that opening our lives and our theologies to the power of the erotic implies serious dangers. Feminist and womanist authors are also increasingly frank in acknowledging the risks and conflicts that erotic forces bring with them. Opening more and more aspects of our lives to the quickening influence of eros means, as Judith Plaskow writes, "living dangerously."[17] Tillich's biography shows that cultivating the creative power of the erotic and the joy it brings also means exposing oneself and others to the ambiguous and potentially destructive energies that eros can unleash.

The potential gain is worth the risk involved. And the consequence of failing to recognize honestly the force of the erotic is a deepened alienation from who we really are as human beings. Whereas living in conscious touch with eros implies risk, failing to acknowledge ourselves as erotic beings and to use creatively the powers that eros puts at our disposal is certain to be destructive. As Tillich writes, an attitude of "condescension" or of simple repression toward the non-rational dynamics of our "vital life" leads to an existence that is ultimately less fulfilling and less secure:

> It is not sufficient, and almost a caricature, if pastoral preaching and counseling recommend the "innocent pleasures of life," thus opening

---

[17]Plaskow, *Standing Again at Sinai*, 204.

the way to the wrong assumption that some pleasures are in themselves innocent and others guilty instead of encouraging a recognition of the ambiguity of creativity and destruction in every pleasure as well as in everything that is called serious. . . . Condescension toward the vital life of man together with a kind of permissiveness toward childish pleasures is worse than genuine asceticism; it leads to continual explosions of the repressed and only superficially admitted forces in the totality of man's being. And such explosions are personally and socially destructive.

Drawing out and naming explicitly the deep and ambiguous powers of eros may well be a frightening step. This is especially true, of course, within the framework of religious traditions that have struggled for centuries to bind and limit the forces of the erotic, to keep them from emerging into full view. But Tillich and feminist authors both insist that the danger involved in recognizing erotic feeling openly is less than that connected with repression and denial. "He who admits the vital dynamics in man," Tillich writes, "as a necessary element in all his self-expressions (his passions or his eros) must know that he has accepted life in its divine-demonic ambiguity." It is "the triumph of the Spiritual Presence" to direct these powers toward creative and life-enhancing ends, "rather than replacing them with the help of suppression by the niceties of 'harmless' pleasures" (*ST* 3:241).

To lead a fully human life means to take up the challenge of realizing our creative potential as erotic beings. It means to recognize the ambiguities of the "vital dynamics" that shape our biological and social existence, and to focus the power of our vital energies in just, creative, and life-sustaining ways. Undoubtedly, this way of being in the world is "living dangerously." Struggling to lead the whole of one's life according to the standard set by the experience of erotic joy brings one inevitably, as Audre Lorde writes, into conflict with the debilitating norms set by those who hold power through oppression and intimidation. The alternative, however, is to refuse all participation in the creative dimensions of existence, to accept without question or criticism the mediocrity, the preprogrammed roles and attitudes imposed by outside authorities. Living in touch with the erotic, as Lorde insists and as Tillich also saw, means daring to demand more from life than oppressive traditions and structures would like to allot to us. Security from risk can be bought only at the price of renouncing creativity and struggle: that is, sacrificing our capacity to live as responsible members of the human community.

For theologies and religious traditions, as well as for individual persons, recognizing and beginning to draw on the power of eros implies dangers and uncertainties. In the case of Christian theology, affirming eros means breaking with ideas and attitudes that have been portrayed as cornerstones of Christian doctrine. Yet the alternative to this transformation of traditional attitudes and discourses is insularity and stagnation, the admission that Christianity can no longer offer a word of life to the world, but can only deny and withdraw from it. Feminist authors name erotic empowerment, erotic connectedness as the "only basis of our hope for the world" (Heyward, 18). If they cannot affirm and embrace the reality of the "erotic as power," Christian theologies and religious communities will lose their capacity to make their proclamation of hope convincing for those who seek in religion not a justification for flight from the world, but a way to love the world better, and more effectively.

Denouncing and struggling to subdue what Tillich called the "vital forces" of eros has been one of the most constant occupations of Christian theologians, from the ascetic church Fathers to Anders Nygren and beyond. Yet today, in feminist and womanist theologies, a radically new approach to the erotic is emerging, and with it, a new vision of what Christian theology and even Christian life could become. Feminists and womanists have claimed that the risk of drawing the power of eros into the center of theological thinking is a risk that must be taken. They affirm that no truly healthy, life-giving spirituality is possible on the basis of repression and denial of the erotic forces essential to our humanness. The future of Christian theology will be decisively influenced by the unfolding of the eros concept and by the ability (or inability) of traditional theological structures to adapt themselves to new understandings of the role of the erotic in our lives as individuals and as communities.

The affirmation of eros in feminist and womanist theologies does not demand that we reject everything the Christian tradition has stood for, nor all the voices that have spoken for and through that tradition. The new image of eros enables us to look at parts of the tradition in a new way, and to discern there the seeds of positive and creative, as well as repressive approaches to erotic power in human life. In Tillich's writings, we find a voice supporting the feminist claim that the risk involved in honoring and using the power of eros, in theological work as in other areas of our existence, is a risk that must be accepted. Feminist and womanist theologies engage and bring out the theme of eros in Tillich's writings.

Opened up through conversation with feminist and womanist understandings of the erotic, Tillich's work points toward the tasks and challenges that will shape the theological future: drawing the full consequences of a fundamental affirmation of sexuality and embodiment; exploring relationality as the central characteristic of human personhood, and human relationships as a primary vehicle of divine revelation; developing approaches to justice and community which maintain the erotic tension between individual agency and communal connectedness; empowering oppressed communities for concrete struggles for justice; emphasizing the interdependence not only of individual persons, but of all human groups; acknowledging the creative interdependence of humanity and the divine. The concept of eros as explored by Tillich and by feminists and womanists has crucial implications for theology as it attempts to address these tasks.

Eros demands a vision that places human experiences of shared pleasure and creativity at the center of theological thinking, instead of looking at embodied pleasure and human relationships generally as peripheral to theological inquiry. In experiences of erotic joy, the meaning of life is revealed to us immediately. Such joy—rooted in a matrix of relational connections to other people and to the world—*is* that meaning. Theological or philosophical glosses coming after the fact can help us to understand and explain the phenomenon. Analytic thought can help us organize our common existence in such a way as to offer greater opportunities for joy to greater numbers of people. But it is in the sharing of this erotic joy itself that our lives together are justified. In the joy that springs from "reaching others and their world in a genuine relation," we enter into the "dimension of the eternal." In our lives as embodied persons, joy means that, "the meaning of creation and the end of salvation are attained" (*NB*, 146, 150–51). It is on the basis of their capacity or incapacity to foster such experience that religious communities and their theological systems must stand or fall.

The concept of the erotic urges Christian theology to affirm authentic embodied pleasure, to honor such life-giving pleasure, as Alice Walker says, "regardless." Heyward's explicitly theological challenge must be taken with the utmost seriousness: "A sex-affirming ethic is morally imperative. Only if we know our erotic power as sacred can we imagine, much less embody among ourselves, the transformation of alienated power into right relation." Erotic joy—including sexual pleasure—does not need to be apologized for. It is a moral good, an end in itself without need of further justification. And as a foundational moral good, eros provides the basis for a new theological vision. "The erotic as our sacred power in mutual relation" is itself, Heyward affirms, the "source of our redemption from evil" (Heyward, 121–22). The central theological function must be reconceived. Theology can no longer proceed by fabricating abstract metaphysical systems and focusing attention on a world beyond this one. It must take up as its central task the development of concrete strategies to maximize the sharing of erotic fulfillment among people here and now.

Eros requires a reorganization of theological discourses around our concrete experience of embodied love and fulfillment, of "rightness" in relationships. A new Christian concept of love, one that embraces all "faces" of love experience from sex to the love of ideas to aesthetics and communion with nature to committed political struggle and the love of God must be articulated. In all of these experiences, estrangement can be conquered. In all of them, we can touch the essence of divine-human strength. In and through a matrix of life-enhancing, empowering relationships, we come to know the power that creates and sustains all life in the world. This matrix connects us to human beings, to other creatures, to inanimate "things," in which Tillich also sensed a living, erotic force. God is revealed to us simultaneously in/as our "eros toward the world," in/as the passion that grounds us in human communities striving to embody the ideal of justice.

Erotic relationality is the mark and source of our humanness, and of our ability to enter into relation with the divine. For those who take seriously this concept of erotic power, all forms of human praxis must be understood and described—ethically, politically, and theologically—not in terms of isolated facts, choices, actions, but in terms that give primary importance to relationship and participation. The thoughts and actions of individuals are always woven into and shaped by a network of erotic connections. Thus theological reflection must proceed on the basis of an awareness of the interconnectedness of the different dimensions, spiritual, sexual, and political, of life. A theology of eros acknowledges that our relationship to the divine cannot be made whole apart from the weave of material, affective, social, political, and economic relations that bind us to other members of the human community. The healing of existential alienation is not merely a private psychological or spiritual question. Political and economic concerns are central to the issue.

With this perception in mind, a new understanding emerges of the relationship between our religious lives and the struggle for political, social, and economic justice. Work for justice can no longer be looked at as at best an auxiliary activity in which Christians can choose to engage once they have taken care of the primary business of achieving a proper personal relationship to God. A view of human life and of human spirituality based on eros asserts that there is no private, personal relationship to the divine outside of the complex tissue of relational connections and responsibilities linking individuals to their communities and to their world. The quality of our relational involvement with others is the quality of our relationship to God. "The presence and revelation of erotic power is the divine dimension of human existence. It grows and moves with us as the resilient, flexible vulnerability that reveals our existence in relationship and our co-creation of each other."[18]

Like feminist and womanist authors, Tillich posits an attitude of passionate involvement and erotic care as the basic mode in which human beings encounter one another and the world. Eros, for Tillich as for Heyward, is at root the urge to "be involved" in the world, in the bodies and lives of other persons, in the divine. The striving for objectivity and detachment which shapes our Western concept of scientific knowledge—and which as the culturally dominant paradigm of right knowledge directly influences relations between individuals, social groups, and entire nations—is a refusal of the most basic truth of our existence as revealed by an understanding of eros: that as human beings we are inextricably and inevitably bound up with, involved in one another's lives, and in the destinies of the beings and things that make up the world. We cannot "step back" from the web of passionate relationships in which we as individuals, as societies and as a species are implicated. Our detachment, our supposed independence from other human beings and from the natural world is an illusion, and a dangerous one.

Eros reveals that all aspects of our own and others' lives are interwoven and interdependent. Our participation in community and political structures is animated by the same fundamental energy as our longing to know one another as sexual beings. Our erotic connection to nature springs from the same source as our connection to the divine. Thus, failure to establish nurturing connections in any one of these spheres will lead directly to failures and distortions in the other areas of our being. Our practice of political and racial oppression will influence our relation to the natural world. Our failure to come to terms

---

[18]Rita Nakashima Brock, *Journeys by Heart: A Christology of Erotic Power* (New York: Crossroad, 1988), 46.

with aspects of our sexuality will have consequences for our understanding of the divine and our ability to interpret and live out the values that we think of as rooted in the divine nature.

Our efforts to free ourselves as individuals from existential alienation are doomed to failure. Within the close tissue of erotic connections linking selves to one another and to the world, the concept of individual salvation becomes meaningless. Even as in our own lives we begin to have a sense of being liberated from certain aspects of estrangement, a deepened perception of the weave of erotic connections shows us that private solutions do not work: others' suffering and alienation is our suffering, and the struggle against it our task. We cannot hope to escape, either through spiritual asceticism or through "feeling good about ourselves," from our direct responsibility for and involvement in the lives of others. Affirmed in many passages of Tillich's work but implicitly undermined in others, this perception has been given an unequivocally central place in feminist and womanist work on the erotic. The idea of erotic connectedness in community will be crucial for new theologies as they strive to integrate the political dimension of human existence more fully with spirituality and religious practice.

An understanding of human life as unified by the force of eros implies that theology must no longer proceed on the basis of dualistic separations, either in its discussions of love, or in its attempts to grapple with other topics. We must reject the antithetical oppositions that traditional theology has constructed between female and male, matter and spirit, body and mind, feeling and rational thought, politics and religion, the human community and the divine. Christian world views must be reshaped to reflect new understandings based not on separation and antagonism, but on erotic connection. Only on this basis can new theological discourses emerge which will do justice to the complex unity of human being.

By acknowledging clearly the erotic interconnection among different forms of human practice, theology can begin to come to terms both with its dependence on and with its potentially transformative impact in other areas of life: politics, socioeconomic structures, prevailing cultural attitudes toward nature and sexuality. The theories of eros shaped by Tillich and by feminist and womanist authors challenge theology to begin to take seriously the full scope of healing, creative potentials that erotic power implies, and to begin at the same time to assume its responsibility for helping to make these potentials a reality in society. Only by developing a new, affirming relationship to the power of eros can theology and religious institutions and practices counter their own very real tendency to degenerate into a "moralistic turning away from the creative potentialities in nature and in man."

The capacity of liberal Christian theology and of the institutions rooted in the liberal theological tradition to understand, assimilate, and transform themselves in accordance with these new perspectives will be a crucial test of the viability of the tradition in a world in the throes of radical change. Conversation between feminist and womanist theologies and more traditional theological perspectives is clearly indispensable to this work of transformation. The concern with eros shared by Tillich and such authors as Carter Heyward, Dorothee Sölle, Beverly Harrison, and Rita Nakashima Brock could help provide a foundation for this vital dialogue. Tillich's ideas and his theological vocabulary may help to make feminist positions more accessible to those whose theological frame of reference is not an explicitly feminist one. In Tillich's writings on eros, a voice emerges from within the liberal Christian tradition itself and echoes many of the claims about the erotic made by feminist and womanist theorists. This point is an important one for those who recognize the necessity of transforming existing structures and attitudes, but who wish at the same time to do this in a way that honors and preserves the liberatory perspectives that the tradition itself provides.

Together, in dialogue and in tension with one another, Tillich's ideas and those of feminist and womanist authors show that the erotic is a topic that reaches beyond the agenda of any particular community or movement. The power of the erotic and its theological consequences concern women and men, whites and persons of color, and persons of highly different intellectual and theological backgrounds, traditional as well as radical. In dialogue, Tillich and feminist and womanist theologians of the erotic announce a new understanding of love with sweeping implications for theological thinking and ultimately for all dimensions of religious and social practice. The force of this new vision of eros makes itself felt today in a way that Tillich's words on the power of love may best describe. Love, Tillich writes,

> is working even today toward new creation. It is hidden in the darkness of our souls and of our history. But it is not completely hidden to those who are grasped by its reality. "Do you not *perceive* it?" asks the prophet. Do *we* not perceive it? (*SF*, 186)

Index